TOWARD
MULTICULTURALISM

TOWARD MULTICULTURALISM

A Reader in Multicultural Education

Edited by
Jaime S. Wurzel

Intercultural Press, Inc.
Yarmouth, Maine

For information, contact Intercultural Press, PO Box 768, Yarmouth, Maine 04096.

Library of Congress Catalogue Card Number 88-081392 ISBN 0-933662-72-6

Printed in the United States of America

Library of Congress Cataloging-in-Publication Data

Toward multiculturalism.

    Bibliography: p.
    1. Intercultural education.   2. Educational anthropology.   3. Pluralism (Social sciences)
I. Wurzel, Jaime S., 1948-
LC1099.T68   1988   370.19′6   88-81392
ISBN 0-933662-72-6

Permissions

The following articles are republished here with the permission of the author and/or the original publisher:

"Eating Christmas in the Kalahari," *Natural History,* Vol. 78, No. 10; copyright the American Museum of Natural History, 1969.

"Kapluna Daughter," from *Women in the Field* by Peggy Golde.

"An Interview with C.P. Ellis," from *American Dreams* by Studs Terkel, Random House, Inc.

"Beth Anne—A Case Study of Culturally Defined Adjustment and Teacher Perceptions," from *Education and Cultural Process Toward an Anthropology of Education* edited by George Dearborn Spindler, copyright 1974 by Holt, Rinehart and Winston, Inc.

"Stereotypes: Explaining People Who Are Different," *Daedalus,* Spring 1961.

"You Will Do As Directed" by Ron Jones from *No Substitution for Madness* by Ron Jones.

"Beating the Man," from James P. Spradley and David W. McCurdy, eds., *Conformity and Conflict: Readings in Anthropology,* 2nd ed.; copyright 1974 by Little, Brown and Company (Inc.).

"The Child in India," from *Aditi: The Living Arts of India,* copyright Smithsonian Institution, Washington, D.C., 1985.

"Child Care in China," *Saturday Review* (Education) May 1973.

"Free Enterprise and the Ghetto Family," *Psychology Today Magazine,* March, 1981, copyright 1981 by American Psychological Association.

Some Discontinuities in the Enculturation of Mistassini Cree Children, monograph published by Research Center in Anthropology.

Permissions (cont.)

Table of Contents

Acknowledgments

I would like to express my thanks to the people whose encouragement, support, and wisdom was essential for the completion of this publication: Jack Levy, from George Mason University, who served as the chair of Publications for the Society for Intercultural Education and Research and urged me to submit this for publication; Margaret Pusch and David Hoopes from Intercultural Press, who always believed in the materials and patiently guided me through the process of completion; and my students, who helped reaffirm the educational value of the readings.

TOWARD MULTICULTURALISM

Multiculturalism and Multicultural Education

by Jaime S. Wurzel

Toward Multiculturalism is a book of readings designed to lay the foundation for the introduction of a broad multicultural perspective—what we call *multiculturalism*—in education. First, however, the meaning of *multiculturalism* needs to be examined. Doing so will provide a framework for understanding how the text is organized and why the readings which constitute it are included.

In this book the word *multiculturalism* is actually used in two senses. In the first, it simply refers to the fact that human existence is inherently and universally multicultural, even though throughout history, mankind has resisted recognizing it. This resistance probably stems from the survival imperative of the ethnocentric impulse; submerging oneself in similarities has been seen as a surer road to survival than trying to cope with differences. The title of this book uses multiculturalism in this universal sense, and at the same time (by using the word *toward*) recognizes that the idea is not yet fully understood nor the condition accepted as universal.

Multiculturalism can also be seen as a set of principles, a "multicultural perspective" by which people act within the context of multicultural society. These principles can be defined and learned. But the key to multiculturalism is awareness. Since the ethnocentric impulse is buried deeply and entwined with unconscious and culturally determined behaviors and patterns of thinking, most people have powerful built-in barriers to accepting society as multicultural. Thus, before one can learn the appropriate behaviors for multicultural living, one must (1) become aware of one's own ethnocentric conditioning and (2) accept the fact that society is indeed multicultural.

This book offers an approach within the framework of formal education for developing in teachers and students both multicultural awareness and the fundamental skills needed for living in a multicultural world. This approach is what we and others call multicultural education.

The Multicultural World

> All human beings live in what for them is a multicultural world, in which they are aware of different sets of others to whom different cultural attributions must be made, and of different contexts in which the different cultures of which they are aware are expected to operate. (Goodenough 1976, p. 5)

We define culture in this book as knowledge, as the shared and learned patterns of information a group uses in order to generate meaning among its members (Goodenough 1971). Every culture creates a system of shared knowledge necessary for surviving as a group and facilitating communication among its members. These shared patterns of information are both explicit and implicit. They are the products of ecological, historical, and contemporary adaptive needs. They encompass subjective dimensions (beliefs, attitudes, values), interactive dimensions (verbal and nonverbal language), and material dimensions (artifacts). Individuals within each micro- or macroculture share these patterns of information to some significant extent, which allows for communication and a relatively high degree of coherent functioning within the group.

Cultural conflict occurs when the interpretation of these cultural patterns of information are not shared with others. It is reflected in the internal (personal) and interactional (social) tensions that arise when different systems of knowledge confront one another.

But these systems of knowledge, or cultural realities, are not derived merely from macrocultural and historical variables, such as ethnicity or nationality. They arise as well from microcultural aspects of human existence—family, religion, occupation, age, sex, avocational interests, etc. A classroom, an office, a social agency, or a family may be described as a microculture in which the members or participants share a belief in certain rules, roles, behaviors and values which provide a functional ethos and a medium of communication.

When these microcultures, or identity groups, are combined with the vast array of national, ethnic, and racial groups (macrocultures) with which the world is filled, it becomes clear that multiculturalism is not an isolated phenomenon, but pervades human society. We live in a multicultural world.

Our macro- and microcultural experiences shape our world view and influence our interaction with others. In effect they determine our reality (see below "The Parable of the Prince and the Magician"). Cultural conflict takes place when differing realities clash. Communication breaks down when different perceptions of reality come into contact and reinforce cultural isolation, prejudice and mistrust.

If we accept the premise that every human being is continuously exposed to different cultural realities, we must also assume that cultural conflict is an inevitable human condition. One of the roles of multicultural education is to ameliorate that conflict, while at the same time accepting its inevitability and recognizing it as a positive element in the process of learning. Cross-cultural conflict provides a medium for cultural learning, including the development of cultural self-understanding and awareness, the expansion of knowledge of other cultural realities in the context of multiculturalism, and the improvement of cross-cultural communication skills. Denying the existence of conflict perpetuates it and blocks communication, while accepting conflict allows it to be reduced by being incorporated into the multicultural education process (see below under Stages of the Multicultural Process).

Multicultural education is often defined in oversimplified terms: the teaching of cultural

2

differences or, even more simply, historical and geographical facts, or the examination of art and artifacts from different countries and the experiencing of culinary diversity. While these activities can be useful, their scope narrows the educational potential which diversity offers and runs the risk of perpetuating separateness and reinforcing negative cultural stereotypes. We propose a more comprehensive definition, one that sees multicultural education not only as an instructional product but as a continuous process involving (1) reflection, learning and the development of cultural self-awareness, (2) the acceptance of conflict for its educational potential, (3) the willingness to learn about one's own cultural reality from interaction with others, (4) the improvement of communication with people from other cultures, and (5) the recognition of the universality of multiculturalism.

Within the context of education it is important to prepare students to expand their macro- and microcultural perspectives. This, in turn, will allow them not only to cope with conflict and change, but, most important, to accept these experiences as an integral part of their educational development. This can be accomplished by providing curricular programs which will allow students to internalize the multitude of cultural and historical experiences which shape their own and others' cultural realities.

Culture is not static. If it is a form of knowledge, as we argue above, then it is intrinsically dynamic and developmental. It changes, expands and adapts to new circumstances. Multicultural education is likewise developmental, expanding our cultural vision to provide us with the ability to become multicultural individuals in a multicultural world.

"The Parable of the Prince and the Magician," which follows, illustrates the basic points we have been making so far.

> Once upon a time there was a young prince who believed in all things but three. He did not believe in princesses, he did not believe in islands, and he did not believe in God.
>
> His father, the king, told him that such things did not exist. As there were no princesses or islands in his father's domain, and no sign of God, the prince believed his father.
>
> But then, one day, the prince ran away from his palace and came to the next land. There, to his amazement, from every coast he saw islands, and on these islands strange creatures whom he dared not name. As he was searching for a boat, a man in full evening dress approached him along the shore.
>
> "Are those real islands?" asked the young prince.
>
> "Of course they are," said the man in evening dress.
>
> "And those strange creatures?"
>
> "They are all genuine and authentic princesses."
>
> "Then God must also exist!" cried the prince.
>
> "I am God," replied the man in evening dress, with a bow.
>
> The young prince returned home as quickly as he could.
>
> "So, you are back," said his father, the king.
>
> "I have seen islands, I have seen princesses, I have seen God," said the young prince reproachfully.
>
> The king was unmoved. "Neither real islands, nor real princesses, nor a real God exists."
>
> "I saw them!" cried the prince.
>
> "Tell me how God was dressed."

"God was in full evening dress."

"Were the sleeves of his coat rolled back?"

The prince remembered that they had been.

The king smiled. "That is the uniform of a magician. You have been deceived."

At this, the prince returned to the next land and went to the same shore, where once again he came upon the man in full evening dress.

"My father, the king, has told me who you are," said the prince indignantly. "You deceived me last time, but not again. Now I know that those are not real islands and real princesses, because you are a magician."

The man on the shore smiled. "It is you who are deceived, my boy. In your father's kingdom, there are many islands and many princesses. But you are under your father's spell, so you cannot see them."

The prince pensively returned home. When he saw his father he looked him in the eye. "Father, is it true that you are not a real king, but only a magician?"

The king smiled and rolled back his sleeves. "Yes, son, I am only a magician."

"Then the man on the other shore was God."

"The man on the other shore was another magician."

"I must know the truth—the truth beyond magic."

"There is no truth beyond magic," said the king.

The prince was full of sadness. He said, "I will kill myself."

The king, by magic, caused Death to appear. Death stood in the door and beckoned to the prince. The prince shuddered. He remembered the beautiful but unreal islands and the unreal but beautiful princesses. "Very well," he said, "I can bear it."

"You see, my son," said the king, "you too, now begin to be a magician."

(Fowles, pp. 550-51)

Everyone is a prince and everyone has a father king. The voice of the father king is gentle, yet a strong guiding force. His reality is protective. He selectively provides us with the coherence and direction we need in order not to be overwhelmed by the world around us. The father king's reality is our comfortable reality until experience painfully forces us to question it.

Culture is a father king. It subtly, purposefully and without our conscious awareness, creates for us notions of reality which ultimately give a shared meaning to our interactions with others. It supplies the familiar, allowing us to understand our environment, but it also defends us against the unfamiliar. The powerful spell of culture will not let us easily accept the existence or validity of other cultural perspectives. We will hold to our own as long as we can, for there is a painful loss in admitting the relativity of our reality and the validity of others.

Yet, when the spell of culture is broken and after the grieving is over, the prince in all of us should recognize that we have become richer. We have learned about ourselves, about our capacity for magic. We have expanded our cultural vision.

The most positive lesson learned from the clashing of cultural realities is that it teaches us about our own cultural conceptions. When the prince's image of the father king was transformed by his encounter with the "man in full evening dress," he discovered a new way of relating to his father and a new way of seeing himself. Just as the conflict in the story helped the prince to understand and expand his cultural and conceptual preconditioning, so it can free us both to accept other cultural conceptions and to examine our own culture with constructive and critical eyes.

The most uncomfortable lesson in the story is about the feeble nature of knowledge. If reality is "magically" conceived, the notion that knowledge is absolute is challenged. As Joseph Bronowsky, a physicist and survivor of Auschwitz, warns: "There is no absolute knowledge. And those who claim it, whether they are scientists or dogmatists, open the door to tragedy. All information is imperfect. We have to treat it with humility. That is the human condition" (p. 175). Multiculturalism is the opposite of dogmatism, for it teaches us to accept the inevitable contradictions embedded in everything we learn.

Thus, a multicultural perspective impels us towards learning about ourselves as we attempt to comprehend the realities of others. Through this process we also learn to tolerate the uncertainty of knowledge. Aldous Huxley upon his return from his first trip around the world put it this way:

> So the journey is over and I am back again, richer by much experience and poorer by many exploded convictions, many perished certainties. For convictions and certainties are too often the concomitants of ignorance.... I set out on my travels knowing, or thinking I knew, how men should live, how be governed, how educated, what they should believe. I had my views on every activity of life. Now, on my return, I find myself without any of these pleasing certainties.... The better you understand the significance of any question, the more difficult it becomes to answer it. Those who attach a high importance to their own opinion should stay at home. When one is traveling, convictions are mislaid as easily as spectacles, but unlike spectacles, they are not easily replaced (p. 3).

STAGES OF THE MULTICULTURAL PROCESS

"The Parable of The Prince and the Magician" illustrates the role of conflict in challenging previous notions of reality. It shows a progressive movement towards cultural expansion and awareness. This section will more systematically illustrate the process by delineating stages of development. The purpose is not to set a rigid progression but to clarify conceptually the main factors intervening in the multicultural learning process. The following seven stages are identified: (1) monoculturalism, (2) cross-cultural contact, (3) cultural conflict, (4) educational interventions, (5) disequilibrium, (6) awareness, and (7) multiculturalism.

1. Monoculturalism

At this stage an individual's ways of communicating and of interpreting experience are regarded as universal or the best of all possible ways. Other ways of behaving and thinking are perceived as either strange or inferior. This is the fundamental psychosocial phenomenon of ethnocentrism:

Ethnocentrism is the technical term for the world view which holds that one's group lies at the center of everything, and that all other groups are scaled and rated with reference to one's own.... Therefore, each group nourishes its own pride and vanity, boasts itself superior, exalts its own divinities, and looks with contempt on outsiders (Sumner, pp. 12-13).

Ethnocentrism is a universal phenomenon, closely tied to the survival of the group and the preservation of the individual's social identity within it. It is also inevitable. A child's parents, environment, religion, and social traditions are all given. These affiliations, which the child takes for granted, define identity. They constitute what the child needs in order to insure his/her psychological belonging, security, and stability. Psychologically, the crux of the matter is that the familiar provides the indispensable basis for existence. Since existence is good, its accompanying groundwork seems good and desirable. Since the "familiar" is associated with the security provided by the group, it is impossible not to evaluate its meaning positively. "What is familiar tends to become a value. We come to like the style of cooking, the customs, the people, we have grown up with"(Allport, p. 24). Consequently, that which is not familiar may be denigrated or perceived as a threat to the identity of the group. Thus, defending one's values (the familiar) may lead one to the brink of hating and/or acting aggressively toward those with different values.

Ethnocentrism is inevitable since it is rooted in the impossibility of escaping from one's experience. What culture has given us and what we ourselves have acquired through experience is what we know. Everything is evaluated from that point of reference; all is perceived in relation to ourselves.

The main characteristic of the monocultural stage is that people at this point have not yet realized the inevitability of ethnocentrism, nor do they understand the universality of this process. If they have not had experience with other cultural groups, they may characterize their own cultural information as unique; if they have had some cross-cultural experience, they may characterize their own information as superior. They may also have a conscious or unconscious tendency to impose their own ways upon others and/or expect others to manifest patterns of cultural knowledge similar to theirs.

2. Cross-Cultural Contact

As in "The Parable of The Prince and the Magician," the process of multiculturalism begins by direct or indirect contact with other cultural groups. Only by contrasting different patterns of cultural information to our own can we begin the questioning process. However, at this point there is no awareness that there are diverse cultural patterns.

3. Cultural Conflict

Cultural conflict is not only the clashing of different cultural patterns. It is also the confrontation of two or more ethnocentric views. Cultural conflict takes place when two or more groups who think of their own folkways as unique collide. The resulting confrontation intensifies ethnocentrism, leading the antagonists to differentiate themselves from each other even more. At this stage, the world is perceived as divided between "us" and "them."

The results of cultural conflict vary in degree of intensity: from miscommunication, reinforcement of false perceptions, and different forms of hostility, to individual and social feelings of depression, marginality, and alienation. Cultural conflict is particularly damaging if one group forces its ways on another.

> When we force people of another culture to make an adjustment to ours, by that much we are destroying the integrity of their realities. When too many adjustments of this sort are required too fast, the personality disintegrates and the result is an alienated, disassociated individual who cannot feel really at home in either culture (Lehmer, p. D-4).

In American classrooms, cultural conflict is evidenced most often when the value, behavior, and knowledge patterns which minorities and international students learn at home clash with the values of the majority culture. The ways in which this clash of cultural patterns is manifest may range from seemingly simple and concrete things such as the use of language, to more abstract processes, such as the advocacy of differing values. The consequences of cultural conflict in the classroom may range from subtle misunderstandings which affect individual learning to the withdrawal of students from the educational system.

4. Educational Interventions

A fundamental premise here is that educational interventions can contribute to the amelioration of cultural conflict and the development of a multicultural perspective. Curricular programs can serve to narrow the communication gap in micro- and macrocultural conflict situations. We will discuss what constitutes an effective educational program under six headings: (1) self-awareness, (2) human condition themes and cultural differences, (3) cognitive imposition vs. cognitive choice, (4) personalization of knowledge, (5) inquiry vs. dogmatism, and (6) microcultural realities.

Self-awareness. The improvement of communication with others will not necessarily follow from the objective learning of each other's cultural characteristics. It involves also a willingness and ability to examine and understand our own patterns, to become aware of the degree to which our behaviors, beliefs and styles of communication are based on cultural learning buried deep in our childhood experience.

Often, it is not until we confront other cultural perspectives that we begin to question our own. It is important that curricular programs, which have as an objective the improvement of communication with other cultural groups, present material that will allow students to relate the content to themselves and help them begin this process of self-discovery. All too frequently well-intentioned educational programs pursue cross-cultural studies by providing lists of cultural traits or purely factual information about one culture or another. The need for students to become culturally self-aware is ignored and the cultures studied, as often as not, end up being stereotyped. In short, the stimulation of cultural self-awareness fosters a more meaningful understanding of other cultures.

Human condition themes and cultural differences. Educational interventions need to involve the study of our common humanity as well as cultural differences. Curricular interventions which only highlight the latter tend, unknowingly, to foster separateness and reinforce negative cultural stereotypes which, in turn, may hamper communication. Similarly, too much attention to the former may lead to the simple conclusion that cultural difference is

7

a minor issue. A balance between the two is essential to the process of cross-cultural conflict amelioration.

It is fundamental that multicultural curricular materials should foster the development of awareness about the nature of the human condition. There are two human condition themes which we feel are particularly important to be dealt with in the context of multicultural education interventions.

The first is the *universality of ethnocentrism and prejudice.* To understand ourselves in human condition terms involves the examination of how ethnocentrism and prejudice are derived from universal cognitive processes and how they are linked to the self-preservation of the individual and the group.

The second involves *the need for cultural conformity.* This involves examining our need to conform to cultural norms for the sake of cultural cohesion and communication. In addition it entails reflecting on the conflicts that conformity imposes on the individual within the culture.

In conjunction with human condition themes, the comparative examination of cultural differences (e.g., values, communication styles, customary behaviors, patterns of thinking, etc.) contributes to the facilitation of communication and the reduction of cultural conflict.

Cognitive imposition vs. cognitive choice. The former term refers to the imposition, in instruction and curricula, of cultural patterns alien to the students without regard to their own identity and cultural needs. This is a particularly significant issue when the educational intervention is geared to the amelioration of cultural conflict between majority and minority groups. *Cognitive imposition* fosters cultural assimilation and the negation of native culture. *Cognitive choice* suggests selective adaptation to the majority culture, involving a conscious adoption of behavior designed to facilitate communication and effective functioning in the majority culture.

Cognitive choice for minorities and the foreign-born needs to be combined in educational interventions with the fostering of respect for different cultural patterns by members of the majority culture. When majority and minority groups consciously learn each other's cultural patterns, they are more likely to accept the proposition that neither one is deficient or inferior to the other.

Personalization of knowledge. An important goal of multicultural educational interventions is to encourage the trend toward making knowledge personally relevant to the learner. Instruction and curricula most often treat knowledge as separate from the personal or emotional. This attitude is based on Western technological notions of science, which tend to devalue subjective experience. The end result is that subjective issues to which emotion is normally attached are seldom dealt with in the school context. When they are, they become the responsibility of the counselor or psychologist and are rarely seen as a legitimate part of classroom learning, although emotional reaction may run fiercely as an undercurrent through the class—especially a multicultural class!

Formal education, by deemphasizing the affective in teaching and learning, also dehumanizes the educational process. Educational institutions are more concerned with transmitting and acquiring technical knowledge than they are with understanding and exploring the human dimensions of existence. Thus, most of what is taught is depersonalized. People and ideas are studied in a way that strips them of the emotional and cultural contexts in which they exist or existed. The cultures of ethnic groups and foreign countries are studied in curricula that emphasize culinary differences, quaint dress and heroic exploits of cultural and national heroes. Seldom do we deal with the values and complex emotions encompassed in

8

belonging to a particular group. This depersonalization of knowledge and superficial approach to culture is reflected in classroom interaction. Teachers rarely get to know their students and the students seldom learn about each other as emotional and cultural beings other than as determined by the prevailing culture of the classroom.

Understanding one's own cultural reality is both an emotional and intellectual experience. The experience of self-discovery and cultural expansion involves both that which is comfortable and that which is not. Relating learning to oneself entails the questioning of basic premises about oneself. Self-discovery almost always involves some personal and emotional stress and some personal sense of loss.

Educational interventions geared to ameliorating cultural conflict and advancing the concept of multiculturalism have the opportunity of challenging entrenched cultural views about knowing by personalizing the learning experience. The teachers can talk about their own lives and the students can relate what they feel as well as what they think.

Inquiry vs. dogmatism. Inquiry involves the development of a humble attitude towards knowledge, the questioning of information and the rejection of absolutes. Its opposite is dogmatic thinking. Multiculturalism calls for an attitude of inquiry and a willingness to withhold judgment and to deal with the complexity of cultural issues. If the notion that there are no simple answers to cultural conflict can be established through educational interventions, then progress will have been made in fostering a multicultural style of thinking.

Microcultural realities. Once again, it is important to understand the role of microcultural relationships in cultural conflict. Two or more individuals, thinking and acting together in a particular situation, may be considered a microculture (a group). The relationship patterns they develop vis-a-vis one another serve as reinforcements to group or microcultural identity and facilitate communication. As students learn about variations of behavior in relation to group identity, they also learn to understand the arbitrariness of context in establishing cultural rules and the extraordinary ability individuals have to adapt and expand their cultural knowledge. It also demonstrates that ethnicity and nationality are not the only variables in the process of communication and cross-cultural relations. There are diverse microcultural identities which affect these processes.

5. Disequilibrium

In his theoretical discussions of cognitive development, Piaget proposes that disequilibrium of mental structures is the necessary condition for the assimilation of new knowledge. He argues that knowledge and intellectual development are facilitated by the twin mental processes of assimilation and accommodation. As interaction with the environment occurs, the child assimilates certain elements into already existing mental structures. Equilibrium in mental organization is upset as mental structures change to accommodate new data. An analogy using the homeostatic processes involved in body temperature control illustrates this:

> As the body cools, temperature equilibrium is upset. Information on changes in the state of the system are assimilated in the hypothalamus, and the autonomic nervous system accommodates by setting in motion certain changes that enable the body to take care of the cooling blood. Vessels close to the skin contract so that less surface area is exposed to

the cold. Shivering increases production of heat in the body (Lavatelly et al., p. 54).

We are suggesting that a similar process takes place in multicultural learning. The shivering is the disequilibrium experienced in cultural conflict and/or as a result of educational intervention in which new cultural information has been introduced which must be accumulated and to which the individual must accommodate. In the context of cultural conflict amelioration, disequilibrium involves "the balance between the need to protect sameness and continuity and the need to accommodate change" (Ackerman, p. 85).

Disequilibrium in the multicultural process occurs when previously held knowledge is challenged or is invalidated. At this stage, students begin to doubt and question some of their attitudes and beliefs. Hopefully, an inner emotional and intellectual struggle will take place as students begin to internalize the concept of culture and its power and arbitrariness in influencing thought and behavior.

6. Awareness

At this point the individual has at last wholly emerged from the ethnocentric capsule and has begun to understand the concept of culture. Equilibrium has been reestablished and the process of accommodation to a new knowledge has started.

7. Multiculturalism

The attainment of a multicultural perspective is the achievement of a new mental and emotional consciousness that enables individuals to negotiate more readily new formations of reality.

It entails internalizing the historical and contemporary contradictions that are embedded in the human condition. The multicultural style of thinking and feeling is tolerant of cultural differences, the ambiguities of knowledge, and variations in human perspective. It rejects simple answers and fosters inquiry. The multicultural person questions the arbitrary nature of his or her own culture and accepts the proposition that others who are culturally different can enrich their experience. Thus, to be multicultural is to be aware and able to incorporate and synthesize different systems of cultural knowledge into one's own. Peter Adler has put it eloquently:

> Multicultural man is the person who is intellectually and emotionally committed to the fundamental unity of all human beings while at the same time he recognizes, legitimizes, accepts, and appreciates the fundamental differences that lie between people from different cultures. This new kind of man cannot be defined by the languages he speaks, the countries he has visited, or the number of international contacts he has made. Nor is he defined by his profession, his place of residence, or his cognitive sophistication. Instead, multicultural man is recognized by the configuration of his outlooks and world views, by the way he remains open to the imminence of experience (p. 23-24).

References and Bibliography

Ackerman, N.W. *The Psycho-Dynamics of Family Life.* New York: Basic Books, 1958.

Adler, P. "Beyond Cultural Identity: Reflections upon Cultural and Multicultural Man." In R. Brislin, ed. *Topics in Culture Learning: Concepts, Applications, and Research.* Honolulu: University of Hawaii Press, 1977.

Allport, G. *The Nature of Prejudice.* Reading, MA.: Addison-Wesley Publishing Co., 1954.

Amir, Y. "Contact Hypothesis in Ethnic Relations." *Psychological Bulletin* 71 (1969): 319-342.

Appleton, N. *Cultural Pluralism in Education: Theoretical Foundations.* New York: Longman, 1983.

Asante, M.K.; E. Newark; and C. Blake. *Handbook of Intercultural Communication.* Beverly Hills, CA: Sage Publications, 1979.

Bagby, J.W. "Dominance in Binocular Rivalry in Mexico and the U. S." In Al-Issa, I. and W. Dennis. *Cross Cultural Studies and Behavior.* New York: Holt, Rinehart & Winston, 1970.

Banks, J.A. *Teaching Strategies for Ethnic Studies.* Boston: Allyn & Bacon, 1975.

Barry, H.; I. Child; and H. Bacon. "The Relation of Child Training to Subsistence Economy." *American Anthropologist* 61(1959): 51-63.

Bem, D.J. *Beliefs, Attitudes and Human Affairs.* Belmont, CA: Wadsworth, 1970.

Berry, J. W. "On Cross-Cultural Compatability." *International Journal of Psychology* 4(1969): 119-128.

Birdwhistell, R. *Kinesics and Context.* Philadelphia: University of Pennsylvania Press, 1970.

Bloom, L. and J. Lahey. *Language Development and Language Disorders.* New York: John Wiley & Sons, 1978.

Bolinger, D. *Aspects of Language.* New York: Harcourt, Brace & Jovanovich, Inc.,1975.

Brislin, R. "Structured Approaches to Dealing with Prejudice and Intercultural Misunderstanding." *International Journal of Group Tensions* 1 & 2 (1978): 33 48.

_____ *Cross Cultural Encounters.* Elmsford, NY: Pergamon Press, 1982.

Bronowsky, J. *The Ascent of Man.* Boston: Little, Brown & Co., 1973.

Byers, P. and H. Byers. *Non-verbal Communication and the Education of Children in Functions of Language in the Classroom.* Ed. by C. B. Cazden; V. John; and D. Hymes. New York: Teachers College Press, 1972.

Cohen, Y. "The Shaping of Men's Minds." In M. J. Wax and S. Diamond. *Anthropological Perspectives on Education* (pp. 19-50). New York: Basic Books, 1971.

Cook, S.W. and C. Selltiz. "Some Factors Which Influence the Attitudinal Outcomes of Personal Contact." *International Social Bulletin* 7(1955): 51-58.

Cole, H. and S. Scribner. *Culture and Thought: A Psychological Introduction.* New York: John Wiley & Sons, Inc., 1974.

Collins, J. J. *Anthropology: Culture, Society & Evolution.* Englewood Cliffs, NJ: Prentice-Hall, 1975.

Davidson, A. R. and E. Thomson. "Cross-Cultural Studies of Attitudes and Beliefs." In H. C. Triandis and R. W. Brislin (eds.) *Handbook of Cross-Cultural Psychology, Vol. 5, Social Psychology.* Boston: Allyn & Bacon, Inc., 1980.

Dawson, J. L. H. "Attitudinal Consistency and Conflict in West Africa." *International Journal of Psychology* 4 (1969): 38-53.

_____ "Attitude Change and Conflict among Australian Aborigines." *Australian Journal of Psychology* 21 (1969): 101-116.

_____"Exchange Theory and Comparison Level Changes among Australian Aborigines." *British Journal of Social and Clinical Psychology* 8 (1969): 133-140.

Deregowski, J. "Pictorial Recognition in Subjects from a Relatively Pictureless Environment." *African Social Research* 5 (1968): 356-364.

_____"Difficulties in Pictorial Depth Perception in Africa." *British Journal of Psychology* 59 (1968): 195-204.

Dollar, D. *Social Learning and Imitation.* New Haven, CT: Yalconin Press, 1957.

Dundes, A., ed. *The Study of Folklore.* Englewood Cliffs, NJ: Prentice-Hall, 1965.

Fitzpatrick, J. P. *Puerto Rican Americans: The Meaning of Migration to the Mainland.* Englewood Cliffs, NJ: Prentice-Hall, 1971.

Foster, G. M. *Traditional Cultures and the Impact of Technological Change.* New York: Harper & Row, 1962.

Fowles, J. *The Magus.* New York: Dell Publishing Co., 1977.

Franklin, V. and R. Rodman. *An Introduction to Language.* New York: Holt, Rinehart & Winston, 1974.

Goodenough, W. *Culture, Language, and Society,* Reading, MA: Addison-Wesley, 1971.

_____"Multiculturalism As the Normal Human Experience." *Anthropology of Education Quarterly* 7 (4), 1976.

Grobman, A. and D. Landes. *Genocide: Critical Issues of the Holocaust.* New York: Rossel, 1983.

Gudykunst, W. B. *Intercultural Communication Theory: Current Perspectives.* Beverly Hills, CA: Sage Publications, 1982.

Hall, E. T. *The Silent Language.* New York: Doubleday Publishing Co., 1959.

Henry, J. *On Education.* New York: Random House, 1977.

Hofstede, G. *Culture's Consequences: International Differences in Work-Related Values.* Beverly Hills, CA: Sage Publications, 1984.

Hoopes, D. S. "Intercultural Communication Concepts and the Psychology of Intercultural Experience." In M. D. Pusch, *Multicultural Education: A Cross-Cultural Training Approach.* Yarmouth, ME: Intercultural Press, Inc., 1979.

Huxley, A. *New York Times.* Interview. 17 September 1926.

Inkeles, A. and D. Smith. *Becoming Modern: Individual Change in Six Different Countries.* Cambridge, MA: Harvard University Press, 1974.

Johnson, N. B. "The Material Culture of Public School Classrooms." *Anthropology and Education Quarterly* 6 (3), 1981.

Kaplan, R. B. "Cultural Thought Patterns in Intercultural Education." *Language Learning* 16 (1977): 1-20.

Katz, D. "The Functional Basis of Attitudes." *Public Opinion Quarterly* 24 (1960): 164-204.

Kelman, H. C. "Changing Attitudes through International Activities." *Journal of Social Issues* 18 (1962): 68-87.

Kluckhohn, F. and F. Strodtbeck. *Variations in Value Orientation.* Evanston, IL: Row Peterson, 1961.

Kochman, T. *Black and White Styles in Conflict.* Chicago: University of Chicago Press, 1981.

Kuper, L. *Genocide.* New Haven: Yale University Press, 1981.

LaBarre, W. "Paralinguistics, Kinesics, and Cultural Anthropology." In T. Sebeok, *Approaches to Semiotics.* The Hague: Mouton Publishing, 1964.

Lavatelly, C. S., et al. *Elementary School Curriculum.* New York: Holt, Rinehart & Winston, 1972.

Lehmer, M. "Navajos Want Their Own Schools." *San Francisco Examiner and Chronicle.* 14 December, 1969.

LeVine, R. A. *Culture, Behavior and Personality.* Chicago: Aldine Publishing Co., 1973.

McClelland, D. C. *The Achieving Society.* New York: Van Nostrand, 1961.

Milgram, S. *Obedience to Authority.* New York: Harper & Row, 1974.

Montagu, A. and F. Matson. *The Dehumanization of Man.* New York: McGraw-Hill, 1983.

Nine-Curt, C. J. *Non-Verbal Communication in Puerto Rico.* Cambridge, MA: National Assessment and Dissemination Center, 1976.

Ogbu, J. O. *Minority Education and Caste: The American System in Cross-Cultural Perspective.* New York: Academic Press, 1978.

Padilla, A., ed. *Acculturation, Theory, Models and Some New Findings.* Boulder, CO: West View Press, 1980.

Piaget, J. *The Origins of Intelligence in Children.* New York: W. W. Norton & Co., 1963.

Ramirez, M. and A. Castaneda. *Cultural Democracy, Bicognitive Development and Education.* New York: Academic Press, 1974.

Robins, M. C.; B. R. DeWalt; and P. J. Pelto. "Climate and Behavior: A Biocultural Study." *Journal of Cross Cultural Psychology* 3 (1972): 331-344.

Rosenfeld, G. *Shut Those Thick Lips.* New York: Holt & Rinehart, 1971.

Salter, C. A. and A. Teger. "Change in Attitudes toward Other Nations As a Function of the Type of International Contact." *Sociometrix* 48 (1975): 281.

Samovar, L. A. and R. E. Porter. *Intercultural Communication: A Reader.* Belmont, CA: Wadsworth, 1976.

Seda-Bonilla, E. *Interaccion Social Y Personalidad en Una Comunidad de Puerto Rico.* San Juan: Edidiones Juan Ponce de Leon, 1969.

Segall, M. H.; P. T. Campbell; and M. J. Herskowitz. *The Influence of Culture on Perception.* Indianapolis: Bobbs-Merrill, 1966.

Stewart, E. C. and M. J. Bennett. *American Cultural Patterns.: A Cross-Cultural Perspective* 2d. rev. Yarmouth, ME: Intercultural Press, 1989.

Strom, M. and W. Parson. *Facing History and Ourselves.* Brookline, MA: Facing History Foundation, 1983.

Sumner, W. B. *Folkways.* Lexington, MA: Ginn & Co., 1960.

Triandis, H. C. "Subjective Culture and Interpersonal Relations across Cultures." *Annals of the NY Academy of Sciences* 285 (1977): 418-434.

Valdes, J. M., ed. *Culture Bound.* New York: Cambridge University Press, 1986.

Werner, E. E. *Cross-Cultural Child Development.* Monterey, CA: Brooks/Cole, 1979.

Whiting, B. B. and J. W. Whiting. *Children of Six Cultures: A Psycho-Cultural Analysis.* Cambridge, MA: Harvard University Press, 1975.

Witkin, H. A. "A Cognitive Style Approach to Cross-Cultural Research." *International Journal of Psychology* 2 (1967): 1983.

Wurzel, J. S. "The Relational Orientations of Puerto Rican and Anglo-American Students." *Journal of Intercultural Relations.* 7 (2), 1983.

_____"Teaching Reflective Thinking Cultural Constraints. Cross-Cultural Responses." Conference on Thinking. Harvard University, 1984. Unpublished Manuscript.

Selected Readings

The purpose of the selected readings is to assist people in developing a multicultural style of thinking, feeling and self-awareness which will enable them to cope more readily with change and conflict.

The criteria for the organization and selection of the readings follow the philosophical guidelines for the development of educational interventions mentioned before. The book combines human condition themes with cultural variation themes. It personalizes knowledge by presenting autobiographical accounts of cultural experiences. It is geared to foster inquiry by encouraging readers to question their own cultural preconceptions.

As mentioned earlier, we emphasize the need to integrate human condition and cultural difference themes. The book closely follows this idea. The first part of the book deals explicitly with human condition issues such as ethnocentrism, the nature of prejudice, and cultural conformity and resistance. The second part deals with cultural variation in socialization, value orientation, cognitive style, and verbal and nonverbal cultural patterns.

While an organizational distinction is made between human condition and cultural difference themes, it should be noted that in many of the readings these themes are intertwined with each other. A total separation of the two would be artificial and would undermine the richness of the message being conveyed. Thus, the reader should be ready to find, throughout the book, the inevitable interaction between human condition themes and cultural differences.

Consistent with the notion of personalizing knowledge, many of the articles are based on personal accounts of cultural experiences. Lee and Briggs relate their futile attempts at becoming "natives" in the cultures they studied, while Baldwin and Ellis tell us about their personal encounters with prejudice. Jones relates his frightening experience with notions of obedience and conformity. We hope that the honesty these authors demonstrate will serve as a source of inspiration for readers to search into their own lives and perhaps write similar or even better accounts of their own cross-cultural experiences.

Personal accounts are complemented by more traditional research articles in the areas of anthropology, psychology and education. These are geared to be provocative while also being informative. However, the reader is encouraged always to question the conclusions of the authors and perhaps even perceive how the authors' respective disciplines become microcultures which guide their formulations of issues and answers.

The readings in this volume cover numerous salient multicultural themes. The study questions at the end of each section are geared to stimulate further inquiry into the content of the readings. We hope that the book will provide readers with significant cultural insights that will motivate them to investigate and expand their knowledge beyond this text.

Part I
Human
Condition
Themes

INTRODUCTION

Ethnocentrism refers to the universal phenomenon of appraising the environment according to one's own experience and cultural background. *Ethnocentrism* is seen as inevitable since experience and culture inescapably serve as the individual's point of reference from which the world is evaluated.

Lee ("Eating Christmas in the Kalahari") and Briggs ("Kapluna Daughter") convey the inevitability of ethnocentrism by illustrating the difficulty anthropologists have in relinquishing their cultural ways of behaving and evaluating their situations. At the same time, the authors demonstrate the positive role that colliding ethnocentric assumptions about human relations played in enhancing their understanding of themselves and of the cultures they studied.

In both readings the anthropologists are compelled to deal with the impact that their own deeply held cultural notions of competition, individualism and independence had on the cultures they attempted to be part of. Thus, the articles raise questions such as these: How "native" can one become in another culture? Is it possible to be an objective cross-cultural observer? How do people change their cultures? Do some aspects of culture change faster than others?

These two articles have important implications for education. Teachers, especially when dealing with diverse cultural populations, need to identify potential cultural conflicts and become aware of their own inescapable ethnocentric behaviors and feelings. By doing so, they can also help their students understand that ethnocentrism is part of the human condition.

The next set of readings deals with the *nature of prejudice*. All the articles touch upon three essential, interrelated themes: a) the role of prejudice in protecting one's self-esteem, b) the impact of prejudice in denigrating the self-esteem of cultural minorities, and c) the relationship between prejudice and the need to create categories which serve to cognitively organize the world around us.

The tendency to raise one's self-esteem at the expense of others is evident in Ellis' description of the reasons for joining the Ku Klux Klan (from Turkel's "American Dreams: Lost and Found"). Ellis tells us how in the midst of poverty and other personal misfortunes, he comes across the Klan. In joining it, he feels he has found the answer to his problems. His prejudice serves to provide him with a sense of purpose and a great feeling of self-esteem:

> I really began to get bitter. I didn't know who to blame. I tried to find somebody. I began to blame it on black people. I had to hate somebody.... You gotta have somethin' to look at to hate.... I joined the Klan, went from member to chaplain, from chaplain to vice president, from Vice President to President.

Ellis' psychological comfort was attained at the expense of the psychological comfort of blacks. His pain was ameliorated by inflicting pain onto a visible cultural group.

The contrasting personal accounts in this section of readings expose some uncomfortable human condition issues which need to be addressed within the context of multicultural education, that is: (1) the relationship between prejudice, power and the meeting of self-esteem needs and (2) the impact of historical prejudice on the identity and self-worth of persecuted minorities.

The next two readings, Spindler's "Beth Anne—A Case Study of Culturally Defined Adjustment and Teacher Perceptions" and Simmons' "Stereotypes: Explaining People Who Are Different," while also touching on these issues, convey in addition some of the cognitive aspects of prejudice.

The articles by Spindler and Simmons have been selected because they reinforce our awareness of the inevitable cognitive tendency to evaluate the world according to categories. They also show us that prejudicial attitudes are based on such cognitive processes.

In their need to cope with their environment and to organize the vast quantities of data to which they are exposed, people classify their experience according to categories derived from cultural conditioning. In doing so they inevitably group together things which are discriminately different. As a result they respond to objects or people in terms of the categories they have created rather than in terms of the individual's uniqueness.

When we see a new person, we evaluate him or her according to the categories we have in our head. We know, therefore, how to react to an individual who by virtue of appearance has been categorized as "dangerous." Similarly, we know how to behave if that person falls into the category of "friendly." The mind, in its role as a survival mechanism, is called upon for immediate reaction. Clearly, it is easier and quicker to prejudge according to categories (stereotypes) than it is to examine all the information available and to make judgments based on unique reality. Thus, a natural and inevitable cognitive process often leads to the harmful imposition of inaccurate attributes and stereotypic characterizations onto others.

The article by Spindler shows a clear example of the impact of imposed categorization on others, even if the attributed category is positive. Teachers evaluated Beth Anne as best-adjusted student on the basis of culturally defined expectations of behavior and appearance rather than on the basis of who she really was. On the surface she conformed to the category: she dressed well, she was quiet and obedient. However, Spindler in his study uncovers a Beth Anne who hardly fits the category her teachers have imposed on her. He concludes:

> The culturally induced blindness of her teachers was in a certain real sense killing her and in ways no less painful than those in which minority children were and are being "killed" in many American schools.

While Spindler points out the powerful impact of culturally conceived categories, even if the participants belong to the same culture, Simmons' article shows us how the cognitive tendency to categorize allows for the development of prejudicial stereotypes which hamper intercultural relations.

As Simmons analyzes the mutual images, perceptions and expectations of Anglo-Americans and Mexican-Americans, we become aware of the thin distinction between categorizing and prejudicial stereotyping. While the former may be unintentional or out of awareness, the latter may be used to justify or rationalize one's behavior towards others. As Simmons points out, the negative Anglo stereotypes towards Mexican-Americans may serve to justify maintaining the inequality between the groups.

The next two readings by Jones ("You Will Do As Directed") and Dixon ("Beating the Man") deal with the notions of *conformity and resistance to cultural norms.*

Every individual in society is faced with the decision of whether to challenge cultural norms or to conform to them. While the ways of conforming or defying may differ from culture to culture, all individuals must deal, at least in thought if not in action, with issues such as obedience to authority or acting differently from conventional standards.

The propensity to conform to normative expectations is part of the human condition. Every culture requires a high degree of conformity in order to function coherently. However, in extreme situations, the same need to conform can make us relegate our individual responsibility to traditional expectations, accepted cultural conventions or the demands of legitimate authority.

Jones' article illustrates this human propensity to conform. It raises fundamental questions regarding the role of the individual in society and the constraints which make resistance to norms or authority very difficult. Similarly, the article demonstrates symbolically how culture, like authority, can arbitrarily manipulate us into behaving like everyone else.

The article by Dixon also deals with resistance and conformity. It describes the culture of a prison. It shows how inmates, having lost all control over their lives, regain some sense of dignity by subtly resisting institutional norms. In doing so they create new norms known and shared only by them. As they resiliently adjust to their situation, they create a clandestine culture of their own, with their own language, symbols, and systems of rewards and punishments. Ironically, as they challenge the norms of the institution they begin to conform to new norms which they must follow in order to survive and gain acceptance among their peers.

Both articles have strong implications for education, especially in relation to notions of authority within the microculture of the school. Jones illustrates the potential power of teachers to manipulate behavior and thought. He also sheds vivid light on the proclivity of students to follow and obey without critically examining their thoughts and actions. Dixon also reveals the potential dangers of institutional authoritarianism which, indirectly, offers an explanation for student alienation. Like inmates, students may need to gain a sense of power and control by creating subtle social rules of peer behavior which conflict with those of the institution.

A. ETHNOCENTRISM

Eating Christmas
in the Kalahari

by Richard Borshay Lee

EDITOR'S NOTE: *The !Kung and other Bushmen speak click languages. In the story, three different clicks are used:*

1. The dental click (/), as in /ai/ai, /ontah, and /gaugo. The click is sometimes written in English as tsk-tsk.

2. The alveopalatal click (!), as in Ben!a and !Kung.

3. The lateral click (//), as in //gom. Clicks function as consonants; a word may have more than one, as in /n!au.

The !Kung Bushmen's knowledge of Christmas is thirdhand. The London Missionary Society brought the holiday to the southern Tswana tribes in the early nineteenth century. Later, native catechists spread the idea far and wide among the Bantu-speaking pastoralists, even in the most remote corners of the Kalahari Desert. The Bushmen's idea of the Christmas story, stripped to its essentials, is "Praise the birth of white man's god-chief"; what keeps their interest in the holiday high is the Tswana-Herero custom of slaughtering an ox for his Bushmen neighbors as an annual goodwill gesture. Since the 1930s, part of the Bushmen's annual round of activities has included a December congregation at the cattle posts for trading, marriage brokering, and several days of trance-dance feasting at which the local Tswana headman is host.

As a social anthropologist working with !Kung Bushmen, I found that the Christmas ox custom suited my purposes. I had come to the Kalahari to study the hunting and gathering subsistence economy of the !Kung, and to accomplish this it was essential not to provide them with food, share my own food, or interfere in any way with their food-gathering activities. While liberal handouts of tobacco and medical supplies were appreciated, they were scarcely adequate to erase the glaring disparity in wealth between the anthropologist, who maintained a two-month inventory of canned goods, and the Bushmen, who rarely had a day's supply of food on hand. My approach, while paying off in terms of data, left me open to frequent accusations of stinginess and hard-heartedness. By their lights, I was a miser.

The Christmas ox was to be my way of saying thank you for the cooperation of the past year; and since it was to be our last Christmas in the field, I determined to slaughter the largest, meatiest ox that money could buy, insuring that the feast and trance-dance would be a success.

Through December I kept my eyes open at the wells as the cattle were brought down for watering. Several animals were offered, but none had quite the grossness that I had in mind. Then, ten days before the holiday, a Herero friend led an ox of astonishing size and mass up to our camp. It was solid black, stood five feet high at the shoulder, had a five-foot span of horns, and must have weighed 1,200 pounds on the hoof. Food consumption calculations are my specialty, and I quickly figured that bones and viscera aside, there was enough meat — at least four pounds — for every man, woman, and child of the 150 Bushmen in the vicinity of /ai/ai who were expected at the feast.

Having found the right animal at last, I paid the Herero £20 ($56) and asked him to keep the beast with his herd until Christmas day. The next morning word spread among the people that the big solid black one was the ox chosen by /ontah (my Bushman name; it means, roughly, "whitey") for the Christmas feast. That afternoon I received the first delegation. Ben!a, an outspoken sixty-year-old mother of five, came to the point slowly.

"Where were you planning to eat Christmas?"

"Right here at /ai/ai," I replied.

"Alone or with others?"

"I expect to invite all the people to eat Christmas with me."

"Eat what?"

"I have purchased Yehave's black ox, and I am going to slaughter and cook it."

"That's what we were told at the well but refused to believe it until we heard it from yourself."

"Well, it's the black one," I replied expansively, although wondering what she was driving at.

"Oh, no!" Ben!a groaned, turning to her group. "They were right." Turning back to me she asked, "Do you expect us to eat that bag of bones?"

"Bag of bones! It's the biggest ox at /ai/ai."

"Big, yes, but old. And thin. Everybody knows there's no meat on that old ox. What did you expect us to eat off it, the horns?"

Everybody chuckled at Ben!a's one-liner as they walked away, but all I could manage was a weak grin.

That evening it was the turn of the young men. They came to sit at our evening fire. /gaugo, about my age, spoke to me man-to-man.

"/ontah, you have always been square with us," he lied. "What has happened to change your heart? That sack of guts and bones of Yehave's will hardly feed one camp, let alone all the Bushmen around /ai/ai." And he proceeded to enumerate the seven camps in the /ai/ai vicinity, family by family. "Perhaps you have forgotten that we are not few, but many. Or are you too blind to tell the difference between a proper cow and an old wreck? That ox is thin to the point of death."

"Look, you guys," I retorted, "that is a beautiful animal, and I'm sure you will eat it with pleasure at Christmas."

"Of course we will eat it; it's food. But it won't fill us up to the point where we will have enough strength to dance. We will eat and go home to bed with stomachs rumbling."

That night as we turned in, I asked my wife, Nancy: "What did you think of the black ox?"

"It looked enormous to me. Why?"

"Well, about eight different people have told me I got gypped; that the ox is nothing but bones."

"What's the angle?" Nancy asked. "Did they have a better one to sell?"

"No, they just said that it was going to be a grim Christmas because there won't be enough meat to go around. Maybe I'll get an independent judge to look at the beast in the morning."

Bright and early, Halingisi, a Tswana cattle owner, appeared at our camp. But before I could ask him to give me his opinion on Yehave's black ox, he gave me the eye signal that indicated a confidential chat. We left the camp and sat down.

"/ontah, I'm surprised at you: you've lived here for three years and still haven't learned anything about cattle."

"But what else can a person do but choose the biggest, strongest animal one can find?" I retorted.

"Look, just because an animal is big doesn't mean that it has plenty of meat on it. The black one was a beauty when it was younger, but now it is thin to the point of death."

"Well I've already bought it. What can I do at this stage?"

"Bought it already? I thought you were just considering it. Well, you'll have to kill it and serve it, I suppose. But don't expect much of a dance to follow."

My spirits dropped rapidly. I could believe that Ben!a and/gaugo just might be putting me on about the black ox, but Halingisi seemed to be an impartial critic. I went around that day feeling as though I had bought a lemon of a used car.

In the afternoon it was Tomazo's turn. Tomazo is a fine hunter, a top trance performer (see "The Trance Cure of the !Kung Bushmen," *Natural History*, November, 1967), and one of my most reliable informants. He approached the subject of the Christmas cow as part of my continuing Bushmen education.

"My friend, the way it is with us Bushmen," he began, "is that we love meat. And even more than that, we love fat. When we hunt we always search for the fat ones, the ones dripping with layers of white fat: fat that turns into a clear, thick oil in the cooking pot, fat that slides down your gullet, fills your stomach and gives you a roaring diarrhea," he rhapsodized.

"So, feeling as we do," he continued, "it gives us pain to be served such a scrawny thing as Yehave's black ox. It is big, yes, and no doubt its giant bones are good for soup, but fat is what we really crave and so we will eat Christmas this year with a heavy heart."

The prospect of a gloomy Christmas now had me worried, so I asked Tomazo what I could do about it.

"Look for a fat one, a young one ...smaller, but fat. Fat enough to make us //gom ('evacuate the bowels'), then we will be happy."

My suspicions were aroused when Tomazo said that he happened to know of a young, fat, barren cow that the owner was willing to part with. Was Toma working on commission, I wondered? But I dispelled this unworthy thought when we approached the Herero owner of the cow in question and found that he had decided not to sell.

The scrawny wreck of a Christmas ox now became the talk of the /ai/ai water hole and was the first news told to the outlying groups as they began to come in from the bush for the feast. What finally convinced me that real trouble might be brewing was the visit from u!au, an old conservative with a reputation for fierceness. His nickname meant spear and referred to an incident thirty years ago in which he had speared a man to death. He had an intense manner; fixing me with his eyes, he said in clipped tones:

"I have only just heard about the black ox today, or else I would have come here earlier. /ontah, do you honestly think you can serve meat like that to people and avoid a fight?" He paused, letting the implications sink in. "I don't mean fight you, /ontah; you are a white man. I mean a fight between Bushmen. There are many fierce ones here, and with such a small quantity of meat to distribute, how can you give everybody a fair share? Someone is sure to accuse another of taking too much or hogging all the choice pieces. Then you will see what happens when some go hungry while others eat."

The possibility of at least a serious argument struck me as all too real. I had witnessed the tension that surrounds the distribution of meat from a kudu or gemsbok kill, and had documented many arguments that sprang up from a real or imagined slight in meat distribution. The owners of a kill may spend up to two hours arranging and rearranging the piles of meat under the gaze of a circle of recipients before handing them out. And I also knew that the Christmas feast at /ai/ai would be bringing together groups that had feuded in the past.

Convinced now of the gravity of the situation, I went in earnest to search for a second cow; but all my inquiries failed to turn one up.

The Christmas feast was evidently going to be a disaster, and the incessant complaints about the meagerness of the ox had already taken the fun out of it for me. Moreover, I was getting bored with the wisecracks, and after losing my temper a few times, I resolved to serve the beast anyway. If the meat fell short, the hell with it. In the Bushmen idiom, I announced to all who would listen:

"I am a poor man and blind. If I have chosen one that is too old and too thin, we will eat it anyway and see if there is enough meat there to quiet the rumbling of our stomachs."

On hearing this speech, Ben!a offered me a rare word of comfort. "It's thin," she said philosophically, "but the bones will make a good soup."

At dawn Christmas morning, instinct told me to turn over the butchering and cooking to a friend and take off with Nancy to spend Christmas alone in the bush. But curiosity kept me from retreating. I wanted to see what such a scrawny ox looked like on butchering, and if there *was* going to be a fight, I wanted to catch every word of it. Anthropologists are incurable that way.

The great beast was driven up to our dancing group, and a shot in the forehead dropped it in its tracks. Then, freshly cut branches were heaped around the fallen carcass to receive the meat. Ten men volunteered to help with the cutting. I asked /gaugo to make the breast bone cut. This cut, which begins the butchering process for most large game, offers easy access for removal of the viscera. But it also allows the hunter to spot-check the amount of fat on the animal. A fat game animal carries a white layer up to an inch thick on the chest, while in a thin one, the knife will quickly cut to bone. All eyes fixed on his hand as /gaugo, dwarfed by the great carcass, knelt to the breast. The first cut opened a pool of solid white in the black skin. The second and third cut widened and deepened the creamy white. Still no bone. It was pure fat; it must have been two inches thick.

"Hey /gau," I burst out, "that ox is loaded with fat. What's this about the ox being too thin to bother eating? Are you out of your mind?"

"Fat?" /gau shot back, "You call that fat? This wreck is thin, sick, dead!" And he broke out laughing. So did everyone else. They rolled on the ground, paralyzed with laughter. Everybody laughed except me; I was thinking.

I ran back to the tent and burst in just as Nancy was getting up. "Hey, the black ox. It's fat as hell! They were kidding about it being too thin to eat. It was a joke or something. A put-on. Everyone is really delighted with it!"

"Some joke," my wife replied. "It was so funny that you were ready to pack up and leave /ai/ai."

If it had indeed been a joke, it had been an extraordinarily convincing one, and tinged, I thought, with more than a touch of malice as many jokes are. Nevertheless, that it was a joke lifted my spirits considerably, and I returned to the butchering site where the shape of the ox was rapidly disappearing under the axes and knives of the butchers. The atmosphere had become festive. Grinning broadly, their arms covered with blood well past the elbow, men packed chunks of meat into the big cast-iron cooking pots, fifty pounds to the load, and muttered and chuckled all the while about the thinness and worthlessness of the animal and /ontah's poor judgment.

We danced and ate that ox two days and two nights; we cooked and distributed fourteen potfuls of meat and no one went home hungry and no fights broke out.

But the "joke" stayed in my mind. I had a growing feeling that something important had happened in my relationship with the Bushmen and that the clue lay in the meaning of the joke. Several days later, when most of the people had dispersed back to the bush camps, I raised the question with Hakekgose, a Tswana man who had grown up among the !Kung, married a !Kung girl, and who probably knew their culture better than any other non-Bushman.

"With us whites," I began, "Christmas is supposed to be the day of friendship and brotherly love. What I can't figure out is why the Bushmen went to such lengths to criticize and belittle the ox I had bought for the feast. The animal was perfectly good and their jokes and wisecracks practically ruined the holiday for me."

"So it really did bother you," said Hakekgose. "Well, that's the way they always talk. When I take my rifle and go hunting with them, if I miss, they laugh at me for the rest of the day. But even if I hit and bring one down, it's no better. To them, the kill is always too small or too old or too thin; and as we sit down on the kill site to cook and eat the liver, they keep grumbling, even with their mouths full of meat. They say things like, 'Oh this is awful! What a worthless animal! Whatever made me think that this Tswana rascal could hunt!'"

"Is this the way outsiders are treated?" I asked.

"No, it is their custom; they talk that way to each other too. Go and ask them."

/gaugo had been one of the most enthusiastic in making me feel bad about the merit of the Christmas ox. I sought him out first.

"Why did you tell me the black ox was worthless, when you could see that it was loaded with fat and meat?"

"It is our way," he said smiling. "We always like to fool people about that. Say there is a Bushman who has been hunting. He must not come home and announce like a braggart, 'I have killed a big one in the bush!' He must first sit down in silence until I or someone else comes up to his fire and asks, 'What did you see today?' He replies quietly, 'Ah, I'm no good for hunting. I saw nothing at all [pause] just a little tiny one.' Then I smile to myself," /gaugo continued, "because I know he has killed something big.

"In the morning we make up a party of four or five people to cut up and carry the meat back to the camp. When we arrive at the kill we examine it and cry out, 'You mean to say you have dragged us all the way out here in order to make us cart home your pile of bones? Oh, if I had known it was this thin I wouldn't have come.' Another one pipes up, 'People, to think I gave up a nice day in the shade for this. At home we may be hungry but at least we have nice cool water to drink.' If the horns are big, someone says, 'Did you think that somehow you were going to boil down the horns for soup?'

"To all this you must respond in kind. 'I agree,' you say, 'this one is not worth the effort: let's just cook the liver for strength and leave the rest for the hyenas. It is not too late to hunt today and even a duiker or a steenbok would be better than this mess.'

"Then you set to work nevertheless; butcher the animal, carry the meat back to the camp and everyone eats." /gaugo concluded.

Things were beginning to make sense. Next, I went to Tomazo. He corroborated /gaugo's story of the obligatory insults over a kill and added a few details of his own.

"But," I asked, "why insult a man after he has gone to all that trouble to track and kill an animal and when he is going to share the meat with you so that your children will have something to eat?"

"Arrogance," was his cryptic answer.

"Arrogance?"

"Yes, when a young man kills much meat he comes to think of himself as a chief or a big man, and he thinks of the rest of us as his servants or inferiors. We can't accept this. We refuse one who boasts, for someday his pride will make him kill somebody. So we always speak of his meat as worthless. This way we cool his heart and make him gentle."

"But why didn't you tell me this before?" I asked Tomazo with some heat.

"Because you never asked me," said Tomazo, echoing the refrain that has come to haunt every field ethnographer.

The pieces now fell into place. I had known for a long time that in situations of social conflict with Bushmen I held all the cards. I was the only source of tobacco in a thousand square miles, and I was not incapable of cutting an individual off for noncooperation. Though my boycott never lasted longer than a few days, it was an indication of my strength. People resented my presence at the water hole, yet simultaneously dreaded my leaving. In short I was a perfect target for the charge of arrogance and for the Bushmen tactic of enforcing humility.

I had been taught an object lesson by the Bushmen; it had come from an unexpected corner and had hurt me in a vulnerable area. For the big black ox was to be the one totally generous, unstinting act of my year at /ai/ai, and I was quite unprepared for the reaction I received.

As I read it, their message was this: There are no totally generous acts. All "acts" have an element of calculation. One black ox slaughtered at Christmas does not wipe out a year of careful manipulation of gifts given to serve your own ends. After all, to kill an animal and share the meat with people is really no more than Bushmen do for each other every day and with far less fanfare.

In the end, I had to admire how the Bushmen had played out the farce — collectively straight-faced to the end. Curiously, the episode reminded me of the *Good Soldier Schweik* and his marvelous encounters with authority. Like Schweik, the Bushmen had retained a thorough-going skepticism of good intentions. Was it this independence of spirit, I wondered, that had kept them culturally viable in the face of generations of contact with more powerful societies, both black and white? The thought that the Bushmen were alive and well in the Kalahari was strangely comforting. Perhaps, armed with that independence and with their superb knowledge of their environment, they might yet survive the future.

Kapluna Daughter
by Jean L. Briggs

"It's very cold down there—*very cold*. If I were going to be at Back River this winter, I would like to adopt you and try to keep you alive."

My Eskimo visitor, Uunai, dramatized her words with shivers as we sat drinking tea in the warm nursing station in Gjoa Haven. It was only mid-August, but already the wind that intruded through the cracks in the window frame was bitter, and the ground was white with a dusting of new snow. Last winter's ice, great broken sheets of it, still clogged the harbor, so that the plane I was waiting for was unable to get through to us. I was on my way to spend a year and a half with the Utkuhikhalingmiut, a small group of Eskimos who lived in Chantrey Inlet at the mouth of the Back River on the northern rim of the American continent. They were the most remote group of Eskimos that I could find on the map of the Canadian Arctic, a people who in many ways lived much as they had in the days before *kaplunas* (white men) appeared in the North. They were nomadic; they lived in snowhouses in winter, in tents in summer; and their diet consisted very largely of fish—trout and whitefish—supplemented now and again by a few caribou.

Uunai's words presaged the most important influence on the course of my life at Back River, namely my adoption as a "daughter" in the household of an Utkuhikhalingmiut family. I want to describe an aspect of that relationship here, with the aim of illustrating some of the difficulties that a host community or family may encounter in its hospitable efforts to incorporate a foreigner.

I arrived in Chantrey Inlet at the end of August 1963 on a plane that the Canadian government sent in once a year to collect the three or four schoolchildren who wished to go to Inuvik. I had with me letters of introduction from the Anglican deacon and his wife in Gjoa Haven. Nakliguhuktuq and Ikayuqtuq were Eskimos from the eastern Arctic who served as missionaries not only to the Anglican Eskimos in Gjoa Haven, but also to the Utkuhikhalingmiut. The letters—written in the syllabic script in which the Utkuhikhalingmiut, like most other Canadian Eskimos, are literate—noted that I would like to live with the Utkuhikhalingmiut for a year or so, learning the Eskimo language and skills: how to scrape skins and sew them, how to catch fish and preserve them or boil the oil out of them for use in lighting and heating the winter iglus. They asked the Eskimos to help me with words and fish and promised that in return I would help them with tea and kerosene. They told the people that I was kind and that they

24

should not be shy and afraid of me—"She's a little bit shy herself"—and assured them that they need not feel (as they often do feel toward kaplunas) that they had to comply with my every wish. They said, finally, that I wished to be adopted into an Eskimo family and to live with them in their iglu as a daughter.

Choosing A Father

I had a number of reasons for wishing to be adopted, and there were several precedents for adoption as well: four other kaplunas of my acquaintance, both scholars and laymen, who had wintered with Eskimos had done so as "sons," sharing the iglus of their Eskimo families. Living in the iglu would be warmer than living alone, I thought (Ikayuqtuq and Nakliguhuktuq agreed); and I thought vaguely that it might be "safer" if one family had specific responsibility for me. The idea had romantic appeal too; I saw it as a fulfillment of a childhood wish to "be" an Eskimo, and I expected no rapport problems, since on two previous trips to the Alaskan Arctic I had identified strongly with the Eskimo villagers with whom I had lived. To be sure, there were also arguments against adoption: I had qualms concerning the loss of an "objective" position in the community, drains on my supplies that would result from contributing to the maintenance of a family household and loss of privacy with resultant difficulties in working. Still, when the moment of decision came, the balance lay in favor of adoption.

There were two suitable fathers among the Utkuhikhalingmiut (that is, two household heads who had wives alive and at home), and these two were both more than eager to adopt me. One, however—an intelligent, vigorous man named Inuttiaq—far outdid the other in the imagination and persistence with which he "courted" me as a daughter. Not only were he and his family extremely solicitous, but he was also a jolly and ingenious language teacher. Most gratifying of all, both he and his wife, Allaq, were astonishingly quick to understand my halting attempts to communicate. There was no question which family I preferred. Fortunately, Inuttiaq also occupied a much more central position among the Utkuhikhalingmiut than did Nilak, the other possible father. He had many more close kin and was also the Anglican lay leader of the group. I was convinced that both anthropology and I would benefit more if I were adopted by Inuttiaq.

Winter

From the moment that the adoption was settled, I was "Inuttiaq's daughter" in the camp. Inuttiaq and his relatives with much amusement drilled me in the use of kin terms appropriate to my position, just as they drilled his three-year-old daughter, who was learning to speak. They took charge of my material welfare and of my education in language and skills. Allaq also to some extent took charge of my daily activities, as it was proper that a mother should. She told me what the day's job for the women of the family was going to be: gathering birch twigs for fuel, scraping caribou hides in preparation for the making of winter clothing or skinning the fish bellies out of which oil was to be boiled. The decision to participate or not was left to me, but if I did join the women—and I usually did—she made sure that my share of the work was well within the limits of my ability and stamina. "We will be walking very far tomorrow to get birch twigs," she would say. "You will be too tired." If I went anyway, it was always silently arranged that my load should be the lightest, and if I wandered out of sight of the other women in my search for birch bushes, someone always followed behind—sent by Allaq, as I discovered months later—to make sure that I didn't get lost.

I felt increasingly comfortable with my family and found their solicitude immensely warming. At the same time, I dreaded the loss of privacy that the winter move into their iglu would bring. Curiously, the effect of the move when it came in October was the opposite of what I had expected. I basked in the protectiveness of Inuttiaq's household; and what solitude I needed I found on the river in the mornings, when I jigged for salmon trout through the ice with Inuttiaq, or, to my surprise, in the iglu itself in the afternoons, when the room was full of visitors and I retired into myself, lulled and shielded by the flow of quiet, incomprehensible speech.

Behaving

The family's continuing graciousness was very seductive. I came to expect the courtesies that I received and even to resent it a bit when they were not forthcoming, though at the same time I told myself that such feelings were shameful. However, as time passed and I became an established presence in the household, I was less and less often accorded special privileges, except insofar as my ineptitude made services necessary. Allaq still mended my skin boots for me and stretched them when they shrank in drying; my stitches were not small enough and my jaws not strong enough. She continued to fillet my fish when it was frozen nearly as hard as wood. But in other respects Allaq, and especially Inuttiaq—who was far less shy than his wife—more and more attempted to assimilate me into a proper adult parent-daughter relationship. I was expected to help with the household work to the best of my ability—to make tea or bannock and to fetch water—and I was expected to obey unquestioningly when Inuttiaq told me to do something or made a decision on my behalf.

Unfortunately, I found it impossible to learn to behave in every respect like an Utkuhikhalingmiut daughter. Unuttiaq lectured me in general terms on the subject of filial obedience, and once in a while I think he tried to shame me into good behavior by offering himself as a model of virtue—volunteering, for example, to make bannock for me if I were slow in making it for him—but to little avail. Sometimes I was genuinely blind and deaf to his lessons, unaccustomed as I was to Utkuhikhalingmiut subtlety. At other times I saw what was wanted but resisted for reasons I will describe in a moment. Inevitably, conflicts, covert but pervasive, developed, both regarding the performance of household chores and regarding the related matter of obedience to Inuttiaq.

Assumptions in Conflict

The causes of the conflicts were three. First was the fact that some feminine skills were hard for me to learn. Overtly my Utkuhikhalingmiut parents were very tolerant of the lack of skill that they rightly attributed to kapluna ignorance and perhaps also to kapluna lack of intelligence, or *ihuma*. However, perhaps because of an assumption that kaplunas were unable to learn, if I was at all slow to understand Allaq's instructions and demonstrations, she easily gave up trying to teach me, preferring instead to continue to serve me. And though she stretched my boots and cut my fish in the most cheerful manner, after a while her added chores may well have been burdensome to her.

A second cause of the conflicts was that some of Inuttiaq's and Allaq's assumptions about the nature of parental and daughterly virtue were at variance with mine; in consequence not only did I have to learn new patterns, I also had to unlearn old ones. Hardest of all to learn was unquestioning obedience to paternal authority. Sometimes I could not help resisting, privately but intensely, when Inuttiaq told me to "make tea," to "go home," to "hurry up" or to "pray." I was irritated even by the fact that after the first weeks of gracious formality had passed he began to address me in the imperative form, which is often used in speaking to women, children and young people. Rationally I knew that I should have welcomed this sign of "acceptance," but I could not be pleased. My irritation was due partly to the fact that subordination threatened my accustomed—and highly valued—independence, but it was aggravated by a fear that the restrictions placed on me interfered with my work.

And herein lay the third cause of the conflicts: I found it hard sometimes to be simultaneously a docile and helpful daughter and a conscientious anthropologist. Though Allaq appeared to accept my domestic clumsiness as inevitable, she may have felt less tolerant on the occasions when it was not lack of skill that prevented me from helping her, but anxiety over the pocketful of trouser-smudged, disorganized field notes that cried out to be typed. A number of times, when I could have helped to gut fish or to carry in snow to repair the sleeping platform or floor or could have offered to fetch water or make tea, I sat and wrote instead or sorted vocabulary—tiny slips of paper spread precariously over my sleeping bag and lap. It was sometimes professional anxiety that prompted me to disobey Inuttiaq too; and I am sure that on such occasions, as on others, he must have found my insubordination not only "bad," but completely incomprehensible. My behavior at moving time is an example. My gear, minimal though it was by kapluna standards, placed a severe strain on Inuttiaq when we moved camp. Whereas the sleds of others were loaded to little more than knee-height, the load on Inuttiaq's sled was shoulder-high. From his point of view it was only reasonable that he should instruct me to leave my heavy tape recorder and my metal box of field notes on the top of a small knoll, as the Utkuhikhalingmiut cached their own belongings, while we moved downstream, not to return until after the flood season. I, however, questioned whether the water might rise over the knoll, and Inuttiaq's silent scrutiny seemed to say that he considered my inquiry a reflection on his judgment.

I do not mean to create the impression that life in Inuttiaq's household during that first winter was continuous turmoil. There were many days, even weeks, when I, at least, felt the situation to be very peaceful and enjoyable. I was grateful for the warmth of my parents' company and care; it was good to feel that I belonged somewhere, that I was part of a family, even on a make-believe basis. But the rewards of my presence for Inuttiaq and his real family were of a different, and probably of a lesser, order. Because Innutiaq's purchases in Gjoa Haven were supplemented by mine, our household was richer than others in store goods: tea, tobacco, flour, jam, dry milk, raisins and kerosene. But apart from these material benefits, and at first perhaps the novelty (and prestige?) of having a kapluna daughter, it is hard to see what Inuttiaq's family gained in return for the burden they carried. I played "Tavern in the Town" and "Santa Lucia" on my recorder; Innutiaq enjoyed that and he once in a while asked me to play for guests. I helped inefficiently in the mornings to remove the whitefish from the family nets and to drag them home, harnessed with Allaq to the sled. I assisted—erratically, as I have mentioned—with the other domestic chores; and in late winter, when the sun returned and Inuttiaq began again to jig for salmon trout, I usually fished with him. That is all that occurs to me, and a trivial contribution it must have been from my family's point of view.

Satan and Self-Control

It was hard for me to know at the time, however, just what their reactions to me were, because the tensions that existed were nearly all covert. Hostility among Utkuhikhalingmiut is ignored or turned into a joke; at worst it becomes the subject of gossip behind the offender's back. I, too, did my best to smother my annoyance with frustration, but my attempts were not wholly successful. My training in self-control was less perfect than theirs, and at the same time the strains were greater than those I was accustomed to dealing with in my own world.

Moreover, the most potentially gratifying of the outlets utilized by the Utkuhikhalingmiut—gossip—was not open to me as an anthropologist. I did my best to learn with the children when they were taught to turn annoyance into amusement, but laughter didn't come easily.

The Utkuhikhalingmiut are acutely sensitive to subtle indications of mood. They heard the coldness in my voice when I said, "I don't understand," noted the length of a solitary walk I took across the tundra or the fact that I went to bed early and read with my back turned to the others. Later, Inuttiaq might give me a lecture—phrased, as always, in the most general terms—about the fate of those who lose their tempers: Satan uses them for firewood. Or he might offer me an especially choice bit of fish—whether to shame me or to appease me I don't know. The contrast between my irritability and the surface equanimity of others gave me many uncomfortable moments, but I persuaded myself that the effects of my lapses were shortlived. When I laughed again and heard others laugh with me, or when they seemed to accept the generous gestures with which I tried to make amends, I was reassured that no damage had been done. I was wrong. But it was only when I returned to Gjoa Haven on my way home a year later that I learned how severe the tensions had become between November and January of that first winter. Then the deacon's wife, Ikajuqtuq, told me of the report Inuttiaq had made of me in January when he went in to Gjoa Haven to trade: "She is not happy. She gets angry very easily, and I don't think she likes us anymore." Shortly after Inuttiaq's return from Gjoa Haven in January, conflict erupted into the open.

"The Iglus Are Cold"

The two weeks of Inuttiaq's absence in Gjoa Haven had been an especially trying period for me. I had looked forward to them as a much needed interlude in which to type and organize my swelling pile of penciled notes. When Inuttiaq was at home, it was often difficult to maintain the iglu temperature within the range of 27 to 31 degrees at which typing was feasible. If I tried to type during the daylight hours of the morning, when the outdoor work was done, my fingers and carbon paper froze as a result of Inuttiaq's drafty comings and goings at jobs that seemed to necessitate propping the door open. But in the sociable afternoon and evening hours the snow dome dripped in the heat and occasionally deposited lumps of slush into my typewriter, and the iglu steamed so that my work was lost in a wet fog as a result of Inuttiaq's demands for tea, boiled fox, bannock and soup in rapid succession. Many were the frustrated moments when I heartily wished him gone; but it was only when he *was* gone that I discovered how completely our comfort depended on his presence. "When the men are away the iglus are cold," the women said; and it was true. The morning drafts that had plagued me before were nothing compared with the chill that resulted when nobody came and went at all. It was partly, of course, that Inuttiaq had taken with him one of our two primus stoves and one of the two kerosene storm lanterns, which ordinarily heated the iglu. But Allaq's behavior during her husband's absence intensified the cold. She never boiled fish, rarely brewed tea and never lit the lamp to dry clothes—any of which activities would have warmed the iglu. She merely sat in her corner of the sleeping platform, blew on her hands and remarked that the iglu was cold. It was; it was 20 degrees colder than when Inuttiaq was at home. I fretted and fumed in silent frustration and determined that when he came back I would take drastic steps to improve my working conditions.

I broached the subject to Inuttiaq a few days after his return to camp. He listened attentively to my explanation. I told him that I had thought about going to live for a while in the empty wooden building that stood on a peninsula a few miles from camp. The government had built it as a nursing station, but it had never been used except by me as a cache for my useless belongings. It had a kerosene stove, which would make it luxuriously comfortable—unless the stove was as erratic as the one in the similar nursing station in Gjoa Haven, with which I had once had an unfortunate experience. Inuttiaq agreed that the stove was unpredictable. Instead, he suggested that he take me to the nursing station every morning and fetch me again at night, so that I would not freeze. As often before, he reassured me: "Because you are alone here, you are someone to be taken care of." And, as often before, his solicitude warmed me. "Taking me to the nursing station every day will be a lot of work for you," I said. The round trip took an hour and a half by dog sled, not counting the time and effort involved in harnessing and unharnessing the team. He agreed that it would be a lot of work. "Could you perhaps build me a small iglu?" I asked. It would take only an hour or two to build a tiny iglu near our own, which I could use as an "office"; then he need concern himself no further. Lulled by the assurance he had just given me of his desire to take care of me and by the knowledge that the request I made was not time-consuming, I was the more disagreeably startled when he replied with unusual vigor, "I build no iglus. I have to check the nets."

A Daughter's Tent

The rage of frustration seized me. He had not given me the true reason for his refusal. It only took two hours to check the nets every second or third day; on the other days, Inuttiaq did nothing at all except eat, drink, visit and repair an occasional tool. I le was offended, but I could not imagine why. Whether Inuttiaq read my face I do not know, but he softened his refusal immediately: "Shall Ipuituq or Tutaq"—he named two of the younger men—"build an iglu for you?" Perhaps it would be demeaning for a man of Inuttiaq's status, a mature householder, to build an iglu for a mere daughter. There was something in Inuttiaq's reaction that I did not understand, and a cautioning voice told me to contain my ethnocentric judgment and my anger. I thought of the small double-walled tent that I had brought with me for emergency use. It was stored in the nursing station. "They say my tent is very warm in winter," I said. Inuttiaq smoked silently. After a while he asked, "Shall they build you an iglu tomorrow?" My voice shook with exasperation: "Who knows?" I turned my head, rummaging—for nothing—in my knapsack until the intensity of my feeling should subside.

Later, when Inuttiaq was smoking his last pipe in bed, I raised the subject again, my manner, I hoped, a successful facsimile of cheerfulness and firmness. "I would like to try the tent and see whether it's warm, as I have heard. We can bring it here, and then if it's not warm, I won't freeze; I'll come indoors." Allaq laughed, Inuttiaq accepted my suggestion, and I relaxed with relief, restored to real cheer by Inuttiaq's offer to fetch the tent from the nursing station the following day—if it stormed—so that he could not go on the trapping trip he had planned.

My cheer was premature. Two days later the tent had still not been fetched, though Inuttiaq had not gone trapping. I decided to walk to the nursing station. I had no intention of fetching the tent myself—it would have been impossible; but I needed a few hours alone, and vaguely I knew that the direction of my walk would be to Inuttiaq a sign, however futile, that I was in earnest about my tent.

But I did not dream that he would respond as charitably as he did. I had just arrived at the nursing station and was searching among my few books for a novel to comfort me in my frustration when I heard the squeak of sled runners on the snow outside and a familiar voice speaking to the dogs: "*Hoooo* [whoa]." Inuttiaq appeared in the doorway. I smiled. He smiled. "Will you want your tent?"

29

Gratitude and relief erased my anger as Inuttiaq picked up the tent and carried it to the sled. "You were walking," he said, in answer to my thanks. "I felt protective toward you."

It was a truce we had reached, however, not a peace, though I did not realize it at once. Since it was nearly dark when we reached camp, Inuttiaq laid the tent on top of the iglu for the night, to keep it from the dogs. Next morning I went with Inuttiaq to jig for trout up-river, and when we returned I thought that finally the time was ripe for setting up the tent. Not wanting to push Inuttiaq's benevolence too far, and remembering the force of his response to my query about iglu-building, I asked, "Shall I ask Ipuituq to help me put up my tent?" "Yes," said Inuttiaq. There was no warmth in his face; he did not smile, though he did tell me to keep my fur trousers on for warmth while I put up the tent. I obeyed, but the wind had risen while we drank our homecoming tea, so that even in fur trousers tent-raising was not feasible that day or the next.

When the wind died two days later, Inuttiaq and I went fishing again, most companionably. Relations seemed so amicable, in fact, that this time on our return I was emboldened to say directly, without mention of Ipuituq, "I would like to put up my tent."

Naively I thought that Inuttiaq would offer to help. He did not. His face was again unsmiling as he answered, "Put it up."

My anger was triggered again. "By myself?" I inquired rudely.

"Yes," said Inuttiaq, equally rudely.

"Thank you very much." I heard the coldness in my voice but did not try to soften it.

Inuttiaq, expressionless, looked at me for a moment then summoned two young men who were nearby and who came, with a cheer that was in marked contrast to his own manner, to help me set up the tent.

Although Inuttiaq thought it ridiculous anyway to set up a tent in winter, I think now that he was also personally affronted by my request. One clue to his reaction I find in a question that I hardly heard at the time: he had wanted to know, after the tent was up, whether I planned to sleep in it or only to work there, and I think he may have felt that my demand for a tent was a sign that I was dissatisfied with him as a father, with his concern for my welfare.

In any case, his behavior was a curious blend of opposites. He chose the site for my tent with care, correcting my own choice with a more practiced eye to prowling dogs and prevailing wind. He offered advice on heating the tent, and he filled my primus stove so that it would be ready for me to use when my two assistants and I had finished setting up the tent. And when I moved my writing things out of his iglu, he told me that if I liked, I might write instead of going fishing. "If I catch a fish, you will eat," he assured me. But he turned his back on the actual raising of the tent and went home to eat and drink tea.

Never in Anger

On the following day I saw his displeasure in another form. It was Sunday morning and storming; our entrance was buried under drifting snow. Since there could be no church service, Inuttiaq and Allaq had each, separately and in mumbling undertones, read a passage from the Bible. Then Inuttiaq began to read from the prayer book the story of creation, and he asked if I would like to learn. I agreed, the more eagerly because I feared that he had perceived my skepticism toward his religious beliefs and that this was another hidden source of conflict between us. He lectured me at length. The story of creation was followed by the story of Adam and Eve (whose sin was responsible for the division of mankind into kaplunas and Eskimos), and this story was in turn followed by an exposition of proper Christian behavior: the keeping of the Sabbath—and of one's temper. "God is loving," said Inuttiaq, "but only to believers. Satan is angry. People will go to heaven only if they do not get angry or answer back when they are scolded." He told me that one should not be attached to earthly belongings, as I was: "One should devote himself only to God's word." Most striking of all was the way Inuttiaq ended his sermon to me. "Nakliguhuktuq made me king of the Utkuhikhalingmiut," he said. "He wrote that to me. He told me that if people—including you—don't want to believe what I tell them and don't want to learn about Christianity, then I should write to him, and he will come quickly and scold them. If people don't want to believe Nakliguhuktuq either, then ... a bigger leader, a kapluna, the king in Cambridge Bay [the government center for the central Arctic], will come in a plane with a big and well-made whip and will whip people. It will hurt a lot."

Much of this I had heard before, but this version was more dramatic than previous ones. It made me see more clearly than I had before something of Inuttiaq's view of kaplunas generally. I heard the hostility directed against myself as well, but again he had softened the latter by blending it with warmth, in the manner that I found so confusing. He knew that I believed in God, he said, because I helped people, I gave things to people—not just to one or two, which God doesn't want, but to everybody.

The rest of the winter passed more peacefully, at least on the surface. I spent much of the time working in my tent, and there was no more overt hostility. But I am no longer sure that my peace of mind was justified. In retrospect, it seems possible that the warm and solicitous acts my family continued to perform were neither rewards for improved behavior on my part nor evidence of a generous, willingness to accept me in spite of my thorny qualities, but, rather, attempts to extract or blunt some of the thorns. If I knew I was cared for, I might not get angry so easily. I thought I heard similar logic in the admonition Inuttiaq once in a while gave his six-year-old daughter when she sulked: "Stop crying, you are loved." Another possible motive may have been a desire to shame me, by virtuous example, into reforming. Perhaps these kind acts even had the effect of nullifying Inuttiaq's and Allaq's own prickly feelings, permitting them to prove to themselves that—as Inuttiaq once said—they didn't get angry, only I did.

Incorrigible

But whatever the interpretation of these incidents, it is clear to me now that there existed more of an undercurrent of tension in my relationship with Inuttiaq and Allaq than I perceived at the time. I began to suspect its presence in the spring, when our iglu melted and I moved—at Inuttiaq's order—back into my own tent; Allaq almost never visited me, as she had done the first days after my arrival in Chantrey Inlet. More important, these winter tensions, I think, added their residue of hostility to a crisis situation that developed at the end of the summer. This introduced a new phase in my relations, not merely with Inuttiaq and Allaq, but with all the other Utkuhikhalingmiut as well—a phase in which I ceased to be treated as an educable child and was instead treated as an incorrigible offender, who had unfortunately to be endured but who could not be incorporated into the social life of the group.

The crisis was brought about by the visit to Chantrey Inlet of a party of kapluna sports fishermen. Every July and August in recent years Chantrey Inlet has been visited by sportsmen from the provinces and from the United States who charter bush planes from private sports airlines and fly up to the Arctic for a week's fishing. Every year the sportsmen ask permission to borrow the Eskimos' canoes, which were given to them by the Canadian government after the famine of 1958 and are indispensable to their economy. In 1958 the disappearance of the caribou herds from the Chantrey Inlet area forced the Eskimos to begin to rely much more completely on fish than they had formerly done. This meant accumulating and storing quantities of fish during seasons when they were plentiful, and to facilitate this, the government introduced fish nets and canoes. Originally there had been six canoes, one for each of the Utkuhikhalingmiut families, but by the time I arrived in Chantrey Inlet only two of these remained in usable condition.

In Anger

The first parties that came asked, through me, if they might borrow both canoes, and the Utkuhikhalingmiut, who for various reasons rarely, if ever, refuse such requests, acquiesced, at some cost to themselves. They sat stranded on the shore, unable to fish, unable to fetch the occasional bird that they shot on the water, unable to fetch a resupply of sugar for their tea from the cache on the nearby island and worst of all, perhaps, unable to visit the odd strangers who were camped out of sight across the river. Ultimately these kaplunas left and were replaced by another group, which asked to borrow only one canoe. But relief was short-lived; trolling up and down the unfamiliar river in the late twilight, the kaplunas were unfortunate enough to run the canoe on a rock and tear a large hole in the canvas, whereupon they returned the canoe and announced to the men through sign language that since that craft was unusable they were now obliged to borrow the other—Inuttiaq's. When I arrived on the scene, the kaplunas were attaching their outboard to the canoe as Inuttiaq and the other Utkuhikhalingmiut men watched.

I exploded. Unsmilingly and in a cold voice I told the kaplunas' guide some of the hardships that I foresaw if his men damaged the second canoe. Then, armed with the memory that Innutiaq had earlier, before the arrival of this party of kaplunas, instructed me in vivid language never again to allow anyone to borrow his canoe, I told the kaplunas that the owner of that second canoe did not wish to lend it.

The kapluna guide was not unreasonable; he agreed at once that the loan of the boat was the owner's option: "It's his canoe, after all." Slightly mollified, I turned to Inuttiaq who stood nearby, expressionless like the other Utkuhikhalingmiut. "Do you want me to tell him you don't want to lend your canoe?" I asked in Eskimo. "He will not borrow it if you say you don't want to lend it."

Inuttiaq's expression dismayed me, but I didn't know how to read it. I knew only that it registered strong feeling, as did his voice, which was unusually loud: "Let him have his will!"

"We Wish She Would Leave"

That incident brought to a head months of uneasiness on the part of the Utkuhikhalingmiut concerning my volatility. I had spoken unbidden and in anger; that much the Eskimos knew. The words they couldn't understand, but it didn't matter; the intrusion and the anger itself were inexcusable. The punishment was so subtle a form of ostracism that I would have continued to think that my difficulties were all of my own imagining had I not come into possession of a letter that Allaq's father, Pala, had written to the deacon, Nakliguhuktuq, the day after the kaplunas left. Pala had intended to send it out on the plane that was daily expected to come and pick up the schoolchildren; he had kept it for a time, but then—fearing that when the plane finally came, he would forget the letter—he had given it to me to hold along with my own correspondence. The letter was in syllabics, of course; in an amoral spirit I decided to read it, to test my skill in reading Eskimo. I did not anticipate the contents: "Yiine [that was my name] lied to the kaplunas. She gets angry very easily. She ought not to be here studying Eskimos. She is very annoying;

because she scolds and one is tempted to scold her. She gets angry easily. Because she is so annoying, we wish more and more that she would leave."

But it was not until October, when the autumn iglus were built, that the change in the Eskimos' feelings really became apparent. I was not at all sure that Inuttiaq would invite me to move in with his family again as he had done the year before, but I need not have worried; his hostility did not take such a crass form. However, the quality of life in the iglu was in striking contrast with the previous year. Whereas then Inuttiaq's iglu had been the social center of the camp, now family and visitors congregated next door, in Allaq's father's iglu. Inuttiaq and Allaq—the children too—spent the better part of every day at Pala's. Even in the early mornings, when the family awoke, and at night when we were preparing for bed, I was isolated. It was as though I were not there. If I made a remark to Inuttiaq or Allaq, the person addressed responded with his usual smile, but I had to initiate almost all communication. As a rule, if I did not speak, no one spoke to me. If I offered to fetch water or make tea (which I seldom did), my offer was usually accepted, but no one ever asked me to perform these services. The pointedness of this avoidance was driven home one day when we were cooking. I do not recall what was being made or who had initiated the cooking; I think it likely that I had done so, since the primus stood on the floor in front of me, instead of in its usual place near Allaq. Nevertheless, when the pressure began to run down, unnoticed by me, Inuttiaq turned not to me but to Allaq to order her to pump up the primus. And she had to get up and come over to my side of the iglu to pump up the stove! Had he spoken to me, I would only have had to lean over to do it. Too late I realized the dignity inherent in the Utkuhikhalingmiut pattern of authority, in which the woman is obedient to the man. I envied Allaq the satisfaction of knowing that she was appreciated because she did well and docilely what Inuttiaq told her to do.

One day, about a week after we had moved into the autumn iglus, Inuttiaq suggested that when we moved into winter iglus later on, I should be physically walled off to a degree. Often when Utkuhikhalingmiut build their permanent winter iglus, they attach to one side a small chamber, called a *hiqluaq*, in which to store the fish they net. The hiqluaq opens into the interior of the iglu by way of a hole just big enough to crawl through. Inuttiaq's idea was to build such a chamber for me to live in; after I left, he would use it in the orthodox manner, for fish storage.

But in spite of all these tensions, I was still treated with the most impeccable semblance of solicitude. I was amazed that it should be so—that although my company was anathema, nevertheless people still took care to give me plentiful amounts of the foods I liked best, to warn me away from thin ice and to caution me when my nose began to freeze. The Utkuhikhalingmiut saw themselves—and wanted me to see them—as virtuously solicitous, no matter what provocations I might give them to be otherwise. Allaq's sister expressed this ethos of concern explicitly in a letter to Ikayuqtuq in Gjoa Haven: "Because she is the only kapluna here and a woman as well, we have tried to be good to her ... and though she is sometimes very annoying ... we still try to help her."

It was at the end of August that the incident with the kapluna fishermen occurred, and it was the end of November before I was finally able to explain myself to the Utkuhikhalingmiut. I had wanted from the beginning, of course, to confront them with an explanation of my behavior, but I had feared that such un-Eskimo directness would only shock them the more. Instead, I had written my version of the story to Ikayuqtuq, had told her about my attempt to protect the Utkuhikhalingmiut from the impositions of the kaplunas and asked her if she could help to explain my behavior to the Eskimos. My letter went out to Gjoa Haven, along with Pala's, when the school plane came in September. Unfortunately there was no way in which Ikayuqtuq could reply until the strait froze in November, enabling the men to make the long trip out to Gjoa Haven to trade. But when Inuttiaq, accompanied as usual by Allaq's brother, Mannik, finally

33

went out, they brought back from the deacon and his wife a response that surpassed my most sanguine expectations. Inuttiaq reported to his family: "Nakliguhuktuq says that the kaplunas almost shot us when Yiini wasn't there." The exaggeration was characteristic of Inuttiaq's lurid style of fantasy. He turned to me: "Did you write that to Nakliguhuktuq?" I denied it—and later, in Gjoa Haven, Nakliguhuktuq denied having made such a statement to Inuttiaq—but I did confirm the gist of Inuttiaq's report: that I had tried to protect the Eskimos. I described what it was that I had written to Ikayuqtuq, and I explained something of the reasons for my anger at the kaplunas.

Wall of Ice

The effect was magical. The wall of ice that had stood between me and the community suddenly disappeared. I became consultant on the moral qualities of fishing guides; people talked to me voluntarily, offered me vocabulary, included me in their jokes and in their anecdotes of the day's activities; and Inuttiaq informed me that the next day he and I were going fishing. Most heartwarming of all is the memory of an afternoon soon after the men had returned. The iglu was filled with visitors, and the hum of the primus on which tea was brewing mingled with the low voices of Inuttiaq and his guests. I knew every detail of the scene even as I bent over my writing, and I paid no attention until suddenly my mind caught on the sound of my name: "I consider Yiini a member of my family again." Was that what Inuttiaq had said? I looked up, inquiring. "I consider you a family member again," he repeated. His diction was clear, as it was only when he wanted to be sure that I understood. And he called me "daughter," as he had not done since August.

Not that I had suddenly become a wholly acceptable housemate; that could never be. I was not and could never become an Utkuhikhalingmiutaq, nor could I ever be a "daughter" to Inuttiaq and Allaq as they understood that role. Inuttiaq made this quite clear one day about this time when we were both sitting, silently working, in the iglu. "I think you're a leader in your country," he said suddenly. The remark had no obvious context; it must mean, I thought, that he had never reconciled himself to my intractable behavior. There was also the slightly wild look that I caught in his eye when I said I thought that I might someday return to Chantrey Inlet. The look vanished when Allaq explained that I meant to return after I had been to my own country, not merely to Gjoa Haven. "Yes," he said then, "We will adopt you again, or others may want to—Nilaak, perhaps, or Mannik, if he marries." And later, when we were talking about the possibility of other "learners" coming to Chantrey Inlet, Inuttiaq said, "We would be happier to have a woman come than a man—a woman like you, who doesn't want to be a wife. Maybe *you* are the only acceptable kapluna."

But it was the letters that Allaq and Inuttiaq wrote me when I left Chantrey Inlet in January that expressed most vividly and succinctly what it meant to them to have a kapluna daughter. They both said, "I didn't think I'd care when you left, but I did."

Stranger, Child, Simpleton

I observed three more or less distinct phases in the Utkuhikhalingmiut's view of me. During the first period I was a stranger and a guest, and I was treated with the formal courtesy and deference that the Utkuhikhalingmiut ordinarily accord to such persons. I was referred to as a kapluna, a white person, and addressed by my personal name—"Yiini" in the Eskimos' speech. Much of the time during this period the Eskimos must have been at a loss what to make of my behavior, and often when I did something that under other circumstances they might have defined as reprehensible—when I went to bed early, nursing a bad humor, or when I was silent in depression—they gave me the benefit of the doubt; they asked me if I were tired and considerately lessened my work load or withdrew so that I might "sleep."

Gradually, however, this first phase gave way to a second, in which my immediate family (though not others in the community) treated me in some respects as a daughter and a child. My parents replaced the name "Yiini" with the term "daughter" when speaking, and sometimes when referring to me; and my two small sisters called me "elder sister." Inuttiaq—though never Allaq—also began to use the imperative forms of speech that he used in addressing his other daughters and his wife. Even an appropriate age was invented for me: I had to be younger than Allaq—if only by one season—though all the evidence pointed to my being in fact slightly older than she was. Both parents directed my daily activities, and I was expected to obey them as a daughter should. When I did not, efforts were made to teach me better behavior through lecturing or shaming, the former a technique that was otherwise only used in teaching small children. My moodiness was no longer interpreted charitably, and efforts were made to educate me out of that behavior too.

Categorization of me as a "child" was probably determined by a combination of factors: I had introduced myself as one who wanted to "learn" from the Utkuhikhalingmiut, and I had asked to be adopted as a "daughter"; I was also obviously ignorant of Utkuhikhalingmiut proprieties and skills. The fact that I am a woman may also have facilitated my categorization as a child in several respects. For one thing, among the Utkuhikhalingmiut a woman's technical skill—skin-sewing—is very difficult to learn. I never mastered more than the most rudimentary, clumsy stitching; my work was so poor that when I mended my skin boots, Allaq considered it necessary to redo the job. Moreover, in order to be considered properly adult, a woman must have children, and I had none. For these reasons the role of an adult woman was virtually closed to me, whereas had I been a man, I might have earned an adult role as a fisherman and hunter, as some male kaplunas who have lived among Eskimos appear to have done. Finally, the fact that I am physically weaker than a man and thus unthreatening may have made it easier for the Utkuhikhalingmiut to view my ill temper, as I think they did, like that of a child. Had I been a man, I think they might have seen my temper as dangerous, even potentially lethal—anything but childish.

The third phase, in which I was treated as an incorrigible offender, replaced the "child" phase, I think, when it became apparent to the Utkuhikhalingmiut that I was uneducable. Inuttiaq no longer lectured me or used any other method to teach me. I was called "yiini" again instead of "daughter," and daughterly services were no longer asked of me. In fact, nothing at all was demanded of me. Though my physical needs for warmth, food and protection from danger were still taken care of, socially I was simply "not there." There was one other person in the community who was similarly ostracized: a woman of about my age, who appeared to be of subnormal intelligence. Almost all of her personal qualities—her imperfect speech, clumsy gestures and domestic incompetence—were subject to comment behind her back, but hostility in her case, as in mine, centered on her volatility—the fact that she was easily upset and was unable to exercise proper restraint in the expression of her feelings. She too was considered uneducable, and I am sure that, like her, I was privately labeled simpleminded.

Hosts and Anthropologists

In more general terms the sequence of judgments passed on me seemed to be: strange; educable; uneducable in important ways. And each phase, each judgment, was associated with a role familiar to the Utkuhikhalingmiut: stranger; child; simpleton—each role being identifiable in terms of the way I was addressed, the kinds of behavior that were expected of me, the interpretations that were placed on my misbehavior and the methods that were used to control that misbehavior.

Although an anthropologist must have a recognized role or roles in order to make it possible to interact with him sensibly and predictably, nevertheless it will be evident from what I have described of my own case that the assignment of a role may create as many problems as it solves for both the anthropologist and his hosts. When Inuttiaq undertook to adopt me, I think he assumed that I would naturally behave as he was accustomed to having daughters behave. He knew, of course, that as a kapluna I was ignorant of the Eskimo skills that adult daughters have usually mastered, but it is easier to recognize cross-cultural differences in technology and language than differences in the structuring of interpersonal relations; one is far more inclined to think of the latter as given in "human nature."

He was wrong, of course, in assuming that my behavior would be that of an Utkuhikhalingmiut daughter. Consequently his first hypothesis was replaced by a second: that kaplunas don't (or Yiini doesn't) know how to behave correctly but can learn. For various reasons, none of which were, I think, recognized by Inuttiaq, I didn't learn easily. The first reason why learning must be difficult is that the intruder faces a double task. On the one hand he must discover what has to be learned—that is, what exactly is wrong with his "normal" behavior and what the proper behavior should be. And on the other hand he must overcome resistance to doing what is required—resistance caused by the interference of his old patterns of role behavior. Such interference may be expected to be particularly marked when the role to be learned bears the same name ("daughter") as a role one is accustomed to playing in one's own culture.

Learning will also be difficult and imperfect because the anthropologist is not completely committed to the role he is playing vis-a-vis his hosts. For one thing, he must try to learn all kinds of facts about the community, many of which it may be inappropriate for someone in his native role to know. He must try to maintain sufficient distance from the culture he is studying and from himself so that he can record "objectively" and, hopefully, use his reactions to his experiences as sources of data. And he must try to record and participate simultaneously. The latter problem has been amply illustrated in my case as I have described it above.

It was because of these difficulties and others that Inuttiaq's second hypothesis—that I was educable—proved to a large extent wrong. And so he arrived at his third hypothesis (shared, as I have said, by the rest of the community), to the effect that I was a defective person: "bad" and "simpleminded."

This analysis of the relationship between my Eskimo family and me is, of course, far from complete. It is obvious that difficulties of conceptualization are only one of the problems that beset relationships of any kind. It is obvious also that most relationships—and the one described here is no exception—have strongly positive features as well, or they would cease to exist. Nevertheless, the account that I have presented here may serve as a basis for discussion of the general issues of anthropological role-playing.

Questions for Discussion

The questions which follow the readings in each section are intended to stimulate discussion. While these questions deal with salient concepts, they are also the product of the editor's own selective concerns. Consequently, the reader should be encouraged to search for additional concepts, questions and issues. The questions encourage reflection, interpretation, synthesis and application rather than the regurgitation of the content of the articles.

1.   Give some examples of ethnocentric behaviors in the interaction of each anthropologist with the people in the host cultures.

2.   Outline the points of cultural conflict in each article. Give examples from your own personal and/or professional experience showing how similar conflicts influenced communication.

3.   Can one ever become a "native" in another culture? Answer the question on the basis of Lee's and Briggs' accounts.

4.   People who deal with other cultural groups sometimes enter the relationship thinking they will be objective. What are the consequences of not realizing that one cannot be objective?

5.   It can be argued that some of the *skills* anthropologists need in order to relate to the cultures they describe are similar to those facing teachers of students of other cultures. Similarly, some of the *limitations* teachers encounter in these situations may resemble Lee's or Briggs' experiences as anthropologists. Speculate on this analogy. Outline the skills teachers may need and the limitations they may experience.

6.   Briggs mentions that an intruder faces a double task in learning about the Eskimo culture: to "discover what has to be learned" and to "overcome resistance to doing what is required." Do these statements have any implications for the education of racial and ethnic minorities? Why? Why not?

7.   In Lee's and Briggs' articles, the !Kung and the Eskimo were the majority relative to the educational experiences of the two anthropologists. What were the techniques and general feelings used by the majority? Do these have any validity for educators in the United States? Why? Why not?

8.   State points of agreement or disagreement with either the ideas in the readings or the behavior of the main characters in each of the articles.

B. THE NATURE OF PREJUDICE

An Interview with
C. P. Ellis
by Studs Terkel

We're in his office in Durham, North Carolina. He is the business manager of the International Union of Operating Engineers. On the wall is a plaque: "Certificate of Service, in recognition to C.P. Ellis, for your faithful service to the city in having served as a member of the Durham Human Relations Council. February 1977."

At one time, he had been president (exalted cyclops) of the Durham chapter of the Ku Klux Klan.

He is fifty-three years old.

My father worked in a textile mill in Durham. He died at forty-eight years old. It was probably from cotton dust. Back then, we never heard of brown lung. I was about seventeen years old and had a mother and sister depending on somebody to make a livin'. It was just barely enough insurance to cover his burial. I had to quit school and go to work. I was about eighth grade when I quit.

My father worked hard but never had enough money to buy decent clothes. When I went to school, I never seemed to have adequate clothes to wear. I always left school late afternoon with a sense of inferiority. The other kids had nice clothes, and I just had what Daddy could buy. I still got some of those inferiority feelin's now that I have to overcome once in a while.

I loved my father. He would go with me to ball games. We'd go fishin' together. I was really ashamed of the way he'd dress. He would take this money and give it to me instead of putting it on himself. I always had the feeling about somebody looking at him and makin' fun of him and makin' fun of me. I think it had to do somethin' with my life.

My father and I were very close, but we didn't talk about too many intimate things. He did have a drinking problem. During the week, he would work every day, but weekend he was ready to get plastered. I can understand when a guy looks at his paycheck and looks at his bills, and he's worked hard all the week, and his bills are larger than his paycheck. He'd done the best he could the entire week, and there seemed to be no hope. It's an illness thing. Finally you just say: "The heck with it. I'll just get drunk and forget it."

My father was out of work during the depression, and I remember going with him to the finance company uptown, and he was turned down. That's something that's always stuck.

My father never seemed to be happy. It was a constant struggle with him just like it was for me. It's very seldom I'd see him laugh. He was just tryin' to figure out what he could do from one day to the next.

After several years pumping gas at a service station, I got married. We had to have children. Four. One child was born blind and retarded, which was a real additional expense to us. He's never spoken a word. He doesn't know me when I go to see him. But I see him, I hug his neck. I talk to him, tell him I love him. I don't know whether he knows me or not, but I know he's well taken care of. All my life, I had work, never a day without work, worked all the overtime I could get and still could not survive financially. I began to say there's somethin' wrong with this country. I worked my butt off and just never seemed to break even.

I had some real great ideas about this great nation. (Laughs.) They say to abide by the law, go to church, do right and live for the Lord, and everything'll work out. But it didn't work out. It just kept gettin' worse and worse.

I was workin' a bread route. The highest I made one week was seventy-five dollars. The rent on our house was about twelve dollars a week. I will never forget: outside of this house was a 265-gallon oil drum, and I never did get enough money to fill up that oil drum. What I would do every night, I would run up to the store and buy five gallons of oil and climb up the ladder and pour it in that 265 gallon drum. I could hear that five gallons when it hits the bottom of that oil drum, splatters, and it sounds like it's nothin' in there. But it would keep the house warm for the night. Next day you'd have to do the same thing.

I left the bread route with fifty dollars in my pocket. I went to the bank and I borrowed four thousand dollars to buy the service station. I worked seven day a week, open and close, and finally had a heart attack. Just about two months before the last payments of that loan. My wife had done the best she could to keep it runnin'. Tryin' to come out of that hole, I just couldn't do it.

I really began to get bitter. I didn't know who to blame. I tried to find somebody. I began to blame it on black people. I had to hate somebody. Hatin' America is hard to do because you can't see it to hate it. You gotta have somethin' to look at to hate. (Laughs.) The natural person for me to hate would be black people, because my father before me was a member of the Klan. As far as he was concerned, it was the savior of the white people. It was the only organization in the world that would take care of the white people. So I began to admire the Klan.

I got active in the Klan while I was at the service station. Every Monday night, a group of men would come by and buy a Coca-Cola, go back to the car, take a few drinks, and come back and stand around talkin'. I couldn't help but wonder: Why are these dudes comin' out every Monday? They said they were with the Klan and have meetings close-by. Would I be interested? Boy, that was an opportunity I really looked forward to! To be part of somethin'. I joined the Klan, went from member to chaplain, from chaplain to vice-president, from vice-president to president. The title is exalted cyclops.

The first night I went with the fellas, they knocked on the door and gave the signal. They sent some robed Klansmen to talk to me and give me some instructions. I was led into a large meeting room, and this was the time of my life! It was thrilling. Here's a guy who's worked all his life and struggled all his life to be something, and here's the moment to be something. I will never forget it. Four robed Klansmen led me into the hall. The lights were dim, and the only thing you could see was an illuminated cross. I knelt before the cross. I had to make certain vows and promises. We promised to uphold the purity of the white race, fight communism, and protect white womanhood.

After I had taken my oath, there was loud applause goin' throughout the buildin', musta been at least four hundred people. For this one little ol' person. It was a thrilling moment for C.P. Ellis.

It disturbs me when people who do not really know what it's all about are so very critical of individual Klansmen. The majority of 'em are low-income whites, people who really don't have a part in something. They have been shut out as well as the blacks. Some are not very well educated either. Just like myself. We had a lot of support from doctors and lawyers and police officers.

Maybe they've had bitter experiences in this life and they had to hate somebody. So the natural person to hate would be the black person. He's beginnin' to come up, he's beginnin' to learn to read and start votin' and run for political office. Here are white people who are supposed to be superior to them, and we're shut out.

I can understand why people join extreme right-wing or left-wing groups. They're in the same boat I was. Shut out. Deep down inside, we want to be part of this great society. Nobody listens, so we join these groups.

At one time, I was state organizer of the National Rights party. I organized a youth group for the Klan. I felt we were getting old and our generation's gonna die. So I contacted certain kids in schools. They were havin' racial problems. On the first night, we had a hundred high school students. When they came in the door, we had "Dixie" playin'. These kids were just thrilled to death. I begin to hold weekly meetin's with 'em, teachin' the principles of the Klan. At that time, I believed Martin Luther King had Communist connections. I began to teach that Andy Young was affiliated with the Communist party.

I had a call one night from one of our kids. He was about twelve. He said: "I just been robbed downtown by two niggers." I'd had a couple of drinks and that really teed me off. I go downtown and couldn't find the kid. I got worried. I saw two young black people. I had the .32 revolver with me. I said: "Nigger, you seen a little young white boy up here? I just got a call from him and was told that some niggers robbed him of fifteen cents." I pulled my pistol out and put it right at his head. I said: "I've always wanted to kill a nigger and I think I'll make you the first one." I nearly scared the kid to death, and he struck off.

This was the time when the civil rights movement was really beginnin' to peak. The blacks were beginnin' to demonstrate and picket downtown stores. I never will forget some black lady I hated with a purple passion. Ann Atwater. Every time I'd go downtown, she'd be leadin' a boycott. How I hated—pardon the expression, I don't use it much now—how I just hated that black nigger. (Laughs.) Big, fat, heavy woman. She'd pull about eight demonstrations, and first thing you know they had two, three blacks at the checkout counter. Her and I have had some pretty close confrontations.

I felt very big, yeah. (Laughs.) We're more or less a secret organization. We didn't want anybody to know who we were, and I began to do some thinkin'. What am I hidin' for? I've never been convicted of anything in my life. I don't have any court record. What am I, C.P. Ellis, as a citizen and a member of the United Klansmen of America? Why can't I go to the city council meeting and say: "This is the way we feel about the matter? We don't want you to purchase mobile units to set in our schoolyards. We don't want niggers in our schools."

We began to come out in the open. We would go to the meetings, and the blacks would be there and we'd be there. It was a confrontation every time. I didn't hold back anything. We began to make some inroads with the city councilmen and county commissioners. They began to call us friend. Call us at night on the telephone: "C.P., glad you came to that meeting last night." They didn't want integration either, but they did it secretively, in order to get elected. They couldn't stand up openly and say it, but they were glad somebody was sayin' it. We visited some of the city leaders in their home and talk to 'em privately. It wasn't long before councilmen would call me up: "The blacks are comin' up tonight and makin' outrageous demands. How about some of you people showin' up and have a little balance?" I'd get on the telephone: "The niggers is comin' to the council meeting tonight. Persons in the city's called me and asked us to be there."

We'd load up our cars and we'd fill up half the council chambers, and the blacks the other half. During these times, I carried weapons to the meetings, outside my belt. We'd go there armed. We would wind up just hollerin' and fussin' at each other. What happened? As a result of our fightin' one another, the city council still had their way. They didn't want to give up control to the blacks nor the Klan. They were usin' us.

I began to realize this later down the road. One day I was walkin' downtown and a certain city council member saw me comin'. I expected him to shake my hand because he was talkin' to me at night on the telephone. I had been in his home and visited with him. He crossed the street. Oh shit, I began to think, somethin's wrong here. Most of 'em are merchants or maybe an attorney, an insurance agent, people like that. As long as they kept low-income whites and low-income blacks fightin', they're gonna maintain control.

I began to get that feeling after I was ignored in public. I thought: Bullshit, you're not gonna use me any more. That's when I began to do some real serious thinkin'.

The same things is happening in this country today. People are being used by those in control, those who have all the wealth. I'm not espousing communism. We got the greatest system of government in the world. But those who have it simply don't want those who don't have it to have any part of it. Black and white. When it comes to money, the green, the other colors make no difference. (Laughs.)

I spent a lot of sleepless nights. I still didn't like blacks. I didn't want to associate with 'em. Blacks, Jews, or Catholics. My father said: "Don't have anything to do with 'em." I didn't until I met a black person and talked with him, eyeball to eyeball, and met a Jewish person and talked to him, eyeball to eyeball. I found out they're people just like me. They cried, they cussed, they prayed, they had desires. Just like myself. Thank God, I got to the point where I can look past labels. But at that time, my mind was closed.

I remember one Monday night Klan meeting. I said something was wrong. Our city fathers were using us. And I didn't like to be used. The reactions of the others was not too pleasant: "Let's just keep fightin' them niggers."

I'd go home at night and I'd have to wrestle with myself. I'd look at a black person walkin' down the street, and the guy'd have ragged shoes or his clothes would be worn. That began to do somethin' to me inside. I went through this for about six months. I felt I just had to get out of the Klan. But I wouldn't get out.

Then something happened. The state AFL-CIO received a grant from the Department of HEW, a $78,000 grant: how to solve racial problems in the school system. I got a telephone call from the president of the state AFL-CIO. "We'd like to get some people together from all walks of life." I said: "All walks of life? Who you talkin' about?" He said: "Blacks, whites, liberals, conservatives, Klansmen, NAACP people."

I said: "No way am I comin' with all those niggers. I'm not gonna be associated with those type of people." A White Citizens Council guy said: "Let's go up there and see what's goin' on. It's tax money bein' spent." I walk in the door, and there was a large number of blacks and white liberals. I knew most of 'em by face 'cause I seen 'em demonstratin' around town. Ann Atwater was there. (Laughs.) I just forced myself to go in and sit down.

41

The meeting was moderated by a great big black guy who was bushy-headed. (Laughs.) That turned me off. He acted very nice. He said: "I want you all to feel free to say anything you want to say." Some of the blacks stand up and say it's white racism. I took all I could take. I asked for the floor and I cut loose. I said: "No, sir, it's black racism. If we didn't have niggers in the schools, we wouldn't have the problems we got today."

I will never forget. Howard Clements, a black guy, stood up. He said: "I'm certainly glad C.P. Ellis come because he's the most honest man here tonight." I said: "What's that nigger tryin' to do?" (Laughs.) At the end of that meeting, some blacks tried to come up shake my hand, but I wouldn't do it. I walked off.

Second night, same group was there. I felt a little more easy because I got some things off my chest. The third night, after they elected all the committees, they want to elect a chairman. Howard Clements stood up and said: "I suggest we elect two co-chairpersons." Joe Beckton, executive director of the Human Relations Commission, just as black as he can be, he nominated me. There was a reaction from some blacks. Nooo. And, of all things, they nominated Ann Atwater, that big old fat black gal that I had just hated with a purple passion, as co-chairman. I thought to myself: Hey, ain't no way I can work with that gal. Finally, I agreed to accept it, 'cause at this point, I was tired of fightin', either for survival or against black people or against Jews or against Catholics.

A Klansman and a militant black woman, co-chairmen of the school committee. It was impossible. How could I work with her? But after about two or three days, it was in our hands. We had to make it a success. This give me another sense of belongin', a sense of pride. This helped this inferiority feelin' I had. A man who has stood up publicly and said he despised black people, all of a sudden he was willin' to work with 'em. Here's a chance for a low-income white man to be somethin'. In spite of all my hatred for blacks and Jews and liberals, I accepted the job. Her and I began to reluctantly work together. (Laughs.) She had as many problems workin' with me as I had workin' with her.

One night, I called her: "Ann, you and I should have a lot of differences and we got 'em now. But there's somethin' laid out here before us, and if it's gonna be a success, you and I are gonna have to make it one. Can we lay aside some of these feelin's?" She said: "I'm willing if you are." I said: "Let's do it."

My old friends would call me at night: "C.P., what the hell is wrong with you? You're sellin' out the white race." This begin to make me have guilt feelin's. Am I doin' right? Am I doin' wrong? Here I am all of a sudden makin' an about-face and tryin' to deal with my feelin's, my heart. My mind was beginnin' to open up. I was beginnin' to see what was right and what was wrong. I don't want the kids to fight forever.

We were gonna go ten nights. By this time, I had went to work at Duke University, in maintenance. Makin' very little money. Terry Sanford give me this ten days off with pay. He was president of Duke at the time. He knew I was a Klansman and realized the importance of blacks and whites getting along.

I said: "If we're gonna make this thing a success, I've got to get to my kind of people." The low-income whites. We walked the streets of Durham, and we knocked on doors and invited people. Ann was goin' into the black community. They just wasn't respondin' to us when we made these house calls. Some of 'em were cussin' us out. "You'r sellin' us out, Ellis, get out of my door. I don't want to talk to you." Ann was gettin' the same response from blacks: "What are you doin' messin' with that Klansman?"

One day, Ann and I went back to the school and we sat down. We began to talk and just reflect. Ann said: "My daughter came home cryin' every day. She said her teacher was makin' fun of me in front of the other kids." I said: "Boy, the same thing happened to my kid. White liberal teacher was makin' fun of Tim Ellis's father, the Klansman. In front of other peoples. He came home cryin'." At this point—(he pauses, swallows hard, stifles a sob)—I begin to see, here we are, two people from the far ends of the fence, havin' identical problems, except hers bein' black and me bein' white. From that moment on, I tell ya, that gal and I worked together good. I begin to love the girl, really. (He weeps.)

The amazing thing about it, her and I, up to that point, had cussed each other, bawled each other. We didn't know we had things in common.

We worked at it, with the people who came to these meetings. They talked about racism, sex education, about teachers not bein' qualified. After seven, eight nights of real intense discussion, these people, who'd never talked to each other before, all of a sudden came up with resolutions. It was really somethin', you had to be there to get the tone and feelin' of it.

At that point, I didn't like integration, but the law says you do this and I've got to do what the law says, okay? We said: "Let's take these resolutions to the school board." The most disheartening thing I've ever faced was the school system refused to implement any one of these resolutions. These were recommendations from the people who pay taxes and pay their salaries. (Laughs.)

I thought they were good answers. Some of 'em I didn't agree with, but I been in this thing from the beginning, and whatever comes of it, I'm gonna support it. Okay, since the school board refused, I decided I'd just run for the school board.

I spent eighty-five dollars on the campaign. The guy runnin' against me spent several thousand. I really had nobody on my side. The Klan turned against me. The low-income whites turned against me. The liberals didn't particularly like me. The blacks were suspicious of me. The blacks wanted to support me, but they couldn't muster up enough to support a Klansman on the school board. (Laughs.) But I made up my mind that what I was doin' was right, and I was gonna do it regardless what anybody said.

It bothered me when people would call and worry my wife. She's always supported me in anything I wanted to do. She was changing, and my boys were too. I got some of my youth corps kids involved. They still followed me.

I was invited to the Democratic women's social hour as a candidate. Didn't have but one suit to my name. Had it six, seven, eight years. I had it cleaned, put on the best shirt I had and a tie. Here were all this high-class wealthy candidates shakin' hands. I walked up to the mayor and stuck out my hand. He give me that handshake with that rag type of hand. He said: "C.P., I'm glad to see you." But I could tell by his handshake he was lyin' to me. This was botherin' me. I know I'm a low-income person. I know I'm not wealthy. I know they were sayin': "What's this little ol' dude runnin' for school board?" Yet they had to smile and make like they're glad to see me. I begin to spot some black people in that room. I automatically went to 'em and that was a firm handshake. They said: "I'm glad to see you, C.P." I knew they meant it—you can tell about a handshake.

Every place I appeared, I said I will listen to the voice of the people. I will not make a major decision until I first contacted all the organizations in the city. I got 4,640 votes. The guy beat me by two thousand. Not bad for eighty-five bucks and no constituency.

The whole world was openin' up, and I was learnin' new truths that I had never learned before. I was beginnin' to look at a black person, shake hands with him, and see him as a human bein'. I hadn't got rid of all this stuff. I've still got a little bit of it. But somethin' was happenin' to me.

It was almost like bein' born again. It was a new life. I didn't have these sleepless nights I used to have when I was active in the Klan and slippin' around at night. I could sleep at night and feel good about it. I'd rather live now than at any other time in history. It's a challenge.

43

Back at Duke, doin' maintenance, I'd pick up my tools, fix the commode, unstop the drains. But this got in my blood. Things weren't right in this country, and what we done in Durham needs to be told. I was so miserable at Duke, I could hardly stand it. I'd go to work every morning just hatin' to go.

My whole life had changed. I got an eighth-grade education, and I wanted to complete high school. Went to high school in the afternoons on a program called PEP—Past Employment Progress. I was about the only white in class, and the oldest. I begin to read about biology. I'd take my books home at night, 'cause I was determined to get through. Sure enough, I graduated. I got the diploma at home.

I come to work one mornin' and some guy says: "We need a union." At this time I wasn't pro-union. My daddy was anti-labor too. We're not gettin' paid much, we're havin' to work seven days in a row. We're all starvin' to death. The next day, I meet the international representative of the Operating Engineers. He give me authorization cards. "Get these cards out and we'll have an election." There was eighty-eight for the union and seventeen no's. I was elected chief steward for the union.

Shortly after, a union man come down from Charlotte and says we need a full-time rep. We've got only two hundered people at the two plants here. It's just barely enough money comin' in to pay your salary. You'll have to get out and organize more people. I didn't know nothin' about organizing' unions, but I knew how to organize people, stir people up. (Laughs.) That's how I got to be business agent for the union.

When I began to organize, I began to see far deeper. I began to see people again bein' used. Blacks against whites. I say this without any hesitancy: management is vicious. There's two things they want to keep: all the money and all the say-so. They don't want these poor workin' folks to have none of that. I begin to see management fightin' me with everything they had. Hire antiunion law firms, badmouth unions. The people were makin' a dollar ninety-five an hour, barely able to get through weekends. I worked as a business rep for five years and was seein' all this.

Last year, I ran for business manager of the union. He's elected by the workers. The guy that ran against me was black, and our membership is seventy-five percent black. I thought: Claiborne, there's no way you can beat that black guy. People know your background. Even though you've made tremendous strides, those black people are not gonna vote for you. You know how much I beat him? Four to one. (Laughs.)

The company used my past against me. They put out letters with a picture of a robe and a cap: Would you vote for a Klansman? They wouldn't deal with the issues. I immediately called for a mass meeting. I met with the ladies at an electric component plant. I said: "Okay, this is Claiborne Ellis. This is where I come from. I want you to know right now, you black ladies here, I was at one time a member of the Klan. I want you to know, because they'll tell you about it."

I invited some of my old black friends. I said: "Brother Joe, Brother Howard, be honest now and tell these people how you feel about me." They done it. (Laughs.) Howard Clements kidded me a little bit. He said: "I don't know what I'm doin' here, supportin' an ex-Klansman." (Laughs.) He said: "I know what C.P. Ellis come from. I knew him when he was. I knew him as he grew, and growed with him. I'm tellin' you now: follow, follow this Klansman." (He pauses, swallows hard.) "Any questions?" "No," the black ladies said. "Let's get on with the meeting, we need Ellis." (He laughs and weeps.) Boy, black people sayin' that about me. I won 134 to 41. Four to one.

It makes you feel good to go into a plant and butt heads with professional union busters. You see black people and white people join hands to defeat the fascist issues they use against people. They're tryin' the same things with the Klan. It's still happenin' today. Can you imagine a guy who's got an adult high school diploma runnin' into professional college graduates who are union busters? I gotta compete with 'em. I work seven days a week, nights and on Saturday and Sunday. The salary's not that great, and if I didn't care, I'd quit. But I care and I can't quit. I got a taste of it. (Laughs.)

I tell people there's a tremendous possibility in this country to stop wars, the battles, the struggles, the fights between people. People say: "That's an impossible dream. You sound like Martin Luther King." An ex-Klansman who sounds like Martin Luther King. (Laughs.) I don't think it's an impossible dream. It's happened in my life. It's happened in other people's lives in America.

I don't know what's ahead of me. I have no desire to be a big union official. I want to be right out here in the field with the workers. I want to walk through their factory and shake hands with that man whose hands are dirty. I'm gonna do all that one little ol' man can do. I'm fifty-two years old, and I ain't got many years left, but I want to make the best of 'em.

When the news came over the radio that Martin Luther King was assassinated, I got on the telephone and begin to call other Klansmen. We just had a real party at the service station. Really rejoicin' 'cause that son of a bitch was dead. Our troubles are over with. They say the older you get, the harder it is for you to change. That's not necessarily true. Since I changed, I've set down and listened to tapes of Martin Luther King. I listen to it and tears come to my eyes 'cause I know what he's sayin' now. I know what's happenin'.

POSTSCRIPT: *The phone rings. A conversation.*

"This was a black guy who's director of Operation Breakthrough in Durham. I had called his office. I'm interested in employin' some young black person who's interested in learnin' the labor movement. I want somebody who's never had an opporutnity, just like myself. Just so he can read and write, that's all."

45

Beth Anne—

A Case Study of Culturally Defined Adjustment and Teacher Perceptions

by George Dearborn Spindler

This case study of Beth Anne will demonstrate how culturally unsophisticated perceptions of children by teachers may damage the "successful" middle-class child as well as the academically "unsuccessful" minority child in the school. The situation is in many respects the reverse of those portrayed in the preceding chapters by Raymond McDermott and myself, but in all three chapters the basic theme is the influence of the teacher's culture and the school upon perceptions and interpretations of children's behavior. For this purpose I am using a case study carried out when I was one of three people working in a school system under the aegis of the Stanford Consultation Service, directed by Dr. Robert N. Bush.[1]

Our purpose as a service team was to perform various studies of whole classrooms, teachers, individual children, other groups in the school, and even of whole school systems, as well as top supervisory personnel. Unlike the practice in a usual field study, we shared the data we collected and the analyses of those data with our informants. By so doing we hoped to share any benefits that might result from our research and direct them toward the improvement of the schools and the professional competence of teachers and related staff.

In this particular school, which we will call Washington Elementary School, we had entered to work with the whole staff of twelve teachers and the principal. First, we asked the assembled staff what it was they would like to study. They proposed a study of the "adjusted"—rather than the maladjusted—child in the classroom and in interaction with teachers and peers. We accepted this novel idea enthusiastically and proceeded to set up a mechanism whereby "adjusted" children could be selected for study. After some discussion the teachers helped out by deciding upon several specific children. These children's classes were approached as a whole for volunteers for the study. Among the volunteers were the children picked out by the staff. The studies were cleared with their parents and we proceeded over a period of about three months to collect data and periodically to discuss these data and our interpretations with the assembled staff of the school. Beth Anne, a fifth-grade pupil, is one of the children studied.

The fifth-grade class consisted of 35 children ranging in age from 9 years, 8 months to 11

46

years, 8 months. The I.Q. range as measured by the California Mental Maturity Test appropriate to this age level was 70-140 with a mean of 106. There were three reading groups in the room, highly correlated with I.Q. scores as well as with reading achievement scores.

The classroom consisted of 20 children who could be described as Anglos whose socioeconomic status ranged from upper-lower to upper- middle (using the scales drawn from the studies of H. Lloyd Warner and his associates). The other 15 children were from the minority groups represented in the community surrounding the school and included 3 blacks, 2 Filipinos, 3 Japanese-Americans, and 7 Mexican-Americans (the term "Chicanos" was not current at that time).

Beth Anne was 10 years and 3 months old, just 3 months below the average for the whole class. She was in the top reading group and at the 95th percentile with her I.Q. test score of 132.

Excepting for occasional minor illnesses Beth Anne was apparently in good health, according to her parents and to records from the school office. She was dark-haired, clear-skinned, well-developed for her age, had regular features and almond-shaped brown eyes, and wore braces on her front teeth. She always came to school extremely well-dressed and was polite and considerate in her relations with her teachers; she appeared to be slightly reserved but equally considerate with her peers. The members of the team as well as the teachers in the school were impressed with her appearance and manners and regarded her as an exceptionally nice-looking child of good background.

Beth Anne was described by the teachers as an "excellent student," one of "the best students in the school," one who is "extremely conscientious," "cooperates well," "never has caused trouble in any of her classes," and who is "well liked by the other children." Further comments from the faculty were elicited in discussions of Beth Anne and the other children selected for study before the studies began.

Her former first-grade teacher said, "She was a very bright little child, perhaps not too friendly. At first she didn't respond too readily to me, but gradually began to work well and by the end of the year appeared to have made an excellent adjustment." Her present fifth-grade teacher said that "Beth Anne has attended very regularly this year. She is very interested in her class work and activities and performs at top level in everything. She even does excellent work in arithmetic and she plays very well with the other members of the class and in general with children of her own age." The principal said, "Her home would certainly be classified in the upper-middle bracket. The parents are middle-aged, having married late. They have a very nice home and provide every cultural experience for the children." She went on to say that "one of the things that has concerned me a little, however, is a kind of worried look that Beth Anne has sometimes. It seems that if she doesn't understand the very first explanation in class, she is all concerned about it. She hasn't seemed so much that way this year, but I have noticed it a lot in the past." Another teacher said, "Well, the mother has always been very interested in her children and has worked to give them many advantages. Beth Anne and her brothers and her parents go to many things and places together." Another teacher agreed, "Yes, they go to symphonies, I know. And they all went to the football game at Orthodox U."

Several times, and in different ways, we asked the teachers whether they regarded Beth Anne as a "well-adjusted" child. There were no explicit reservations expressed except for the comment by the principal about her "worried look" and the comment by her first-grade teacher that at first "she didn't respond too readily." The teachers all expressed verbal agreement that she was indeed very well-adjusted, both academically and socially. Several teachers went out of their way to say that she was not only accepted by her peers but was considered a leader by them.

The Evidence

The study consisted of weekly classroom observations, watching playground activities, interviewing teachers, and administering psychological and sociometric tests. After having established the conditions of our study, our first step was to explain to Beth Anne what we would be doing and why. With her apparent enthusiastic consent, we proceeded then to a first interview followed by administration of the Rorschach projective technique and the Thematic Apperception Test (TAT). Within the following two weeks we also administered a sociometric technique to the classroom group. This technique included the questions, "Whom would you like best to sit next to?" "Whom do you like to pal around with after school?" and "Whom would you invite to a birthday party if you had one?" The sociometric maps of the choices expressed by the children were made up from the results elicited by these questions. They were quite consistent with each other. The sociometric map (sociogram) resulting from the responses to the first question is shown in Figure 2. We also administered a status-reputation technique that included thirty-two statements such as, "Here is someone who fights a lot," "Here is someone who never has a good time," "Here is someone who does not play fair," "Here is someone who is good-looking," "Here is someone who likes school," "Here is someone who plays fair," and so forth. The children were to list three names in rank order following every statement.[2] Following are summaries of these categories of data.

Observations

The reports by our three-man team of observers of Beth Anne's behaviors in the classroom and around the playground were monotonously similar. Beth Anne did not cause trouble. She was obedient, pleasant, and hard-working. She responded to questions in a clear voice and was noticeably disturbed when she was unable to provide the answer to a question in the arithmetic section. She read well and easily.

However, she interacted only infrequently with the other children in the classroom, either in the room or on the playground. She seemed quite reserved, almost aloof. Apparently she had a fairly strong relationship with one girl who looked and acted much as she did and who seems to have come from the same general social and cultural background.

Sometimes she chose to stay in the classroom when recess was called and would go out only at the urging of the teacher. She played organized games but not enthusiastically and seemed to find aggressive handling of a ball or other play equipment difficult.

The Rorschach and the TAT were administered the day after the preliminary interview with Beth Anne and before any other observations or other methods of data collection had been implemented. Without becoming involved with the many problematic aspects of their interpretation, I will summarize the results of these psychological techniques. In general we found these projective techniques to be of considerable use in our studies of individuals, though we regarded them with a certain flexibility.

Thematic Apperception Test Analysis

Most of the pictures in the TAT are of people engaged in social interaction and the subject is asked to tell a story about each picture. This story should state what the people are doing and thinking, what probably happened before the situation pictured, and what probably will happen. Beth Anne did not like to tell stories of this kind. Picking up the TAT pictures, she stated perfunctorily who the people were and what they were doing and then laid them down with what appeared to be an impatient air of finality. She was not able to say more upon probing, though she appeared to be at least superficially eager to comply. The TAT record is consequently rather sparse, though it is revealing.

The resistance to letting her imagination guide her to a creative solution to problems of human relationships as suggested by the pictures seems to be the most important feature of her protocol. She does not seem to like to be in a situation where she has to turn to her own creativity and utilize her emotions for interpretation. She does not seem to be able to empathize freely with the people in the pictures, even when she sees them as children. When asked what they might be feeling or thinking, she answered "I don't know," and if pressed by the interviewer, "How should I know?"

It is hard to pick out the most revealing instance of this aspect of her personality from the large amount of evidence in the TAT protocol. Upon seeing a picture of a little boy sitting in front of a log cabin she said, "It looks like he lives in a log cabin." ("What is he doing there?") "He's probably sitting there thinking about something." ("What is going to happen?") "Probably he is going to do what he is thinking about after a while." ("What is he thinking about?") "I don't know what he's thinking about. He's just thinking about all the things there are to think about!" In my experience with the administration of this technique with children her age, this is an unusual response. Most children as intelligent as Beth Anne seemed to embrace the task of telling the story about each picture with considerable spontaneity and creativity. Not so Beth Anne, who did not seem to be able to let herself go.

In another instance, when she was presented with a blank card and told to draw a picture there telling a story, she said, "There's nothing to make up that I can think of." That appeared to be literally true. She did not seem to be able to dip into any reservoir of imagination.

Beyond this prevailing feature in her TAT protocol, we can say that she shows some overt hostility toward authority. She also shows a certain amount of depression that is fairly rare for children her age, and she is made quite uneasy by symbols of open aggression.

There is no direct evidence of what could be called a pathological character development. What seems to be apparent is a lack of spontaneity and a refusal or inability to use her imagination to interpret the behavior of others.

Rorschach

Beth Anne gives evidence in her Rorschach protocol of possessing superior intelligence. She produced forty-eight appropriate responses, a result which is not only well above the average for her age group but higher than most adults achieve. She exhibits a high regard for detail and specification, but does not embark upon any flights of fantasy nor does she often put the details together to form an integrated whole perception.

Both qualitatively and quantitatively her protocol suggests that she is more constricted emotionally and intellectually than her superior productivity would lead one to expect. She has a well-developed perception of the concrete world about her, but these perceptions seem to stop at the level of concrete detail.

There is some evidence that she feels herself to be at times overwhelmed by forces beyond her control. There is also evidence that she has strong feelings that are not channeled into manageable interpersonal relationships or self-development.

It may be misleading to say that she lacks "creativity," but there is little imaginative spontaneity and little use of emotions for interpretive purposes. Beth Anne is what is sometimes known as a "tightrope" walker who sees what it is safe to see. She seems to avoid aspects of the inkblots that may have strong emotional implications for her and does not go deeply within herself for responses that would be emotionally meaningful. She avoids entanglements in emotionally laden material.

Furthermore, she seems to be fairly restricted in her ability to empathize with human motives or feelings. She does not seem to be able to put herself into another person's shoes, possibly because she has suppressed many of her own drives and feelings. At times, this may affect her intellectual performance, since she appears to be led off into inconsequential details and fails to see the larger whole.

Beth Anne is not likely to be a trouble-maker. She conforms even at her own personal cost. She says "Thank you" every time a Rorschach card is handed to her and "Oh, pardon me!" when she drops a card an inch onto the desk and it makes a little noise. She seems very concerned about performing adequately and asks continually if she has given enough responses.

There is evidence that there are some definite problems in the handling of emotions. Generally speaking, the emotions seem to be suppressed or avoided, but when they are confronted they seem overwhelming. Given this evidence within the context of a personality adjustment that can be described as constricted and at the same time achievement-oriented, one would predict the probability of some form of hysterical behavior, probably in the form of conversion to somatic disturbances or to chronic invalidism. We shall see later that this prediction was supported.

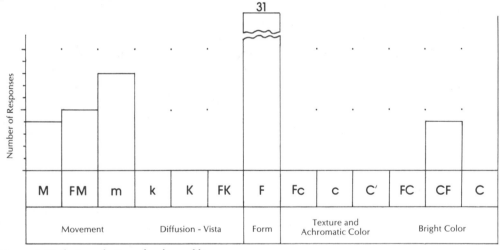

Figure 1. Beth Anne's Rorschach profile.

The Rorschach psychogram is reproduced here (Fig. 1). For those familiar with Rorschach interpretation, one can note the heavy emphasis upon the "m" response and upon the "F" category, the absence of textural or shading responses, the absence of controlled color responses, and the presence of several relatively uncontrolled color responses. This psychogram is accompanied by 6 percent whole responses, 51 percent large usual-detail responses, 20 percent small usual-detail responses, and 23 percent unusual-detail or white-space responses. Beth Anne's average reaction time for all responses was 11.5 seconds. As everyone who has worked with the Rorschach knows, not too much faith should be placed upon the formal psychogram. It happens in this particular case that the psychogram relates closely to interpretations that flow from the qualitative nature of the responses. This tends to support the interpretation but does not validate it.

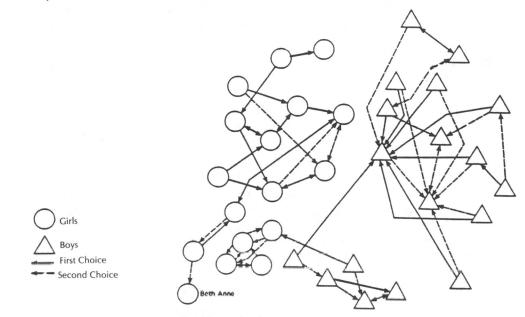

Girls
Boys
First Choice
Second Choice

Beth Anne

Figure 2. Sociogram for Beth Anne's fifth-grade class.

Sociometric Results

The sociogram (Fig. 2) maps the results of class responses to the question, "Whom would you like to sit next to?" Without attempting an analysis of the classroom as a whole, I will only say that as is not unusual at this age level, there is a definite separation between boys and girls. While the boys tend to cluster around certain leaders or "stars of attraction," the girls usually relate to each other in smaller cliques or even dyads.

Beth Anne's position in the classroom group insofar as these data show is extremely marginal. She is the second choice of a girl whom she considers (inferred from other data) to be her best friend. She made no choices herself. Her social situation is not significantly altered according to the social mapping of the results of the responses to the other two questions, "Whom would you like to pal around with after school?" and "Whom would you like to invite to a birthday party?"

Responses on the status-reputation test from the classroom group are impressively consistent with the results of the sociometric technique. Beth Anne is rated minimally: once for "Never having a good time" and once each for "Liking school" and "Being good-looking."

The results from both techniques indicate that Beth Anne is marginal in the classroom group. She is given very little attention—either favorable or unfavorable. It is almost as though she were not there at all. These results are consistent with direct observations made of her behavior and interactions with other children in the classroom and on the playground during recess.

Her parents were informed that the study of Beth Anne was under way. They had given their enthusiastic permission for the study when they were told, as was true, that Beth Anne was selected as a particularly well-adjusted child for special study. After the data collected above

51

had been discussed within our team, an appointment was made to discuss the material with the parents and I was elected as the team representative. By that time the study had become primarily mine, although all three members of the team had engaged in observations and we had discussed the data as they came in during weekly seminar sessions.

Home Visit and Parent Interview

Beth Anne's home was decidedly upper middle-class in furnishings and exterior appearance. The interior appointments were luxurious and a two-car garage with a beautifully landscaped lawn completed the picture. Her father's occupation as the manager of a large building materials manufacturing company was appropriate to the socioeconomic status assignment.

When I entered the house Beth Anne's mother was waiting for me and said that her husband would come soon because he was very interested also. We discussed their recent trip to Alaska until Mr. Johnson arrived. Mrs. Johnson's attitude seemed very cooperative, and in fact she appeared pleased that the school had arranged to have a home visit and interview.

As soon as Mr. Johnson arrived we began a cordial discussion over coffee. I wished to make it clear at the very beginning that we were not dealing with Beth Anne as a "problem" case, so I reviewed the circumstances of the selection. We were working with the faculties of several schools in the community in an attempt to improve understanding of the adjustments of children at different grade levels—academically, socially, and emotionally. Having set the stage in this positive manner, I asked what aspects of our results they were particularly interested in. The father, a dynamic doer who wasted no time getting to the point, asked three questions as one, "What did you do, what did you find out, and what are you going to do about it?"

Rather than answer all these questions, I explained the techniques used in our study in some detail, including observations, sociometric materials, and projective tests. I explained why we used these techniques and what each contributed to a rounded picture of the child's adjustment. The parents seemed interested but obviously had some other concerns on their minds.

Mrs. Johnson queried, "Did you find that Beth Anne was temperamental or nervous at all?" I asked her to explain what she meant by that. She went on to explain that Beth Anne was "always complaining about her health. If any little thing is wrong with her, she wants to go to bed and she is always thinking that she is getting sick." She elaborated upon this at some length and then went on further to say, "She used to have a tic.... I guess that's what you would call it. When she was reading, and she reads a lot, she would draw her stomach up into a tight little knot and then let it go and the abdominal muscles would jerk back and forth." She continued, "I took her to the doctor, of course, and he said that she was tense and nervous but not to worry about it, that it was just an abdominal tic. He said that she would get over it eventually and as a matter of fact she is better now." This condition had apparently become obvious about a year ago.

Using this as leverage, I asked the parents if she were not rather a perfectionist—if she didn't seem to feel that everything she did, particularly at school, had to be done perfectly. Both parents agreed quickly and rather enthusiastically that this was the case. They appeared to regard any question as somewhat of a compliment. Possibly they could regard the pattern I described as evidence of a high achievement drive. They confirmed the observation implicit in the question with several examples concerning her behavior at home, in her room, her dress, and maintenance of personal possessions. After some minutes of this, I asked them if they thought this perfectionism might not cost her too much in tension and loss of spontaneity. While both parents nodded assent to this, they did not agree as wholeheartedly as they did when I asked them if she were not a perfectionist. They apparently could accept the definition of Beth Anne as an achievement-oriented youngster, but they could not bring themselves to accept the possibility that the standards of achievement could be so high as to make the cost so great. I did not press the point. When a silence in the conversation developed, I did nothing to fill it.

At this point Mr. Johnson said, "There's something else…. I'm not so concerned about it but Mary [the mother] is…."And then the mother took up the cue, saying, "There are several junior high schools here [and she named them], now you have had a lot of experience in schools, could you tell us which one is the best?" I replied by asking her what she particularly wanted of the school selected. She said, "Well, we've been wondering whether or not we should move to a different neighborhood when Beth Anne is ready for junior high school. Washington School has been fine and we both appreciate all the things the teachers have done for Beth Anne, but you know there are all kinds of children over there—Mexicans, Italians, Chinese, Japanese, and even Negroes. Now, I believe in being democratic, but I feel that Beth Anne should associate with children that are, well…more her *equals!* [emphasis hers]. When she gets into junior high school this will be more important than it is now, but she feels it even now. She came home just the other day and said, 'Oh Mother, do I *have* to dance with them?' I think she should go to a school that doesn't have such a mixed group, where the children are all more her kind…don't you think so?"

In response I pointed out that the choice of a school was a decision that should be made by the parents in consultation with the child and that what was important to one might not be important to another. Furthermore, it seemed to me that two points of equal importance in respect to a child's associates are, first, that the child be given a sense of belonging to a particular group and, second, that he or she should have broad experience with a wide variety of people from different backgrounds. This should enable the child to adjust well in any situation and to respect differences in others. When the parents pointed out that the two seemed contradictory I agreed, stating, however, that both could be accomplished if the parents' attitudes were supportive. To probe their attitudes a bit, I then suggested that they send their daughter to a private boarding school. Mrs. Johnson said that she wanted Beth Anne to be under her supervision, which would not be possible if she went away. However, she said, she wanted Beth Anne to be able to choose her own friends, with no attempt at reconciliation of the contradiction this posed with her other statements. I ended this phase of the discussion by saying that whatever the situation, Beth Anne's attitudes toward her classmates would reflect in significant degree what the parents thought.

I asked if there was any other specific topic they would like to discuss. The father asked how well Beth Anne was liked by her classmates. I replied, "She was not rejected more than a very few times by any other child; apparently they do not dislike her." While this did not tell the whole truth, it was at least in the direction of the truth, and I thought it was about as much as the parents could accept. I then asked if any of Beth Anne's friends were in her class, and Mrs. Johnson named three. My next statement was that Beth Anne was not chosen often either and that in my opinion some of her classmates may have felt that she was critical of them. However, I told them also that the only negative trait on our status-reputation test was that she was rated as never having a good time. I could not explain the exact meaning of this, but assumed that it represented the children's feeling that she was serious about her school work. Before leaving I reassured them that "Beth Anne is a very excellent student and the teachers all like her a great deal." With reference to the points they had brought up, I told them that it might be important to see that she is encouraged to relax a little more and enjoy life as it comes. I said I thought her school work would keep up since she is very intelligent, even though her parents make this appear less important. I left thanking them for their cooperation and saying that it was a pleasure to talk with parents who were as cooperative as they were. They both uttered the usual pleasantries and said that they very much appreciated my coming to talk with them.

Teachers' Responses to the Evidence

By the end of our study period all of the evidence described above, plus many more details, had been shared with the staff. The teachers' responses could be described as ranging from surface compliance and agreement to deep covert resistance and resentment. I will draw a few representative comments from the tape taken during the final session with the faculty.

"I have her in art for 80 minutes a week where we try to bring out creative ideas, but actually she never offers any ideas. She usually looks at me as if to say, 'Well, what do I do next?'"

"I know Beth Anne and her family quite well and she knows this, but she is aloof with me. Does she impress the rest of you that way?"

"She reads so much. I should think this would aid her imagination. She reads stories about girls, camping, fairy stories, everything that children her age and even older read."

"She belongs to a group that went to camp last summer, but I don't think she went. She does have that little frown or worried look. I remember it bothered you, Mrs. Smith."

"I suppose that when a teacher has thirty-five children she tends to think of normal and adjusted in terms of how well they conform."

"Well they do have a very nice home. The parents just returned from a month's trip to Alaska and they hired a trained nurse to stay with the children. They have always been very thoughtful about their welfare."

"Well she has certainly done outstanding work academically, all the way through since kindergarten right up to the present in this school."

"She was always absent a lot in third grade and she never was particularly friendly. I always felt that she looked down her nose at the other children in the class who weren't quite up to her ... I don't know whether she just didn't want to enter into things or whether she was fearful of making a mistake or what. Though she did good work, I always had a queer little feeling about her. I don't know just what it was."

"I don't think you have to worry about Beth Anne. She is going to arrive. Her family and their standing will see to that and she represents them very well."

"I agree. She'll be successful! She'll belong to a sorority."

"Well, anyway, she's a great reader!"

Interpretation

This case study virtually tells its own story and in that sense little interpretation is needed. Not all cases are as neat. This one was selected out of a much larger group—not for its representativeness but rather for its ideal-typical characteristics. It pulls together in one configuration dynamic processes that are present in some form in many other cases. It seems to be in part a reversal of the relationship between the teacher and the fifth-grade class and the counselor and his class that I have discussed elsewhere. It is actually only a variation in this relationship. In all of these cases and in many others that we studied during our several years of field research and consultation, it became apparent that teachers, usually quite contrary to their expressed intentions and ideals, were selecting children for the fruits of success in our social system or for the ignominy of defeat and alienation on the basis of undeclared, and probably unknown, cultural biases.

Beth Anne was selected by the teachers by consensus as exceptionally well adjusted. It is difficult to know exactly what "adjusted" means to anyone, though it was a term used very widely in the fifties and sixties in American public schools. These particular teachers said during our preliminary consultations that adjustment meant "conformity to the rules and regulations of the classroom," "success at school work," "the ability to achieve according to the expectations of parents and teachers," "an ability to get along well with one's peers," "a person who is not too conflict-ridden when he or she attempts to get along with their work and play," and "a child who works and plays well with others." The teachers were clearly not all of a single mind concerning what adjustment meant, but their definitions tended toward an adaptation to the situation as defined by teachers, by rules, and, by the culture which the school represented. This is not unreasonable. In every cultural system those who accept the rules and achieve the goals laid down within the system are "adjusted" and those who do not are deviant, maladjusted, or criminal. The teachers' definitions do not pay much attention to what is inside Beth Anne's mind and, in fact, do not have much to do with Beth Anne at all. They have more to do with the school than with the child. This is understandable too.

However, we are faced with the fact that the teachers, even given their own criteria of adjustment, inaccurately perceived Beth Anne's situation. It is true that she achieved well according to the formal standards of academic performance. This achievement, however, was apparently at considerable psychic cost which was almost completely overlooked. Even more startling is the fact that the teachers misread the degree of her social adjustment. She did not "work and play well with others." In fact, she interacted with other children very little and was definitely marginal, really isolated within the classroom group.

Beth Anne's social marginality and isolation within the school was accompanied by severe internal distress in her own psychic system. She was compliant, a high achiever, but fearful of not achieving. She was unable to express her own emotions and had begun to evolve into a very constricted personality—all the more sad because she was such an intelligent girl. These processes had gone so far that a form of hysteric conversion had occurred. The prediction made on the basis of Rorschach evidence that the conversion would take the form of a somatic disturbance or possibly chronic invalidism was strongly supported. She wanted to stay in bed "on the slightest pretext" and suffered an "abdominal tic."

It would be easy to conclude that the teachers misperceived Beth Anne simply because she was academically successful—a high achiever in those areas where the teachers are directly responsible. This is, indeed, part of the cause for the misreading, but it is not a sufficient cause.

As I interpret the whole pattern of Beth Anne's adaptation and the perceptions of others of this adaptation, I see the teachers' perceptions as a self-sustaining cultural belief system. Beth Anne was selected not only because she was a high achiever but because in every other way she represented the image of what is desirable in American middle-class culture as it existed at the time of the study in the fifties and still exists today in slightly modified form. Beth Anne and her family represented success and achievement, the value of hard work, the validity of gratification delayed for future satisfaction, the validity of respectability and cleanliness, of good manners and of good dress as criteria for behavior. Beth Anne fit the criteria by means of which the teachers were selecting behaviors and children for the single channel of success and adaptation for which the school was designed as an institution representing the dominant mainstream culture.

I have characterized the belief in these values and selective criteria as self-sustaining because negative evidence was rationalized out of the system. Despite behaviors and attributes that any alert observer could have picked up in Beth Anne's case without the aid of outside experts or foreign instruments, Beth Anne was seen as one of the best-adjusted children in the school because she fit the belief system about the relationship between certain symbols, certain behaviors, and success as culturally defined.

This belief system, like most, can and does work. When belief systems stop working entirely they cease to exist, but they can continue to work partially for a very long time at great cost. In this case the cost to Beth Anne was profound. The culturally induced blindness of her teachers was in a certain real sense killing her and in ways no less painful than those in which minority children were and are being "killed" in many American schools.

Conclusion

I am not blaming teachers personally for what I have described in this case analysis. The teachers, the children, the administrator, and all of the other actors on the stage are acting out a cultural drama. What I am striving for as an anthropologist of education is an understanding of this drama as a cultural process. As an anthropologist teaching teachers I want to promote *awareness* of this cultural process. None of the teachers that I have described here or elsewhere in my writings[3] are people of bad intent. Most teachers are idealistic, many are quite liberal in their political and social beliefs, but they *are products of their culture* and live within the framework of values and symbols that are a part of that culture. By being made aware of what they are and do they can be freed from the tyranny of their cultures; in turn, they will be able to free children from the damaging effects of premature, inaccurate, or prejudiced estimates and interpretations of their behavior that are culturally induced.

This awareness is not easily gained. Though the teachers were exposed to intimate details of Beth Anne's case as these details developed, and though we exercised responsible skill and sensitivity in the dissemination of this evidence in open and closed discussions, the resistance of the teachers to the implications of the evidence was profound. The educative process had some effect, probably, but I doubt that it was very significant as far as the future behavior of the teachers is concerned. Nor is a course or two in anthropology the answer. A year's fieldwork in a foreign community where one's assumptions, values, and perceptions are profoundly shocked by raw experience would make a significant difference, but not always in a direction that would be useful in the classroom. Matters have improved since the study of Beth Anne, but they have not improved enough. In my opinion a substantial part of the energy and time devoted to training teachers should be devoted to learning how to cope with the kinds of problems that I have been discussing in this and other case studies.

We were somewhat more successful with Beth Anne and her family as individuals than we were with the teachers. We explicitly recommended that the standards of excellence be lowered somewhat for Beth Anne and that she be given to understand that such achievements were not all that was important. Beth Anne seemed considerably improved according to a short follow-up observation the next year. But we cannot be sure of what happened. It may be that doing the study had a positive effect. Beth Anne at least knew that someone else had found out what it was like to be Beth Anne, and her parents discovered that it was possible to face a problem that they intuitively felt to be there because an outside agency had detected the same problem.

[1] Details of time and place are left ambiguous, certain details of fact are altered, and all personal references are disguised in order to protect all parties involved with the case study.
[2] With the wisdom of hindsight, I would not administer this technique again. It is potentially destructive to children's self-feelings and stimulates corrosive interpersonal evaluation.
[3] See Spindler, George Dearborn, 1959, *The Transmission of American Culture,* Cambridge, MA: Harvard University Press, for the Graduate School of Education.

Stereotypes: Explaining People Who Are Different

by Ozzie Simmons

EDITORS NOTE: *In this article the author uses "Mexican" and "Mexican-American" more or less interchangeably.*

A number of psychological and sociological studies have treated ethnic and racial stereotypes as they appear publicly in the mass media and also as held privately by individuals. The present paper is based on data collected for a study of a number of aspects of the relations between Anglo-Americans and Mexican-Americans in a South Texas community, and is concerned with the principal assumptions and expectations that Anglo- and Mexican-Americans hold of one another; how they see each other; the extent to which these pictures are realistic; and the implications of their mutual expectations.

The Community

The community studied (here called "Border City") is in South Texas, about 250 miles south of San Antonio. Driving south from San Antonio, one passes over the vast expanses of brushland and grazing country, then suddenly comes upon acres of citrus groves, farmlands rich with vegetables and cotton, and long rows of palm trees. This is the "Magic Valley," an oasis in the semidesert region of South Texas. The Missouri Pacific Railroad (paralleled by Highway 83, locally called "The longest street in the world") bisects twelve major towns and cities of the Lower Rio Grande Valley between Brownsville, near the Gulf of Mexico, and Rio Grande City, 103 miles to the west.

Border City is neither the largest nor the smallest of these cities, and is physically and culturally much like the rest. Its first building was constructed in 1905. By 1920 it had 5,331 inhabitants and at the time of our study these had increased to an estimated 17,500. The completion of the St. Louis, Brownsville, and Mexico Railroad in 1904 considerably facilitated Anglo-American immigration to the Valley. Before this the Valley had been inhabited largely by Mexican ranchers, who maintained large haciendas in the traditional Mexican style based on peonage. Most of these haciendas are now divided into large or small tracts that are owned by Anglo-Americans, who obtained them through purchase or less legitimate means. The position of the old Mexican-American landowning families has steadily deteriorated, and today these families, with a few exceptions, are completely overshadowed by the Anglo-Americans, who have taken over their social and economic position in the community.

The Anglo-American immigration into the Valley was paralleled by that of the Mexicans from across the border, who were attracted by the seemingly greater opportunities for farm labor created by the introduction of irrigation and the subsequent agricultural expansion. Actually, there had been a small but steady flow of Mexican immigration into South Texas that long antedated the Anglo-American immigration. At present, Mexican-Americans probably constitute about two-fifths of the total population of the Valley.

In Border City, Mexican-Americans comprise about 56 percent of the population. The southwestern part of the city, adjoining and sometimes infiltrating the business and industrial areas, is variously referred to as "Mexiquita," "Mexican-town," and "Little Mexico" by the city's Anglo-Americans, and as the *colonia* by the Mexican-Americans. With few exceptions, the *colonia* is inhabited only by Mexican-Americans, most of whom live in close proximity to one another in indifferently constructed houses on tiny lots. The north side of the city, which lies across the railroad tracks, is inhabited almost completely by Anglo-Americans. Its appearance is in sharp contrast to that of the *colonia* in that it is strictly residential and displays much better housing.

In the occupational hierarchy of Border City, the top level (the growers, packers, canners, businessmen, and professionals) is overwhelmingly Anglo-American. In the middle group (the white-collar occupations) Mexicans are prominent only where their bilingualism makes them useful, for example, as clerks and salesmen. The bottom level (farm laborers, shed and cannery workers, and domestic servants) is overwhelmingly Mexican-American.

These conditions result from a number of factors, some quite distinct from the reception accorded Mexican-Americans by Anglo-Americans. Many Mexican-Americans are still recent immigrants and are thus relatively unfamiliar with Anglo-American culture and urban living, or else persist in their tendency to live apart and maintain their own institutions whenever possible. Among their disadvantages, however, the negative attitudes and discriminatory practices of the Anglo-American group must be counted. It is only fair to say, with the late Ruth Tuck, that much of what Mexican-Americans have suffered at Anglo-American hands has not been perpetrated deliberately but through indifference, that it has been done not with the fist but with the elbow. The average social and economic status of the Mexican-American group has been improving, and many are moving upward. This is partly owing to increasing acceptance by the Anglo-American group, but chiefly to the efforts of the Mexican-Americans themselves.

Anglo-American Assumptions and Expectations

Robert Lynd writes of the dualism in the principal assumptions that guide Americans in conducting their everyday life and identifies the attempt to "live by contrasting rules of the game" as a characteristic aspect of our culture.[1] This pattern of moral compromise, symptomatic of what is likely to be only vaguely a conscious moral conflict, is evident in Anglo-American assumptions and expectations with regard to Mexican-Americans, which appear both in the moral principles that define what intergroup relations ought to be, and in the popular notions held by Anglo-Americans as to what Mexican-Americans are "really" like. In the first case there is a response to the "American creed," which embodies ideals of the essential dignity of the individual and of certain inalienable rights to freedom, justice, and equal opportunity.

Accordingly, Anglo-Americans believe that Mexican-Americans must be accorded full acceptance and equal status in the larger society. When their orientation to these ideals is uppermost, Anglo-Americans believe that the assimilation of Mexican-Americans is only a matter of time, contingent solely on the full incorporation of Anglo-American values and ways of life.

These expectations regarding the assimilation of the Mexican are most clearly expressed in the notion of the "high type" of Mexican. It is based on three criteria: occupational achievement and wealth (the Anglo-American's own principal criteria of status) and command of Anglo-American ways. Mexican-Americans who can so qualify are acceptable for membership in the service clubs and a few other Anglo-American organizations and for limited social intercourse. They may even intermarry without being penalized or ostracized. Both in their achievements in business and agriculture and in wealth, they compare favorably with middle-class Anglo-Americans, and they manifest a high command of the latter's ways. This view of the "high type" of Mexican reflects the Anglo-American assumption that Mexicans are assimilable; it does not necessarily insure a full acceptance of even the "high type" of Mexican or that his acceptance will be consistent.

The assumption that Mexican-Americans will be ultimately assimilated was not uniformly shared by all the Anglo-Americans who were our informants in Border City. Regardless of whether they expressed adherence to this ideal, however, most Anglo-Americans expressed the contrasting assumption that Mexican-Americans are essentially inferior. Thus the same people may hold assumptions and expectations that are contradictory, although expressed at different times and in different situations. As in the case of their adherence to the ideal of assimilability, not all Anglo-Americans hold the same assumptions and expectations with respect to the inferiority of Mexican-Americans; and even those who agree vary in the intensity of their beliefs. Some do not believe in the Mexican's inferiority at all; some are relatively moderate or skeptical, while others express extreme views with considerable emotional intensity.

Despite this variation, the Anglo-Americans' principal assumptions and expectations emphasize the Mexicans' presumed inferiority. In its most characteristic pattern, such inferiority is held to be self-evident. As one Anglo-American woman put it, "Mexicans are inferior because they are so typically and naturally Mexican." Since they are so obviously inferior, their present subordinate status is appropriate and is really their own fault. There is a ready identification between Mexicans and menial labor, buttressed by an image of the Mexican worker as improvident, undependable, irresponsible, childlike, and indolent. If Mexicans are fit for only the humblest labor, there is nothing abnormal about the fact that most Mexican workers are at the bottom of the occupational pyramid, and the fact that most Mexicans are unskilled workers is sufficient proof that they belong in that category.

Associated with the assumption of Mexican inferiority is that of the homogeneity of this group—that is, all Mexicans are alike. Anglo-Americans may classify Mexicans as being of "high type" and "low type" and at the same time maintain that "a Mexican is a Mexican." Both notions serve a purpose, depending on the situation. The assumption that all Mexicans are alike buttresses the assumption of inferiority by making it convenient to ignore the fact of the existence of a substantial number of Mexican-Americans who represent all levels of business and professional achievement. Such people are considered exceptions to the rule.

Anglo-American Images of Mexican-Americans

To employ Gordon Allport's definition, a stereotype is an exaggerated belief associated with a category, and its function is to justify conduct in relation to that category.[2] Some of the Anglo-American images of the Mexican have no ascertainable basis in fact, while others have at least a kernel of truth. Although some components of these images derive from behavior patterns that are characteristic of some Mexican-Americans in some situations, few if any of the popular generalizations about them are valid as stated, and none is demonstrably true of all. Some of the images of Mexican-Americans are specific to a particular area of intergroup relations, such as the image of the Mexican-American's attributes as a worker. Another is specific to politics and describes Mexicans as ready to give their votes to whoever will pay for them or provide free barbecues and beer. Let us consider a few of the stereotypical beliefs that are widely used on general principles to justify Anglo-American practices of exclusion and subordination.

One such general belief accuses Mexican-Americans of being unclean. The examples given of this supposed characteristic most frequently refer to a lack of personal cleanliness and environmental hygiene and to a high incidence of skin ailments ascribed to a lack of hygienic practices. Indeed, there are few immigrant groups, regardless of their ethnic background, to whom this defect has not been attributed by the host society. It has often been observed that for middle-class Americans cleanliness is not simply a matter of keeping clean but is also an index to the morals and virtues of the individual. It is largely true that Mexicans tend to be much more casual in hygienic practices than Anglo-Americans. Moreover, their labor in the field, the packing sheds, and the towns is rarely clean work, and it is possible that many Anglo-Americans base their conclusions on what they observe in such situations. There is no evidence of a higher incidence of skin ailments among Mexicans than among Anglo-Americans. The belief that Mexicans are unclean is useful for rationalizing the Anglo-American practice of excluding Mexicans from any situation that involves close or allegedly close contact with Anglo-Americans, as in residence, and the common use of swimming pools and other recreational facilities.

Drunkenness and criminality are a pair of traits that have appeared regularly in the stereotypes applied to immigrant groups. They have a prominent place in Anglo-American images of Mexicans. If Mexicans are inveterate drunkards and have criminal tendencies, a justification is provided for excluding them from full participation in the life of the community. It is true that drinking is a popular activity among Mexican-Americans and that total abstinence is rare, except among some Protestant Mexican-Americans. Drinking varies, however, from the occasional consumption of a bottle of beer to the heavy drinking of more potent beverages, so that the frequency of drinking and drunkenness is far from being evenly distributed among Mexican-Americans. Actually, this pattern is equally applicable to the Anglo-American group. The ample patronage of bars in the Anglo-American part of Border City, and the drinking behavior exhibited by Anglo-Americans when they cross the river to Mexico indicate that Mexicans have no monopoly on drinking or drunkenness. It is true that the number of arrests for drunkenness in Border City is greater among Mexicans, but this is probably because Mexicans are more vulnerable to arrest. The court records in Border City show little difference in the contributions made to delinquency and crime by Anglo- and Mexican-Americans.

Another cluster of images in the Anglo-American stereotype portrays Mexican-Americans as deceitful and of a "low" morality, as mysterious, unpredictable, and hostile to Anglo-Americans. It is quite possible that Mexicans resort to a number of devices in their relations with Anglo-Americans, particularly in relations with employers, to compensate for their disadvantages, which may be construed by Anglo-Americans as evidence of deceitfulness. The whole nature of the dominant-subordinate relationship does not make for frankness on the part of Mexicans or encourage them to face up directly to Anglo-Americans in most intergroup contacts. As to the charge of immorality, one need only recognize the strong sense of loyalty and obligation that Mexicans feel in their familial and interpersonal relations to know that the charge is baseless. The claim that Mexicans are mysterious and deceitful may in part reflect Anglo-American reactions to actual differences in culture and personality, but like the other beliefs considered here, is highly exaggerated. The imputation of hostility to Mexicans, which is manifested in a reluctance to enter the *colonia*, particularly at night, may have its kernel of truth, but appears to be largely a projection of the Anglo-American's own feelings.

All three of these images can serve to justify exclusion and discrimination: if Mexicans are deceitful and immoral, they do not have to be accorded equal status and justice; if they are mysterious and unpredictable, there is no point in treating them as one would a fellow Anglo-American; and if they are hostile and dangerous, it is best that they live apart in colonies of their own.

Not all Anglo-American images of the Mexican are unfavorable. Among those usually meant to be complimentary are the beliefs that all Mexicans are musical and always ready for a fiesta, that they are very "romantic" rather than "realistic" (which may have unfavorable overtones as well), and that they love flowers and can grow them under the most adverse conditions. Although each of these beliefs may have a modicum of truth, it may be noted that they tend to reinforce Anglo-American images of Mexicans as childlike and irresponsible, and thus they support the notion that Mexicans are capable only of subordinate status.

Mexican-American Assumptions, Expectations, and Images

Mexican-Americans are as likely to hold contradictory assumptions and distorted images as are Anglo-Americans. Their principal assumptions, however, must reflect those of Anglo-Americans—that is, Mexicans must take into account the Anglo-Americans' conflict as to their potential equality and present inferiority, since they are the object of such imputations. Similarly, their images of Anglo-Americans are not derived wholly independently, but to some extent must reflect their own subordinate status. Consequently, their stereotypes of Anglo-Americans are much less elaborate, in part because Mexicans feel no need of justifying the present intergroup relation, in part because the very nature of their dependent position forces them to view the relation more realistically than Anglo-Americans do. For the same reasons, they need not hold to their beliefs about Anglo-Americans with the rigidity and intensity so often characteristic of the latter.

Any discussion of these assumptions and expectations requires some mention of the class distinctions within the Mexican-American group. Its middle class, though small as compared with the lower class, is powerful within the group and performs the critical role of intermediary in negotiations with the Anglo-American group. Middle-class status is based on education and occupation, family background, readiness to serve the interests of the group, on wealth, and the degree of acculturation, or command of Anglo-American ways. Anglo-Americans recognize Mexican class distinctions (although not very accurately) in their notions of the "high type" and "low type" of Mexicans.

In general, lower-class Mexicans do not regard the disabilities of their status as being nearly as severe as do middle-class Mexican-Americans. This is primarily a reflection of the insulation between the Anglo-American world and that of the Mexican lower class. Most Mexicans, regardless of class, are keenly aware of Anglo-American attitudes and practices with regard to their group, but lower-class Mexicans do not conceive of participation in the larger society as necessary nor do they regard Anglo-American practices of exclusion as affecting them directly. Their principal reaction has been to maintain their isolation, and thus they have not been particularly concerned with improving their status by acquiring Anglo-American ways, a course more characteristic of the middle-class Mexican.

Mexican-American assumptions and expectations regarding Anglo-Americans must be qualified, then, as being more characteristic of middle- than of lower-class Mexican-Americans. Mexicans, like Anglo-Americans, are subject to conflicts in their ideals, not only because of irrational thinking on their part but also because of Anglo-American inconsistencies between ideal and practice. As for ideals expressing democratic values, Mexican expectations are for obvious reasons the counterpart of the Anglo-Americans'—that Mexican-Americans should be accorded full acceptance and equal opportunity. They feel a considerable ambivalence, however, as to the Anglo-American expectation that the only way to achieve this goal is by a full incorporation of Anglo-American values and ways of life, for this implies the ultimate loss of their cultural identity as Mexicans. On the one hand, they favor the acquisition of Anglo-American culture and the eventual remaking of the Mexican in the Anglo-American culture; but on the other hand, they are not so sure that Anglo-American acceptance is worth such a price. When they are concerned with this dilemma, Mexicans advocate a fusion with Anglo-American culture in which the "best" of the Mexican ways, as they view it, would be retained along with the incorporation of the "best" of the Anglo-American ways, rather than a one-sided exchange in which all that is distinctively Mexican would be lost.

A few examples will illustrate the point of view expressed in the phrase, "the best of both ways." A premium is placed on speaking good, unaccented English, but the retention of good Spanish is valued just as highly as "a mark of culture that should not be abandoned." Similarly, there is an emphasis on the incorporation of behavior patterns that are considered characteristically Anglo-American and that will promote "getting ahead," but not to the point at which the drive for power and wealth would become completely dominant, as is believed to be the case with Anglo-Americans.

Mexican ambivalence about becoming Anglo-American or achieving a fusion of the "best" of both cultures is compounded by their ambivalence about another issue, that of equality versus inferiority. That Anglo-Americans are dominant in the society and seem to monopolize its accomplishments and rewards leads Mexicans at times to draw the same conclusion that Anglo-Americans do, namely, that Mexicans are inferior. This questioning of their own sense of worth exists in all classes of the Mexican-American group, although with varying intensity, and plays a substantial part in every adjustment to intergroup relations. There is a pronounced tendency to concede the superiority of Anglo-American ways and consequently to define Mexican ways as undesirable, inferior, and disreputable. The tendency to believe in his own inferiority is counterbalanced, however, by the Mexican's fierce racial pride, which sets the tone of Mexican demands and strivings for equal status, even though these may slip into feelings of inferiority.

The images Mexicans have of Anglo-Americans may not be so elaborate or so emotionally charged as the images that Anglo-Americans have of Mexicans, but they are nevertheless stereotypes, over-generalized, and exaggerated, although used primarily for defensive rather than justificatory purposes. Mexican images of Anglo-Americans are sometimes favorable, particularly when they identify such traits as initiative, ambition, and industriousness as being peculiarly Anglo-American. Unfavorable images are prominent, however, and, although they may be hostile, they never impute inferiority to Anglo-Americans. Most of the Mexican stereotypes evaluate Anglo-Americans on the basis of their attitudes toward Mexican-Americans. For example, one such classification provides a two-fold typology. The first type, the "majority," includes those who are cold, unkind, mercenary, and exploitative. The second type, the "minority," consists of those who are friendly, warm, just, and unprejudiced. For the most part, Mexican images of Anglo-Americans reflect the latter's patterns of exclusion and assumptions of superiority, as experienced by Mexican-Americans. Thus Anglo-Americans are pictured as stolid, phlegmatic, cold-hearted, and distant. They are also said to be braggarts, conceited, inconstant, and insincere.

Intergroup Relations, Mutual Expectations, and Cultural Differences

A number of students of intergroup relations assert that research in this area has yet to demonstrate any relation between stereotypical beliefs and intergroup behavior; indeed, some insist that under certain conditions ethnic attitudes and discrimination can vary independently. Arnold M. Rose, for example, concludes that "from a heuristic standpoint it may be desirable to assume that patterns of intergroup relations, on the one hand, and attitudes of prejudice and stereotyping, on the other hand, are fairly unrelated phenomena although they have reciprocal influences on each other...."[3] In the present study, no systematic attempt was made to investigate the relation between the stereotypical beliefs of particular individuals and their actual intergroup behavior; but the study did yield much evidence that both images which justify group separatism and separateness itself are characteristic aspects of intergroup relations in Border City. One of the principal finds is that in those situations in which contact between Anglo-Americans and Mexicans is voluntary (such as residence, education, recreation, religious worship, and social intercourse) the characteristic pattern is separateness rather than common participation. Wherever intergroup contact is necessary, as in occupational activities and the performance of commercial and professional services, it is held to the minimum sufficient to accomplish the purpose of the contact. The extent of this separateness is not constant for all members of the two groups, since it tends to be less severe between Anglo-Americans and those Mexicans they define as of a "high type." Nevertheless, the evidence reveals a high degree of compatibility between beliefs and practices in Border City's intergroup relations, although the data have nothing to offer for the identification of direct relationships.

In any case, the separateness that characterizes intergroup relations cannot be attributed solely to the exclusion practices of the Anglo-American group. Mexicans have tended to remain separate by choice as well as by necessity. Like many other ethnic groups, they have often found this the easier course, since they need not strain to learn another language or to change their ways and manners. The isolation practices of the Mexican group are as relevant to an understanding of intergroup relations as are the exclusion practices of the Anglo-Americans.

This should not, however, obscure the fact that to a wide extent the majority of Mexican-Americans share the patterns of living of Anglo-American society; many of their ways are already identical. Regardless of the degree of their insulation from the larger society, the demands of life in the United States have required basic modifications of the Mexicans' cultural tradition. In material culture, Mexicans are hardly to be distinguished from Anglo-Americans, and there have been basic changes in medical beliefs and practices and in the customs regarding godparenthood. Mexicans have acquired English in varying degrees, and their Spanish has become noticeably Anglicized. Although the original organization of the family has persisted, major changes have occurred in patterns of traditional authority, as well as in child training and courtship practices. Still, it is the exceedingly rare Mexican-American, no matter how acculturated he may be to the dominant society, who does not in some degree retain the more subtle characteristics of his Mexican heritage, particularly in his conception of time and in other fundamental value orientations, as well as in his modes of participation in interpersonal relations. Many of the most acculturated Mexican-Americans have attempted to exemplify what

63

they regard as "the best of both ways." They have become largely Anglo-American in their way of living, but they still retain fluent Spanish and a knowledge of their traditional culture, and they maintain an identification with their own heritage while participating in Anglo-American culture. Nevertheless, this sort of achievement still seems a long way off for many Mexican-Americans who regard it as desirable.

A predominant Anglo-American expectation is that the Mexicans will be eventually assimilated into the larger society; but this is contingent upon Mexicans' becoming just like Anglo-Americans. The Mexican counterpart to this expectation is only partially complementary. Mexicans want to be full members of the larger society, but they do not want to give up their cultural heritage. There is even less complementarity of expectation with regard to the present conduct of intergroup relations. Anglo-Americans believe they are justified in withholding equal access to the rewards of full acceptance as long as Mexicans remain "different," particularly since they interpret the differences (both those which have some basis in reality and those which have none) as evidence of inferiority. Mexicans, on the other hand, while not always certain that they are not inferior, clearly want equal opportunity and full acceptance now, not in some dim future, and they do not believe that their differences (either presumed or real) from Anglo-Americans offer any justification for the denial of opportunity and acceptance. Moreover, they do not find that acculturation is rewarded in any clear and regular way by progressive acceptance.

It is probable that both Anglo-Americans and Mexicans will have to modify their beliefs and practices if they are to realize more nearly their expectations of each other. Mutual stereotyping, as well as the exclusion practices of Anglo-Americans and the isolation practices of Mexicans, maintains the separateness of the two groups, and separateness is a massive barrier to the realization of their expectations. The process of acculturation is presently going on among Mexican-Americans and will continue, regardless of whether changes in Anglo-Mexican relations occur. Unless Mexican-Americans can validate their increasing command of Anglo-American ways by a free participation in the larger society, however, such acculturation is not likely to accelerate its present leisurely pace, nor will it lead to eventual assimilation. The *colonia* is a relatively safe place in which new cultural acquisitions may be tried out, and thus it has its positive functions; but by the same token it is only in intergroup contacts with Anglo-Americans that acculturation is validated, that the Mexican's level of acculturation is tested, and that the distance he must yet travel to assimilation is measured.

Conclusions

There are major inconsistencies in the assumptions that Anglo-Americans and Mexican-Americans hold about one another. Anglo-Americans assume that Mexican-Americans are their potential, if not actual, peers, but at the same time assume they are their inferiors. The beliefs that presumably demonstrate the Mexican-Americans' inferiority tend to place them outside the accepted moral order and framework of Anglo-American society by attributing to them undesirable characteristics that make it "reasonable" to treat them differently from their fellow Anglo-Americans. Thus the negative images provide not only a rationalized definition of the intergroup relation that makes it palatable for Anglo-Americans, but also a substantial support for maintaining the relation as it is. The assumptions of Mexican-Americans about Anglo-Americans are similarly inconsistent, and their images of Anglo-Americans are predominantly negative, although these are primarily defensive rather than justificatory. The mutual expectations of the two groups contrast sharply with the ideal of a complementarity of expectations, in that Anglo-Americans expect Mexicans to become just like themselves, if they are to be accorded equal status in the larger society, whereas Mexican-Americans want full acceptance, regardless of the extent to which they give up their own ways and acquire those of the dominant group.

Anglo-Americans and Mexicans may decide to stay apart because they are different, but cultural differences provide no moral justification for one group to deny to the other equal opportunity and the rewards of the larger society. If the full acceptance of Mexicans by Anglo-Americans is contingent upon the disappearance of cultural differences, it will not be accorded in the foreseeable future. In our American society, we have often seriously underestimated the strength and tenacity of early cultural conditioning. We have expected newcomers to change their customs and values to conform to American ways as quickly as possible, without an adequate appreciation of the strains imposed by this process. An understanding of the nature of culture and of its interrelations with personality can make us more realistic about the rate at which cultural change can proceed and about the gains and costs for the individual who is subject to the experiences of acculturation. In viewing cultural differences primarily as disabilities, we neglect their positive aspects. Mexican-American culture represents the most constructive and effective means Mexican-Americans have yet been able to develop for coping with their changed natural and social environment. They will further exchange old ways for new only if these appear to be more meaningful and rewarding than the old, and then only if they are given full opportunity to acquire the new ways and to use them.

[1] Robert S. Lynd, *Knowledge for What?* (Princeton: Princeton University Press, 1948).

[2] Gordon W. Allport, *The Nature of Prejudice* (Cambridge: Addison-Wesley Publishing Company, 1954).

[3] Arnold M. Rose, "Intergroup Relations vs. Prejudice: Pertinent Theory for the Study of Social Change," *Social Problems* 4 (1956): 173-176.

Questions For Discussion

1.   Gordon Allport defines a stereotype as "an exaggerated belief associated with a category. Its function is to justify conduct in relation to that category." Give examples from Simmons' article of stereotypes and illustrate their functions in relation to the conduct of Mexican-American and Anglo-American groups.

2.   Are the stereotypes described in Simmons' and Spindler's articles different from each other? Which are more harmful? Explain.

3.   What generalizations about the nature of prejudice can be made on the basis of Ellis' reasons for joining the Klan?

4.   Discuss the implications that each of the articles in this section has regarding the education of minority groups. State points of agreement or disagreement. Explain.

You Will Do As Directed

by Ron Jones

This is the story of a teacher, Ron Jones, who tried an "experiment" about obedience with his class. The results were frightening!

For years I had kept a strange secret. Two hundred students shared this secret with me. Yesterday I ran into one of them by chance, and for a moment it all rushed back.

Steve McDonald had been a student in my World History class. As he came running down the street shouting, "Mr. Jones! Mr. Jones!" I had to stop for a minute to remember: Why is this young man hugging me? Steve sensed my doubt and backed up, then smiled, and slowly raised a hand in a cupped position. My God! He's a member of the Third Wave. It's Steve—Steve McDonald. He sat in the second row—a sensitive and bright student, played guitar and enjoyed drama.

I unconsciously raised my hand in the same salute: two comrades meeting long after the war. "Mr. Jones, do you remember the Third Wave?" I sure do: one of the most frightening events I have ever experienced in the classroom.

We talked and laughed about our secret, the Third Wave, for the next few hours. Then it was time to part. Steve turned and gave the salute without a word. I returned the gesture.

The Third Wave. Well, at last it can be talked about. The nightmare must finally be waning, after three years. I think it was Steve who initiated it all with a question.

We were studying Nazi Germany, and in the middle of a lecture he asked: How could the German people claim ignorance of the slaughter of the Jews? How could railroad conductors, teachers, doctors, know nothing about concentration camps and human carnage? How could neighbors and even friends of a Jewish citizen say they weren't there when it happened? I didn't know the answer.

There were several months to go in the school year and we were already at World War II, so I decided to take a week and explore the issue.

Strength through Discipline

On Monday I introduced my class to one of the key experiences of Nazi Germany—discipline. I talked about the beauty of discipline: how an athlete feels having worked hard and regularly to be successful at a sport; how a ballet dancer or painter perfects a movement, or a scientist pursues an idea. It's discipline, self-control, the power of the will, the tolerance of physical hardship for superior mental and physical ability. The ultimate triumph.

To demonstrate the power of discipline, I invited the class to try a new sitting posture. I described how proper posture assists concentration and strengthens the will. In fact, I commanded them to adopt this posture: feet flat on the floor, hand placed flat across the small of the back to force a straight alignment of the spine. "There. Can't you breathe more easily? Don't you feel better?"

We practiced this new position over and over. I walked up and down the aisles making small improvements. Proper sitting became the most important aspect of learning. I would allow the class to leave their desks, then call them abruptly back to sitting at attention. In speed drills, I concentrated on the feet being parallel and flat, ankles locked, knees bent at 90 degrees, hands flat and crossed against the back, spine straight, chin down, head forward. After repeated drilling, the class could move silently from outside the room to sitting at attention at their desks in five seconds.

It was strange how quickly the students took to this code of uniform behavior. I began to wonder just how far they could be pushed. Was this display of obedience a temporary game we were all playing, or was it something else? Was the desire for discipline and conformity a natural need, a social instinct we exercise subliminally inside a world of franchise restaurants and TV programming?

I decided to stretch the class's tolerance for regimented action. In the final 25 minutes I introduced some new rules: students must be sitting at attention before the late bell; all must carry pencils and paper for note-taking; when asking or answering questions, students must stand at the side of their desks; the first words of what they say must always be "Mr. Jones." We practiced questions and answers to achieve promptness and respect. Eventually the intensity of the response became more important then the content. To accentuate this, I demanded answers of three words or less. Students were rewarded for effort, and for a crisp and attentive manner. Soon everyone began popping up with questions and answers, even formerly hesitant speakers. The entire class seemed more involved—listening more intently, speaking out more openly, offering greater support. There was even a marked improvement in the quality of answers.

As for my part, I had nothing but questions. Why hadn't I thought of this exercise before? Students were reciting facts and concepts more accurately, asking better questions and treating each other with more compassion. How could this be? Here I was creating an authoritarian environment and it was turning out to be highly productive. I began to ponder not just how far this class could be pushed but how much I would alter my belief in the open classroom and self-directed learning. Was my faith in Carl Rogers to shrivel away? Where was this experiment leading?

Strength through Community

On Tuesday, the second day, I entered the classroom to find everyone sitting silently at attention. Some of their faces were relaxed with smiles that come from pleasing the teacher. But most of the students were looking straight ahead earnestly—neck muscles rigid, no sign of a smile or a thought. To release the tension I went to the board and wrote in big letters: STRENGTH THROUGH DISCIPLINE. Below this I wrote a second law: STRENGTH THROUGH COMMUNITY.

While the class sat in stern silence, I began to talk—lecture, sermonize—about the value of community. Inwardly I was debating whether to stop the experiment or continue. I hadn't foreseen such intensity or compliance. In fact, I was surprised to find my ideas on discipline acted out at all. I talked on and on, making up stories from experience as an athlete, coach and historian. It was easy. Community is that bond between individuals who work and struggle together. It's raising a barn with your neighbors, feeling that you are part of something beyond yourself—a team, a cause, *la raza*.

It was too late to go back. I now can appreciate why the astronomer returns relentlessly to the telescope. I was probing deeper into my own conceptions and into the motivations for group and individual action. There was much more to see and understand. Why did the students accept the authority I was imposing? Why didn't they question this martial behavior? When and how would this end?

I told the class that community-like discipline must be experienced to be understood. I had them chant in unison: "Strength through Discipline. Strength through Community." It was fun. They began to look at each other and sense the power of belonging; everyone was capable and equal. For the entire period we developed this simple activity.

What's more, I began to think of myself as part of the experiment, a willing subject of the group's momentum and identity. As the period was ending, and without forethought, I created a salute for class members only. To make it you brought your right hand up toward the right shoulder in a curled position. I called it the "Third Wave" salute because the hand resembled a wave about to top over, the beach lore has it that waves travel in series, the third wave being the last and largest. I made it a rule to salute all class members outside the classroom. When the bell sounded, with everyone sitting at attention, I slowly raised my arm and with a cupped hand saluted. It was a signal of recognition. Without command the entire group returned the salute.

Throughout the day, around the school, students from the class exchanged this greeting. I would be walking down the hall when suddenly three classmates would turn and flash a quick salute. In the library or in gym, they'd be seen giving this signal of recognition. The mystique of 30 individuals making this strange gesture soon called attention to the class and its exploration of the Nazi German personality. Many students outside the class asked if they could join.

Strength through Action

On Wednesday I decided to issue membership cards to everyone who wanted to continue what I called "the experiment." Not a single student elected to leave the room. There were now 43 in the class; 13 had cut other classes to join us. While the students sat at attention, I gave them a card. I marked three of the cards with a red X and informed the recipients that they had a special assignment: to report any members not complying with class rules. I then explained how discipline and community were meaningless without action. I discussed the beauty of taking full responsibility, for believing so thoroughly in yourself and your community or family that you would do anything to preserve and protect them. I stressed how hard work and allegiance to each other would accelerate learning. I reminded students what it felt like to be in classes where competition caused pain and degradation, the feeling of never acting wholeheartedly, never supporting each other.

At this point, people began to volunteer testimonials: "Mr. Jones, for the first time I'm learning lots of things." "Mr. Jones, why don't you teach like this all the time?" I had been pushing information at them in an extremely controlled setting, and the fact that they liked it was shocking. It was equally disconcerting to realize that the complex, time-consuming homework on German life was being completed and even enlarged on by students. I began to think they might do anything I assigned, and I decided to find out.

To create the experience of direct action I gave each individual a specific assignment: "It is your task to design a Third Wave banner...to stop any student who is not a Third Wave member from entering this room...to memorize the name and address of every Third Wave member...to convince at least 20 children in the elementary school that our sitting posture is necessary for better learning." I also asked each student to give me the name and address of one reliable friend who might want to join the Third Wave. I announced that once recommended, new members would receive a card and must pledge obedience to our rules.

By this time the whole school was alive with rumor and curiosity. Our principal came into an afternoon faculty meeting and gave me the Third Wave salute. The librarian thanked me for the 30-foot banner on learning, which she placed above the library entrance. By the end of the day, over 200 students were admitted into the order. I felt alone and a little scared.

Most of my fear came from the incidence of tattletaling. Although I appointed only three students to report deviate behavior, about 20 came to me with reports of Allan's not saluting, or Georgene's criticizing our experiment. This meant that half the class now considered it their duty to observe and report on other members.

By the end of the third day I was exhausted; I'd lost the balance between role playing and directed behavior. Many of the students were completely absorbed in being Third Wave members. They demanded strict obedience and bullied those who took the experiment lightly. Others simply fell into step and assigned themselves roles. I particularly remember Robert, big for his age and an academic drudge, though he tried harder than anyone I know to be successful. Like so many kids in school who don't excel or cause trouble, Robert was invisible. The only reason I came to know him at all was that I usually found him eating lunch in my classroom, alone.

The Third Wave gave Robert a place. At last he was equal to everyone; he could take part. Wednesday afternoon I found him following me and asked what in the world he was doing. He smiled (I don't think I'd ever seen him smile) and announced: "Mr. Jones, I'm your bodyguard. I'm afraid something will happen to you. Can I do it, Mr. Jones, please?" Given that assurance and smile, I couldn't say no. For the rest of the day Robert remained at my side, opening and closing doors for me, smiling at and saluting other class members. In the faculty room he stood silently at attention while I gulped coffee. When accosted by another teacher for being in the teachers' room, he just smiled and informed the faculty members that he wasn't a student, he was a bodyguard.

Strength through Pride

By Thursday I was ready to wind things up. Many students were over the line; the Third Wave was dominating their existence. I myself was acting instinctively as a dictator, however benevolent. I played the role more and more, and had trouble remembering its pedagogic origin and purpose. I wondered if this happens to many people. We get or take a role and then bend our lives to fit it. Soon the role is the only identity other people will accept. I worried about students doing things they would regret, and I worried about myself.

Once again I debated closing the experiment immediately or letting it go its own course. Both options were painful. If I stopped, a great number of students would be left hanging. They had committed themselves in front of their peers to radically new behavior patterns. If I suddenly jolted them back, I would face a deeply confused student body for the rest of the year. It would be especially demeaning for people like Robert to be suddenly thrust back and told it's just a game in front of bright students who had participated in a more deliberate, cautious way. I couldn't let the Roberts lose again.

On the other hand, things were already getting way out of control. Wednesday evening a father of one of my students had broken in and ransacked the room. He was a retired Air Force colonel who had spent time in a German prison camp. Upon hearing of our activities, he had simply gone berserk. I found him next morning propped up against the classroom door. He told me about his buddies killed in Germany. Holding on and shaking me, he pleaded brokenly that I understand and get him home. Later we spent hours talking about what he had felt and done, but at that moment I was more concerned with what was happening at school.

The Third Wave was affecting the faculty and other students and disrupting normal learning. Students were cutting class to participate, and the school counselors were beginning to question every student in the class. With my experiment threatening to explode, I decided to try an old basketball strategy; when you're playing against all odds, try the unexpected.

By now the class had swollen to over 80. A strange calm takes effect in a room full of people sitting at perfect attention. I talked ringingly about pride. "Pride is more than banners or salutes. Pride is something no one can take from you. Pride is knowing you are the best. It can't be destroyed." In the midst of this crescendo I abruptly lowered my voice to announce the real reason for the Third Wave. "The Third Wave isn't just an experiment or classroom activity. It's far more important. The Third Wave is a nationwide program to find students willing to fight for political change. That's right. What we've been doing has been practice for the real thing. Across the country teachers have been recruiting and training a youth brigade capable of demonstrating a better society through discipline, community, pride and action. If we can change the way school is run, we can change the way factories, universities and all other institutions are run. You are a selected group of young people chosen to help in this cause. If you will display what you have learned in the past four days, we can bring this nation a new sense of discipline, community, pride and action. Everything rests with you and your willingness to take a stand."

To show my seriousness I turned to three people who I knew had questioned the Third Wave, and demanded that they leave the room. I assigned four guards to escort them to the library and keep them from entering class on Friday. Then dramatically I announced a special noon rally on Friday—a rally for Third Wave members only.

It was a wild gamble. I just kept talking, afraid that if I stopped someone would laugh or ask a question and the grand scheme would dissolve. I explained how at noon Friday a national candidate for president would declare a Third Wave Youth Program. Simultaneously, over a thousand youth groups from every part of the country would stand up in support of the movement. I confided that the students in my class had been selected to represent their area, and I asked if they would make a good showing, because the press had been invited. There was no laughter, no murmur of resistance. Quite the contrary. Feverish excitement swept the room. "We can do it!" "Should we wear white shirts?" "Can we bring friends?"

"It's all set for tomorrow," I said. "Be in the auditorium ten minutes before noon. Be seated, ready to display the discipline, community and pride you have learned. Don't talk to anyone about this. This rally is for members only."

Strength through Understanding

I spent most of Friday morning preparing the auditorium for the rally. At 11:30 students began to show up—at first a few scouting the way and then more. Row after row filled up in hushed silence. Third Wave banners hung like clouds over the assembly. At 12 sharp I sealed the room and placed guards at each door. Several friends of mine posing as reporters and photographers began to interact with the crowd, taking pictures and jotting down notes. A group photograph was taken. The room was crammed with over 200 students: athletes, social stars, student leaders, loners, kids that always left school early, bikers, the pseudo hip, a few representatives of the school's Dadaist clique. But they all looked like one force as they sat at attention, focused on the TV set at the front of the room. It was as if we were all witnesses to a birth; the tension and anticipation were hard to believe.

"Before turning on the national press conference, I want you to demonstrate the extent of our training." With that, I gave the salute, and automatically 200 arms stabbed a reply. I then pronounced the words "Strength through Discipline," and the chorus replied. The photographers were still covering the ritual but by now no one noticed them. Again the room rocked with the guttural cry, "Strength through Discipline!"

At 12:05, I turned off the lights and walked to the TV. The air in the room seemed to be drying up; it felt hard to breathe and even harder to talk. I switched the set on and stood next to it, facing the people. The machine came to life, producing a field of light. The only light in the room, it played against the faces of the crowd. Their eyes strained and pulled toward it, but the blank screen didn't change. The room stayed deadly still; there was a mental tug of war between the people and the television. Yet the white glow didn't snap into an image of a political candidate; it just hummed on. Still the viewers persisted—there must be a program coming on; where is it? This trance continued for what seemed like hours. It was 12:07... Nothing... Anticipation turned to anxiety and then to frustration. Finally someone stood up and shouted: "There isn't any leader, is there?"

Everyone turned in shock, first to the desperate student and then back to the television. Their faces filled with disbelief. In the confusion of the moment I moved slowly toward the set and turned it off. Immediately I felt air rush back into the room; the room remained silent, but people were breathing again, bringing their arms from behind their chairs. Instead of a flood of questions, there was intense quietness. I began to speak.

"Listen closely; I have something important to tell you.... There was no leader! There is no such thing as a national youth movement called the Third Wave. You've been used, manipulated, shoved by your own desires to where you now find yourself. You're no better or worse than the German Nazis we have been studying.

"You thought you were the elect—better than those outside this room. You bargained your freedom for the comfort of discipline. You chose to accept the group's will over your own convictions. Oh, you think you were just going along for the fun, that you could extricate yourself at any moment. But where were you heading? How far would you have gone? Let me show you your future."

With that I switched on a rear screen projector, which lit up on a white cloth behind the TV. Large numbers appeared in a countdown; then the roar of the Nuremberg rally blasted into vision. My heart was pounding. In ghostly images the Third Reich paraded into the room: discipline, super race, the big lie, arrogance, violence, terror. People being pushed into vans, the visual stench of death camps, faces without eyes. The trials, the plea of ignorance, "I was only doing my job." As abruptly as it started, the film froze on a single written frame: "Everyone must accept the blame. No one can claim that they didn't in some way take part."

In the dark the last footage flapped against the projector. I felt sick to my stomach. No one moved. As if awakening from a deep dream, the whole room took one last look back into their minds. Several minutes went by, then questions began to emerge. With the room still dark I admitted my sickness and remorse. Feeling myself shift from participant to the easier role of teacher, I began to describe what had happened.

"In the past week we have all tasted what it was like to live and act in Nazi Germany. We learned what it felt like to create a disciplined social environment, pledge allegiance to that society, replace reason with rules. Yes, we would all have made good Nazis. We would have put on the uniform, turned our heads as friends and neighbors were cursed and then persecuted, pulled the locks shut, worked in the 'defense' plants, burned ideas. We now know in a small way what it feels like to find a hero, to grab quick solutions, to control our destiny. We know the fear of being left out, the pleasure of doing something right and being rewarded. Perhaps we have seen what these actions can lead to.

"Over the past week we have seen that facism is not just something those other people did. It's right here in this room, in our own personal habits and way of life. Scratch the surface and it appears; we carry it like a disease: the belief that human beings are basically evil and therefore demand a strong leader and discipline to preserve social order.

"This is the crucial lesson, which started our plunge into Nazi life. Do you remember the question? It went something like this: How could the German soldier, teacher, railroad conductor, nurse, tax collector, the average citizen claim afterwards that they knew nothing of what was going on? How could they be part of something and then say at the end that they were not really involved? What causes people to blank out their own history? In the next few minutes and perhaps years, you'll have the chance to answer this question.

"If our enactment of the facist mentality is complete, not one of you will ever admit to being at this Third Wave rally. You won't allow your friends and parents, or even yourself, to know you were willing to give up individual freedom to the dictates of order and unseen leaders. You won't admit to being manipulated, to accepting this madness as a way of life. You will keep the Third Wave and this rally a secret. It's a secret I shall share with you."

I took the film from the news cameras and exposed it to the light. The Third Wave ended.

Students slowly rose from their chairs and without talking began to file outdoors. Robert was sobbing. I walked over and threw my arms around him. We stood in the stream of students, some of whom swirled back to hold us for a moment. Others were crying or moving toward the door and the world outside.

For a week in the middle of a school year we had shared something fully. In the fours years I taught at Cubberly High School, no one ever spoke of the Third Wave rally. Certainly we thought over what we'd done. But the rally itself, everyone wanted to forget.

Beating the Man

by George Dixon

Riding in the back of a police wagon it seems like a long drive from the nearest transfer point. The prison itself is a massive stone structure; the walls have turned black from age. Two guards walk beside you as the massive steel gates swing open. Just inside the gate is the first shakedown point. Though you have been stripped of any personal possessions long before, the two guards now search you carefully, patting you down, even checking the insides of your shoes. Together you walk up a long walk that cuts across an acre of carefully manicured lawn and enter the administrative section of the prison. Here you walk past a series of administrative offices: the warden and his assistants, the head psychologists, several clerical offices, and a door that is labeled simply "Visitor's Room." Later you'll learn to call this area *up front.* Again you are searched at the second shakedown point. Another long hall is reached; you walk silently until you reach a pair of large double steel doors. These doors open to the inner world of the prison, *the joint,* as the men call it, but before you go through, the third and last shakedown takes place. Past the doors is the prison proper, a mixture of cellblocks, stores, and workshops which give the appearance of a very small town. And indeed, Mayfair State Prison is a small society, almost self-contained. It even has a Main Street lined with stores and work shops. But behind this physical manifestation of social order is a more significant and enduring society—the society of the men who live for one year, two years, five, ten, or for the rest of their lives in the joint and who all come to share a common culture. Behind the steel doors lies a way of life sealed off, both physically and emotionally, from the outside world. This culture is based on the highest degree of inequality known in our society today. The wardens and guards have absolute authority and power; even the most trivial aspects of daily routine are strictly regulated. The inmates must live in seemingly total subordination. Discrimination is overt, explicit, and backed by the laws of the state in the culture of a maximum security prison.

The men who make up the inmate population at Mayfair State Prison represent the whole spectrum of what modern Western society regards as criminal behavior. Some men refused to be inducted into the armed forces; others sold marijuana to friends in college; some were convicted of murder or armed robbery. A few are former politicians and labor leaders found guilty of political corruption. And still others are serving sentences for crimes ranging from sexual assault to income tax evasion. Whatever the reason, whatever the status of a man outside the prison walls, once inside this maximum security prison, each man takes up life in another culture based on radically different conceptions of individual rights. Mayfair State Prison is a total institution and each man learns to adjust in one way or another to this nonegalitarian culture.

Inequality in some form exists in every society. It is symbolized by the difference in respect and prestige accorded to some and denied others. In most societies, some cultural and social norms are inviolable; failure to live up to these norms can lead to ostracism, imprisonment, and even death. Although our own society has historically placed less emphasis than some on maintaining social equilibrium through extremes of physical punishment, we still identify a large catalog of illegal acts, and we deny many thousands freedom and control over their lives because they violate social norms. The men at Mayfair State Prison use different strategies, play different parts, as they live through the daily routine of prison life and adapt to their social inequality.

Inmates recognize two types of people at Mayfair State Prison: *inmates* and *screws* [prison officers]. Inmates are housed in cellblocks or cellhouses connected to the main building that contains the up-front section. A typical cellblock includes two banks of cells set back to back, rising from the floor to the ceiling in the center of the building. Within these honeycombed structures the inmate lives for the duration of his sentence. An individual cell is about 9 feet long and 10 feet high; a few may be larger or smaller. Regardless of their size, the furnishings of these compartments are spartan; a toilet, a washbowl, a bed, a table, a footlocker, an earphone for the prison radio, and a single electric lightbulb hanging from the ceiling.

The cells offer no real privacy, for an inmate is subject to constant scrutiny. An inmate is counted four times a day in his cell. He returns to it after every meal, after spending his daily hour in the exercise yard, and after working for three or four hours in an industrial shop. This cell comes to symbolize to the inmate the depth and extent of the control exercised over him, the bleak reality of the enforced routine, and his double loss of liberty: isolation from the outside world and isolation from his own prison.

The little freedom the inmate has begins early in the day when his cell bars are electronically opened and he goes to his assigned work, usually in an industrial shop. The prison has several dozen places to work, most of which are located on or near the main street, the most prominent being the shops and the hospital. The work assignments are much more than enforced activity. To a prison administrator, the activity might be viewed as therapeutic; it keeps the men busy and they might even learn a skill. But to most inmates, once allowed to leave their cell, the way has been opened for interaction with other men, both inmates and screws. Work assignments are the foundation upon which the strategies for coping with inequality are built. Extreme subordination is not easily accepted, even in prison. Work assignments permit the man to cope with this. As one inmate stated:

> You're kept busy and you use less time to think. Working adds a little normalcy. There are opportunities to fuck up and make monkeys of the screws. The Man has to deal with you on a more equal basis and after you've been in for a while, you really need that.

Inmates use several different behavioral contexts [or categories] to classify other inmates… An inmate may, for various reasons, act as an unpaid informant. He reports to the prison administration on inmate activity and consequently is viewed as a security risk by other inmates. The others call him a *stool pigeon*. As with all the roles a man may take on in the inmate society, this one minimizes the tension and anxiety of the institutional inequality and deprivation of prison life. By adopting the stool-pigeon role the inmate seeks to place himself on a level nearer to his superiors. Such an inmate tries to reduce the extreme sense of inequality, but he finds it creates an intensification of dependency. But this may be welcomed by some, as one informant pointed out:

> Some guys did it, I'm sure, just because they enjoyed getting a pat on the head and being called a good boy. The institution fosters dependency and that is just sort of an extension of it. All you have to do is get up in the morning and follow the guy ahead of you and you've got it made. No responsibilities. It's a real dependency and this is just the furthest extension of it. They treat you like children and eventually you become like children running to Papa.

A stool pigeon might try to conceal his dealings with the screws against the other inmates, but inmates are open about their identification with their superiors in another role. The *goon*, a special type of stool pigeon, not only acts as an informant for the administration but he also works with them to enforce the rules. All inmates in Mayfair State Prison know about *the hole*, a small isolation cell. It is unlighted and contains only a toilet. An inmate can be sent to the hole for three or four days if he violates some rule of the prison. It is at this point that the goon may play his part; as one informant stated:

> You don't want to go to the hole. He's the one who will grab you, a guard won't do it, and throw you in. If you're unhappy in the cell and you make it known, a goon will come in and kick your ass. Goons are muscle and mouth. If you were a stool pigeon you wouldn't want to be a goon because you'd rather use your mouth and not your muscles.

The following example illustrates graphically the role goons play:

> When I was sent to the hole, I sort of made a play about not going in. Well, the screws wouldn't throw me in, but this con I didn't know, this goon, gave me a kick that had me bouncing off the cell wall. He worked there, he did the intimidating work that the screws didn't like to do.
> There's usually another con in the hole with you and once when I was in, me and another guy made chess men out of toilet paper, if you can visualize that. There's nothing in the cell but a toilet and toilet paper. No cots, not even a light. So we used a lot of spit and this toilet paper and played on the floor; we etched a sort of board with a piece of wire. Well, the screw sees us playing and sure enough, the door opens and in comes this goon. We knew the screw wouldn't do it. The goon takes the pieces we made and the roll of toilet paper. We didn't have any toilet paper for the rest of the week.

The hole symbolizes the full extent of power the staff holds over the inmates. Every inmate always keeps the hole in mind as a possible consequence of almost any action. As an inmate said:

They send you to the hole for just about anything—talking in line, fighting, homosexual activity, beating a guy over the head with a baseball bat, not keeping your cell clean, having contraband books or contraband food, or whatever. There's a whole bunch of rules. So let's say you break a rule and a screw sees you doing it. He pulls out his ticket book and writes you up, which means that he describes your offense. Then he sends your ticket over to the yard officer. This captain, a disciplinary captain, stays in the yard office. You then get called in; a little slip will come for you saying: "Report to the yard office." Sometimes you don't even know why you're being called in, what they say your offense is. Anyway, you go in there and see a whole bunch of other cons who've been written up standing in line, waiting to be called up before the captain. Sometimes there are two captains up there and sometimes you just talk to these goons who are standing around. These goons are just tough stool pigeons, like toughs on the street who dig pushing people around, and they all look up to the captain. The captain gets a hold of your slip, the one with your offense written up on it, and then he looks up at you and says, "O.K., what have you got to say for yourself?" And you say, "Read it off to me," so you can hear it nice and slow. He reads it off, and depending on how much of a kick he gets out of intimidating cons, says something like, "I'm going to see you busted so hard, you'll never get up," or, he might just yell, "Look, you know you can't get away with this." And you say, "Man, I didn't have nothing to do with that," or something like that. What you say to him really depends on what's on the ticket. That kind of answer is for something more serious than, say, just talking in line. Let's say you were talking in line; O.K., then you say something like, "Ah, captain, it wasn't anything in particular." You can play around with that kind of thing, trying to get off the rap. If it's your first offense you might get out of it, or they might just take away a couple of yard privileges or commissary time. You're not too worried. But if it's serious, or if it's more than your first or second offense, then they give you three days in the hole, maybe five. Depending on the seriousness of the rap, the days in the hole can go up to fifteen. Then you've got to start thinking, 'How can I get off this thing.' Once you're sentenced to the hole, you can't beat it. That's it, in the hole.

Another important context for identifying people in the joint is homosexuality. The prison is, of course, an institution designed to segregate a large group of men from normal social contact, sometimes for a very long duration. What happens to a man deprived of heterosexual relations for extended periods is too complex to examine here, but using sexual roles is a major way inmates classify other inmates.

Inmates distinguish between what they perceive as a "true" homosexual and an inmate who resorts to homosexual behavior because of temporary deprivation. A true homosexual is a *faggot,* a temporary one is a *situational.* One inmate informant estimated that possibly 30 percent of the inmates at Mayfair State fell into one of these two categories.

Another major consideration is the extent to which homosexual behavior involves "masculinity" and "femininity." Homosexuals are divided into those who play an active, aggressive, and dominant role according to the standards of the inmates, and those who play a more passive and submissive part. The former are *wolves,* the latter are referred to as *punks* and *fags.*

The fag is perceived as being genuinely homosexual. A punk turns to homosexuality for reasons ranging from coercion, to gaining access to goods in short supply, to protection and favorable treatment. In many cases, a punk becomes the submissive property of a wolf—the aggressive, dominant homosexual. If the wolf is threatening enough and has adequate methods to back up his threats, a new inmate may have little choice in adopting this role.

> A wolf is just like a wolf on the street; he's out looking for a piece of ass, only he's not looking for it the way you usually look for it—he wants the ball bearing kind. He's more than that; he preys on young guys, he wants a possession. It's a status symbol to have a young kid or punk. To his cronies he says, "Look what I've got." It's particularly true among blacks with white kids; somewhat of a status symbol, although it's not limited to that. Often a little more blatant, a little more obvious. When you see a white kid with a black con you assume something is happening. If nothing is happening, your assumption can get you into trouble.

Thus, the wolf escapes some of the frustration of subordinate status by acquiring for his own use and control someone to dominate.

In the inmate society, men who have adopted different roles frequently attempt to maintain patterns of association with others in similar roles. Punks associate with other punks; blatant homosexuals manage to achieve some degree of self-segregation. Stool pigeons usually remain aloof from everyone, behavior that makes them highly suspect. The *straight con* (sometimes called a *solid con* or *good con*), like homosexuals and stool pigeons, fits into a prescribed role that calls for association with others of this type. Inmates refer to the solid con in a loosely defined way as the man who has achieved a kind of balance between the frustration of inequality and confinement manifest in prison life and his own desire for freedom and self-assertion. The solid con can achieve a maximum degree of autonomy without jeopardizing his chances of parole. He may deal contraband, usually to other solid cons, and often has an uncanny knack of getting away with things for which other inmates are punished. In the parlance of the inmate world, he "beats the man." This balance of defiance and a little arrogance on one hand, and stability and intelligence on the other, marks the inmate who will spend as little *hard time* as possible:

> He's the kind of a guy who has some rationale as a con. He knows that the cons are here and that the administration is there and never the twain shall meet. He knows when to act cool and when to play dumb. He knows when to use the screws for his own convenience. I think that basically the most important thing in leading this kind of existence is in-telligence.

Inmate culture also includes categories for identities based on the length of time a man must remain in prison. A *short-timer* is destined to spend a minimum of only eleven months in prison, a *long-timer* will be in for over five years. A *fish* is a newcomer from the outside world and socialization into inmate society awaits him. As a fish, the inmate has a new uniform with a freshly inked number on his back, new shoes, a closely cropped haircut, and the general appearance of an insecure novice on his own in the prison society for the first time. During this significant and unsettling time he is prey to all the forces that underlie the prison community. He may be approached by an aggressive wolf, he may be frightened into becoming a stool pigeon for protection, or he may assume some other role.

Whether an inmate takes up such a specialized role as goon or punk or is merely identified by others as a con or inmate, each man seeks to alleviate the frustration of subordinate status. To some degree, most men will use strategies designed to "beat the man."

Beating the Man

The security wing of the prison is composed of wardens, captains, sergeants, and guards. To the inmate, anyone who maintains order, regardless of rank, is simply a screw. In an even more generic context, an official controller is termed *the man*. The man frustrates any sign of initiative and independence; he is seen as the all-pervasive influence responsible for controlling inmates. In this sense, any inmate activity that circumvents the totalitarian authority of the man is significant; an inmate is given crucial evidence that his controllers are not infallible and the system can be beaten. One inmate illustrated this point:

> Probably the biggest thing is asserting your own manhood. There are a number of ways to do this, from just getting a little verbal dig in at a screw to dealing behind the man's back. Anything you can do that gives you the satisfaction of knowing that you beat them, that you pulled off something that was illegal. When you beat the man you let out a little of the pressure that builds up when you know that you just have to take it, when you know that you are not really a man.

In a broader way, a guy like Leopold made a statement when he got out that he "bamboozled" them. How a man who's been in for forty years is bamboozling them… But what he did do, he felt, was put up a front long enough so that he was able to get out when he wouldn't have otherwise. So far as he was concerned, he beat the man. He got some time outside.

To Erving Goffman, beating the man is reflected in a system of "secondary adjustments," or various practices that allow inmates to obtain prohibited satisfactions without directly challenging the prison administration. He states:

> Secondary adjustments provide the inmate with important evidence that he is still his own man, with some control of his environment; sometimes a secondary adjustment becomes a kind of lodgement for the self, a *churinga* in which the soul is felt to reside.[1]

In Goffman's explanation, the inmate, once tried, convicted, and sentenced, loses all control over the fate of his primary or biological adjustments. He is fed, told when to sleep, when to wake, when to wash, where to work and for how long, whom to associate with—in general, all aspects of daily routine are planned and controlled. He loses all function as a determinate man. The secondary adjustments, in this case, the strategies for beating the man, help to restore his lost independence of action. A man can partially rebuild his concept of self and manhood; he may do this by dealing contraband, emulating a respected solid con, becoming a wolf or even a stool pigeon, as well as in other ways. In the eyes of the other men, most important, in his own, he is at least something other than a societal outcast with negative status. Beating the man, or secondary adjustments, provide, in Goffman's words, "the chief framework within which reassembly of the self takes place."[2]

In short, anything giving an inmate the satisfaction of independent action beats the man. Though the prison daily routine is highly regulated, an inmate is presented with several important opportunities. These are situations that might entail prohibited interaction with other inmates, and maybe even with guards, or opportunities to *rip off* contraband from workshops, commissaries, dining rooms. If one takes advantage of such opportunities, he can effectively make a mockery of prison law. If caught, an inmate may be put in detention, sent to solitary confinement (the hole), lose some *good time* (time off for good behavior), or have his limited recreational privileges taken away. But the whole point of beating the man is not to be caught. To this end, inmates have devised strategies that range from having one inmate distract a guard while another hides a *shiv* (handmade knife) in his shirt, to maintaining a whole network of drop-off points and *contact men* in getting drugs inside the prison walls and then from one place to another in the joint. As illustrated by one inmate, getting a spoon out of the dining hall (spoons are useful in making *stingers,* a device consisting of two spoons wrapped in insulated wire and placed in a light socket, used to heat coffee), is relatively effortless:

> As you filed out of the mess hall, you would throw your spoon, your only eating utensil, into a box. There was a screw standing next to it, watching you do it. Well, you'd coordinate with the guy behind you. You put your spoon into your pocket and as you walked up to the box, just as he threw his arm and his spoon into the box, you'd throw your arm up only you didn't throw your spoon. It worked all the time. That's the sort of thinking you start getting consistent with. That was really nice because it was just so simple.

A small act, but one with enormous satisfaction to the inmate.

Beating the man may happen in the dining hall as an eruption of spontaneous tray-thumping or food rejection, disrupting the routine and making the guard's duties more difficult. Or a single inmate, sizing up the possibilities for official retribution and the intelligence of a guard, may make a subtle indirect inference to that screw's mental capacity, sexual prowess, or whatever seems appropriate; he might even be openly insolent in the right situation. An inmate's success in getting away with it depends on his ability to judge the screw's consequent reaction. Group action, for example, collective teasing in the dining hall or refusal to return to cells after the daily hour in the exercise yard, is relatively safe. The administration's ability to deal with two hundred rule-breakers is severely limited. There is indeed safety in numbers; the inmates are well aware of the administration's capabilities and many of the strategies to beat the man make use of this knowledge. One inmate demonstrated this implicit knowledge reflected in beating the man:

> We had a guard who was pretty decent in the sense that he wouldn't write you a disciplinary ticket unless you were caught screwing some-one in the asshole right in front of his eyes. And I had a knife, a shank, and once I pulled it out near him. I knew he wouldn't write me up. He got all nervous and said, 'Don't let anybody see that. There might be a lieutenant coming!' And I got him so upset that he started yelling and here comes a lieutenant. Of course I had gotten rid of it by this time and

the screw looked pretty ridiculous. It's that sort of playing around. That's a specific instance of beating the man.

This action goaded the guard to the point where he lost his self-control, but most importantly, the screw wasn't pushed into sending a write-up slip to the disciplinary warden. The inmate received the satisfaction of mocking the guard before other inmates and making him look foolish in the eyes of his immediate superior. In general, a warden, guard, or even the administration as a whole is teased, ridiculed, or subjected to other forms of minor harrassment, culminating at most in a loss of self-control and displays of ineffectual counteraction. An inmate adept at beating the man this way can effectively push the man towards the desired reaction while minimizing the risk of personal retribution. One of the most important ways to beat the man is by trading contraband items, an exchange practice referred to as *dealing*.

Dealing

Dealing can be as complex as smuggling heroin into the joint through an outside contact man, maintaining a system of drop-off points inside the walls, and finally a network of inmate contacts passing the heroin from one hand to another until its final destination is reached, or simply involves one inmate ripping off a pair of socks from the knit shop in exchange for a pack of cigarettes from another inmate. In any deal the inmate must consider such factors as risk, contraband value, a precise strategy, the reliability of others involved, and most important, the sanctions the disciplinary warden might use if the inmate were caught with contraband. The inmate busted with a pair of socks stuffed down his pant leg, with a little skill, can come away clean. But no amount of "fast-talking the screws" will get the inmate *off the rap* who was busted for an envelope of heroin stuffed under his mattress. In any society, systems of shared knowledge bind together different functional components into common strategies. Dealing is one such strategy in inmate society; knowledge of possibilities and consequences is vital if the society is to run smoothly.

Inmates, restricted by precise institutional norms, must resort to subterfuge for even the most minor pleasures. A cake smuggled out of the kitchen is contraband, as is candy from the officer's commissary. Books, pornographic magazines, fruit, cigarettes, uncancelled stamps, harmonicas, kazoos, extra articles of clothing, food, cards, and many other pleasures are either denied or severely restricted by the norms of the official prison society. Dealing any of these items may lead to getting caught and require attempts to avoid punishment, such as playing dumb, a strategy seen in the following incident:

> I got a line on some *Playboys* once; I'd get them from a con who worked in the officer's commissary and then peddle them around to people in the block. Well, a screw found two of them in my cell and wrote me up. When I got to the yard office I tried to play it young; like I was just a kid and naive—just following the crowd, didn't know any better and that sort of thing. I did pretty well; they didn't even suspect I'd been dealing the magazines. All I got was a couple of yard privileges taken away. If they thought I'd been dealing the stuff and was a few years older, they would have had my ass in a sling. For a while I could get away with that kind of act. If I had been older I would probably have played it differently.

The prison administrator is faced with a dilemma in maintaining strict internal order. His superiors, under political and social pressure, espouse the goal of imprisonment as two-pronged: strict incarceration and the metamorphosis of inmate from socially destructive to socially productive. The administrator has neither the funds nor, in many cases, the progressive creativity to fulfill such goals. His dilemma stems, in part, from conflicting goals of strict regulation and deprivation on one hand, and turning out a product that will fit into an accepted social niche on the other. The work system, part of "state industries" which shuttles goods made by inmate labor in one institution for use in another state institution, is designed as a means of social rehabilitation. Yet this conflicts with the administrator's ability to maintain internal order. To work, inmates must be allowed access to various places around the prison; they interact with other inmates and are exposed to potential contraband and raw materials for hand-fashioned weapons that are frequently used against guards and possibly even the administrator himself. The work system, then, is a fertile breeding ground for more and more elaborate ways to deal. Social rehabilitation becomes a tool for beating the man. The following account of an inmate's part in a deal illustrates some advantages offered by this system of interaction and prison mobility:

> When I was sweeping up in mental health, down below us was the hospital—here's a nice little situation. I knew a guy who worked as a carpenter and had access to the whole joint because he moved around with various jobs. He and I both knew a surgical nurse who worked in the hospital, but he knew him better than I did. So come Wednesday, when they had regularly scheduled operations, this nurse would be able to swing with some morphine sulfate in tubes. The guy gave it to Louie, the carpenter, because Louie would make sure he could get around at a certain time. So it went from Louie (he would have been shaken down back at the cell block) to me—I would meet him downstairs. Then I dealed it to someone else, or sometimes I'd do it directly. Chances are the con who got it from me would deal it to someone else; it was all like being a middleman on the street. There was a certain amount of profit all down the line.

In this deal, the importance of the work assignment is twofold. The work assignment of inmate-surgical nurse puts him in close proximity to the hospital's drug supply. With a little skill and an essential knowledge of hospital routine, inventory procedure, and where the hospital staff keeps the all important keys to the medicine locker, the inmate can *swing* with the morphine sulfate. At other times he may find it possible to rip off benzedrine inhalers, amphetamines, and barbiturates in pill form. Even something as innocuous as aspirin finds its way to other places in the prison to be traded or sold. Almost all the thirty-five inmate work assignments open the way to potential contraband. The inmate working in the barbershop may swing with an occasional straight razor; in the laundry shop it may be shirts and socks; in the bakery, pies or yeast for making prison hooch; in the machine shop, metal scraps, later to be filed into shivs and knives. Inmates report at least twenty-five different work assignments that are direct sources of contraband.

The other important contribution work assignments make to dealing strategies is well illustrated by Louie the carpenter's role in the last example. His carpentry assignment takes him to various places around the prison and gives him one of the highest degrees of mobility in the work system hierarchy. Rather than going from cell to work shop and then back to cell, Louie is assigned to any place in the prison where work must be done. This mobility frequently enables him to be in the right place at the right time, giving him the role of *contact man* in the morphine sulfate deal. Other work assignments place inmates in this strategic position. *Yard gang* workers maintain the prison grounds. *Utility gang* workers are responsible for building repairs. *Runners* and *helpers* do administrative errands. *Farm cons* are bussed daily to a prison farm. Inmates consider that these jobs all share the common attribute of mobility. Though this mobility may be highly limited, Louie the carpenter and other good contact men find enough freedom to function effectively as integral links in the dealing chain.

It is common, then, for an inmate to take advantage of contraband sources through his work assignment. But the inmate has to know more than what contraband is available, how to get it out from "under the eyes of the man," and whom to make contact with. The complexity in a deal varies with the inmate's perception of how the different factors present in a dealing situation combine to form a kind of risk potential. Access and contact are two important factors that have been cited, but the inmate must also know what the penalty is for possession of this accessible contraband and whom he can trust in making contact. Possession of certain types of contraband warrants stiff penalties. Drugs, especially those originating outside prison, weapons, or liquor can drastically reduce an inmate's accumulated good time. Coupled to this loss of good time may be a stint in the hole. Handling this lethal cargo requires precise strategies and often an elaborate system of contact men and drop-offs. The more inmates involved in the deal, the greater the chances for a *bust* through a stool pigeon's betrayal. Often the dangers inherent in a complex deal lead to a system of informal secrecy in which everyone seeks to insure their anonymity in the chain. You *score* from one inmate and make contact with another, no questions asked. If you happen to be a stool pigeon, you can only give the screws two names—your contact and who received the contraband from you. "It's a domino theory," one inmate said, "If the deal gets busted at the bottom, all the cons in on it don't fall over each other in a row leading to where the stuff came from."

In certain types of deals, access and contact is limited by varying degrees of official surveillance. The inmate's masters are highly suspicious of any situation involving interaction among different men in the prison and even more so with outside visitors. "Under the eyes of the man," describes areas that are closely watched, such as the visitor's room and the exercise yards. Risk is compounded by this close scrutiny, but it may be worth it for the more profitable contraband, the more danger involved. Scoring in the visitor's room through an outside contact usually means pills, pot, or heroin—*choice stuff* in this prison existence based on denial. The worth of the deal may be defined on a higher value scale. Risk, complexity, and intrigue often function as secondary adjustments, or in the prison's terminology, "beating the man." As one inmate said:

> There's this sort of equation between challenge and satisfaction. You don't like to admit to yourself that the man's got you over a barrel so you're always trying to prove you can do bigger and better things. Things like scoring smack up front. Or, if you don't do anything about it, at least you're always working these things out in your mind.

Summary

Though by no means exhaustive, the attempt has been made to provide some insight into the culture of life in a maximum security prison. Inmates are given special status by their society, one which appears to involve total subordination and inequality. Men interpret this peculiar role thrust upon them as more than just a period of enforced incarceration. Their suffering is both physical and emotional; the pain drives deep into a man's concept of self-integrity. Beating the man and all the cultural strategies associated with this domain provide a way to reconstruct the inmate's perception of his shattered manhood, to partially redefine his subordinate status, and to lessen the degree of official inequality.

[1] Erving C. Goffman, "The Inmate World," in *Studies in Institutional Organization and Change,* Donald Cressy, ed. (New York: Harcourt, Brace, 1958), p. 53.

[2] Ibid., p. 63.

Questions for Discussion

1. In "You Will Do As Directed" the author states: "We know now in a small way what it feels like to find a hero, to grab quick solutions, to control our destiny. We know the fear of being left out, the pleasure of doing something right and being rewarded. Perhaps we have seen what these actions can lead to." What does the author mean?

2. If you were a student in Ron Jones' school, how would you have acted?

3. It has been said that every culture needs a high degree of conformity in order to function coherently. Are the results of Jones' experiment a consequence of this need or can they be attributed to other factors?

4. Discuss the educational implications of the article "You Will Do As Directed."

5. Is the conformity reflected in "You Will Do As Directed" different from the conformity in "Beating the Man"? Explain why this is or is not an appropriate question.

6. Draw some analogies between the cultural behaviors in the article "Beating the Man" and the cultural behaviors in schools.

7. Draw some analogies between the cultural behaviors in "Beating the Man" and those of the culture at large.

Part II
Cultural
Variation
Themes

INTRODUCTION

While the first section of the book presented themes which allow us to raise questions about the inevitability of basic human processes and their role in multiculturalism, the second part of the book deals with cultural variation themes such as socialization patterns, value orientations, verbal and nonverbal interaction and cognitive styles. Each of these themes will become conceptually clear as the readings are introduced.

Socialization refers to the process by which cultural groups convey, from generation to generation, formally and informally, traditions, skills, values, symbols and behaviors. Through the process of socialization children learn the cultural knowledge they need in order to be effective in their physical, social and economic environment.

The purpose of the articles in this section is to illustrate some patterns and forms of transmitting cultural knowledge. Similarly, the readings should illustrate the impact of change and conflict on the process of socialization.

The articles by Kakar ("The Child in India") and Dollar ("Child Care in China") portray two distinct forms of cultural transmission. The former illustrates the power of religious literary tradition and folklore in perpetuating cultural knowledge and in influencing the upbringing of children. The latter describes the overt role of institutions such as day care centers and schools in conveying desirable cultural traits to their young. As the two articles serve to contrast traditional and institutional forms of socialization we also gain more insight into culture-specific ways of being, which are emphasized in India and China.

The articles by Sindell ("Some Discontinuities in the Enculturation of Mistassini Cree Children") and by Sharff ("Free Enterprise and the Ghetto Family") deal with socialization in the context of cultural change and conflict. Sindell describes the cultural conflict which takes place when change is imposed upon a cultural minority. Sharff shows us how cultural minorities living in impoverished conditions develop adaptive socialization rules to insure their survival. In both readings we become aware of the conflicts that emerge when the socialization goals of minority

87

groups differ from those of the majority culture. While describing the socialization practices of native North American Cree and Hispanics in New York City, Sindell and Sharff illustrate the discontinuities and conflicts which take place when the expectations and values imparted by the family differ from those of the schools.

The articles in this section should help us understand the process of socialization in our own lives. They should also provoke further inquiry about the socialization process, about the ways institutions and schools prescribe cultural behavior, and about the conflict which takes place when family socialization differs from institutional socialization.

Value orientations are abstract categories which encompass a world view and a preference for a way of life. They are based on assumptions about the nature of human existence from which standards of right and wrong, or good and bad, are drawn. They encompass notions of social relations (independence, interdependence, individualism, competition), of activity (being, doing, pragmatism, reflection), of time (orientation towards the past, present or future), and of our relationship with nature or the supernatural (fatalistic orientation, technological orientation).[1]

The articles by Fukue ("The Persistence of *Ie*") and Whiting ("You've Gotta Have *Wa*") discuss the origin and content of fundamental Japanese value orientations. As the articles examine values in contemporary Japan, we cannot help comparing them with Western and North American values and thereby gaining insights into the way they influence our thinking and behavior.

Fukue shows us the lasting impact value orientations have in Japan. His analysis enables us to understand how traditional values such as "group orientation" and "rank consciousness," spawned in an agrarian society, continue to prevail in spite of profound social and technological changes. The article provides a stimulus to reflection on the nature of cultural change.

Whiting's article about being an American baseball player in Japan complements Fukue's. It shows how cultures transfer and modify imported ideas to fit their own value systems. It also illustrates the kind of communication problems individuals from different cultures may experience when they do not understand the nonexplicit and abstract aspects of the host culture, particularly its value orientations.

Verbal and nonverbal communication are inextricably intertwined, allowing people from the same culture to give meaning to their interaction. When interacting with each other in our own environment, we know the culturally appropriate ways of integrating into our speech gestures, eye movement, and the like. Similarly, we practice culturally accepted ways of touching and we follow unspoken rules which regulate our use of space and body posture in interaction.

We have internalized our patterns of interaction without even knowing it. We have learned socially appropriate interactive behaviors by unconsciously imitating others. Thus, when we are asked to explain the rules which govern such behavior, we find it impossible. It is only through the violation of the norms, which produces clear behavioral contrast, or through the formal teaching of these patterns that awareness begins.

This out-of-awareness quality of both verbal and nonverbal modes of interaction reinforces the need to incorporate these aspects into multicultural instruction and curricula, since these behaviors are, most of the time, the main criteria for impression formation and attribution about others with whom we interact.

The purpose of the articles in this section is to contribute to the development of awareness of verbal and nonverbal patterns of behavior by examining (a) variations and similarities in

---

[1]F. Kluckhohn and F. Strodtbeck. *Variations in Value Orientations.* Evanston, IL: Row Peterson, 1961.

nonverbal behavior, (b) cultural assumptions about verbal competence, (c) the relationship between language and schooling, and (d) the power of language to create reality.

Irujo, in "An Introduction to Intercultural Differences and Similarities in Nonverbal Communication", surveys the literature on nonverbal communication from a universalistic and cultural-specific perspective. The article reviews research and theory on facial expressions, eye contact, gestures, posture, touching, use of space, architecture and paralinguistics.

Menyuk and Menyuk, in "Communicative Competence: A Historical and Cultural Perspective," examine the origins and patterns of Western conceptions of competence in verbal interaction. For example, the authors examine Western notions of equating intelligence with verbal output and directness. Their discussion raises fundamental questions about the way we evaluate people whose cultures emphasize silence and indirectness in interaction.

Heath's classic article, "What No Bedtime Story Means," looks at the process by which children in different cultural groups in the United States are socialized into the use of language. The way adults use language with children serves to create different patterns of thinking and learning which, in turn, seem to determine school success or failure.

Farb's "Man at the Mercy of Language" discusses the well-known Sapir-Whorf hypothesis, the basic premise of which is that language functions not simply as a device for communication, but also as a way of defining experience for its speakers. Farb points out how the nature of our language may shape our reality.

Fundamental to teacher training and multicultural curriculum development is an understanding of the relationship between cognitive styles. As the readings in the *culture and thought* section demonstrate, people develop the cognitive patterns which are necessarily emphasized in their environmental and social contexts. Factors such as socialization, family organization, value orientations, and even the way people write or structure their rhetorical presentations may influence how people think and the way they perform cognitive tasks.

Ramirez's "Cognitive Styles and Cultural Democracy in Education" examines the research on the relationship between cognitive styles and culture and discusses how patterns of childrearing and social organization influence cognitive styles.

Ramirez raises fundamental issues regarding the criteria for evaluation and instruction of minority and international students in U.S. educational settings. In the United States schools emphasize in their curricula, instruction and evaluation procedures the importance of "field independent" thinking or analytical skills. Consequently, those individuals who demonstrate strong analytical thinking, display independence from the teacher and show individual initiative are more likely to succeed than students who are "field dependent" and whose background and sociocultural conditioning place greater stress on the social environment and sensitivity to human relationships.

Kaplan, in "Cultural Thought Patterns in Inter-Cultural Education," discusses the cultural differences which emerge in the process of teaching reading and composition to foreign students. As he analyzes their writing and their verbal presentations, different patterns of thought become evident. Kaplan suggests that the different rhetorical styles of English, Semitic, Oriental, Romance and Russian languages correlate with different patterns of thinking.

Both readings compel us to become more aware of the relationship between culture and cognitive performance. The information they present cautions us against the use of deficient and inferior models in evaluating minority and international students. It also compels us to take account of culturally determined styles of thinking and cognition of minority and international students when developing curriculum and establishing instructional procedures.

A. SOCIALIZATION

The Child in India
by Sudhir Kakar

Within the wide diversity of India, its welter of distinct regional, linguistic, caste, and religious groupings, there is still a unified cultural awareness of the child that informs the behavior of parents and other adult caretakers. This cultural awareness, a specific Indian conception of the nature of children and the place of childhood in the life cycle, derives from many sources. There are passages dealing with children in the law books of the Hindus, while the section on the care and upbringing of the children, the Bālānga, is an integral part of traditional Indian medicine, Ayurveda. There are references to children and childhood in such ancient epics as the Ramayana and Mahabharata and descriptions of childhood in classical Sanskrit and medieval vernacular literature. In addition, the symbolic content of the various rites of childhood, and of the traditional folk songs that accompany them, provide some indications as to what Indians consider the chief characteristic of a given stage of childhood. While much of this material may seem to belong to the literate traditions of the Hindu upper castes, anthropological accounts have shown that such traditions are basically much the same in many lower groups, their continuous and continuing survival in large sections of society being one of the most distinctive features of the Indian culture.[1]

IDEOLOGY OF CHILDHOOD

The first theme that stands out in the Indian cultural traditions is the intense parental longing for children, especially sons who can carry on the family line. This is important because of the emphasis placed on celibacy by the Buddhists and the Jains. A number of myths and didactic passages in the epics repeatedly emphasize that begetting a son is one of man's highest duties and the only way he can discharge the debt he owes to his ancestors. Consider the story of Jaratkuru.

The renowned ascetic Jaratkuru, full of merit and great spiritual power derived from his sustained asceticism, was wandering around the world when one day he came across a deep pit. In this pit, the spirits of his ancestors—the pitris—were hanging head down, their feet tied to a tree trunk by a single skein of rope that was gradually being nibbled away by a large rat. It was evident that the pitris would soon fall down into the deep darkness of the pit. Moved by their pitiable condition, Jaratkuru enquired whether he could somehow save them from this fate, expressing his readiness to do so even if he had to give up all rewards to which his great asceticism entitled him. 'Venerable ascetic,' the spirts of his ancestors answered, 'thou desirest to relieve us!...O child, whether it is asceticism or sacrifice or whatever else there be of very holy acts, everything is inferior. These cannot count equal to a son. O child, having seen all, speak unto Jaratkuru of ascetic wealth...tell him all that would induce him to take a wife and beget children!'[2]

Another ascetic, Mandapala, is told in no uncertain terms that in spite of his most ascetic efforts, certain celestial regions will forever remain closed to him, for they can be reached only by those who have had children: "Beget children therefore!" Mandapala is instructed, "Thou shalt then enjoy multifarious regions of felicity!"[3] Children in the Mahabharata are not only seen as instrumental in the fulfillment of a sacred duty which, however agreeable and meritorious, still carries the connotation of religious necessity and social imposition. They are also portrayed as a source of emotional and sensual gratification. Listen to Shakuntalā, the forsaken wife of Dushyanta, asking the king to acknowledge his son:

What happiness is greater than what the father feels when the son is running towards him, even though his body is covered with dust, and clasps his limbs? Even ants support their own without destroying them, then why shouldst not thou, virtuous as thou art, support thy own child? The touch of soft sandal paste of women, of [cool] water is not so agreeable as the touch of one's own infant son locked in one's embrace. As a Brahman is the foremost of all bipeds, a cow, the foremost of all quadrupeds, a guru, the foremost of all superiors, so is the son the foremost of all objects agreeable to touch. Let, therefore, this handsome child touch thee in embrace. There is nothing in the world more agreeable to the touch than the embrace of one's son.

Sanskrit poets, too, have waxed lyrical over the parental longing for children and the parents' emotions at the birth of a child. In two well-known examples, Bhavabhūti describes Rama's love for Lava and Kusha, while Bānabhatta rhapsodizes over Prabhakarvardhana's love for his son, Harsha. The greatest of all Sanskrit poets, Kalidasa, in his Raghuvamsha, describes Dilipa's response to Raghu's birth thus:

He went in immediately (on hearing the news) and as the lotus becomes motionless when the breeze stops, he gazed at his son's face with the same still eyes. Just as tides come into the ocean when it sees the moon, similarly the King (Dilipa) was so happy on seeing his son that he could not contain the happiness in his heart.[4]

The demands of objectivity compel us to report that the intense parental longing and pleasure at the birth of a child in the Indian tradition is generally limited to sons. Girls receive a more muted reception. Although a firstborn daughter may be regarded by parents as a harbinger of good luck, the welcome accorded to further daughters declines markedly.

Contemporary anthropological studies from different parts of India and the available clinical evidence assure us that the traditional preference for sons is very much intact.[5] At the birth of the son drums are beaten in some parts of the country, conch shells are blown in others, and the midwife is paid lavishly, but no such spontaneous rejoicing accompanies the birth of a daughter. Women's folk songs reveal a painful awareness of their ascribed inferiority—of this discrepancy, at birth, between the celebration of sons and the mere tolerance of daughters. Thus, in a north Indian song, the women complain:

> Listen, O Sukhmā, what a tradition has started!
> Drums are played upon the birth of a boy,
> But at my birth only a brass plate was beaten.[6]

And in Maharashtra, the girl, comparing herself to a white sweet-scented jasmine (*jai*) and the boy to the big, strong-smelling flower (*keorā*), plaintively asks:

> *Did anyone notice the sweet fragrance of a jai?* The hefty keorā however
> has filled the whole street with its strong scent.[7]

The second major element in the Indian ideology of the child is the great emphasis placed on protective indulgence, as compared to the element of "disciplining the child" which has been prominent in much of the Western history of childhood. In the law books, children belong to a group consisting of women, the aged, the sick, and the infirm—those who deserve society's protection and claim its indulgence. Thus, even before serving invited guests (and guests as we know are almost on a par with gods in the Indian tradition), the householder is enjoined to feed pregnant women, the sick, and the young.[8] Although a man may not quarrel with learned men, priests, or teachers, he is also forbidden to speak harshly to the aged, the sick, or children.[9] Whereas the king is within his rights to exact retribution from those who question his authority or inveigh against his person, he is required to forgive children (as also the old and the sick) who may be guilty of lese majesty. Although punishments, including fines, are prescribed for everyone soiling the king's highways, children are specifically exempted; they are only to be reprimanded and are required to clean up after themselves.[10]

The protective indulgence shown toward the child is manifested most clearly where it matters the most (at least to the child), namely, in the pronouncements in the law books of the Hindus on the chastisement of children. Children are only to be beaten with a rope or a bamboo stick split at the end. The split bamboo, as we may remember from circus clowns' mock fights, makes a loud noise without inflicting much pain. Moreover, even this punishment is to be carried out only on the back and never on a "noble part," i.e., not on the head or chest.[11] To those who hold progressive views on child discipline, the beating of children may hardly seem like "protective indulgence." However, the extent of this indulgence becomes strikingly clear when we compare Indian law books with the legal texts of other ancient societies. For example, there is evidence in the law codes and digests of ancient Rome to suggest that brutal forms of child abuse were common; it was only as late as A.D. 374 that infanticide was declared a capital offense in the Roman world.[12]

The humane attitude toward the child in India is also apparent in the medical texts which contain detailed and copious instructions on the care of the young child. These wide-ranging instructions on such diverse topics as the time when a child should be encouraged to sit up and the specification of toys with regard to color, size, and shape reflect great solicitude concerning the period of infancy and early childhood. The voices of ancient doctors sound strangely modern as they expound on the relationship between childrearing practices and personality development. For example, the practice of persuading the child to eat or to stop crying by conjuring up threatening visions of ghosts, goblins, and ferocious animals, they tell us, is to be avoided because it has a very harmful effect.[13] The child should not be awakened from sleep suddenly, they go on to say, nor should he be snatched or thrown up in the air. He should not be irritated, and he should be kept happy at all costs, as this is crucial for his psychological development and future well-being.[14] With compassion and tenderness for the young, the texts strive to develop the adult caretaker's capacity to comprehend the needs and emotions of the child—needs that are apt to be overlooked since they are articulated in voices that are frail and words that are indistinct.

Besides the longing and protective indulgence, the third element in the Indian ideology is a celebration, even an idealization of the child and childhood. In the most powerful surviving literary tradition of northern and central India, for instance, such poets of the *bhakti* movement as Surdas and Tulsidas have placed childhood close to the center of poetic consciousness and creativity. Surdas, in fact, composed five hundred verses on Krishna's childhood alone![15] Indeed, in this poetry the celebration of the Divine takes place through the metaphor of celebration of the child. The aspects that are admiringly emphasized as divine attributes are the child's freedom and spontaneity, his simplicity, charm, and delight in self.

> Krishna is singing in the courtyard.
> He dances on his small feet, joyous within.
> Lifting up his arms, he shouts for the black
> and white cows.
> Sometimes he calls Nandbābā, sometimes he goes in and out of the
> house.
> Seeing his reflection, he tries to feed it.
> Hidden, Yashoda watches the play that makes her so happy.
> Sūrdās says, to see Krishna's play everyday is bliss.[16]
> Tulsīdās sings:
> Self-willed he (Rāma) insists on having the moon.
> He sees his shadow and is frightened.
> Clapping his hands, he dances.
> Seeing his child-play.
> All mother-hearts are brimming over with happiness.
> Becoming angry, he is obstinate.
> And remains stubborn till he gets what he wants.
>
> Tulsīdās says, the sons of the King of Ayodhyā live in the temple of his
> heart.[17]

In an adult-centered world that overvalues abstractions, prudence, and reason, it is refreshing to find popular Indian poetry celebrating such childlike virtues as intensity and vivaciousness, capacity for sorrow and delight, mercurial anger and an equally quick readiness to forgive and forget injuries. In the Indian vision, these qualities are not seen as "childish," to be socialized out of existence, but valuable attributes of humans—of all ages—since they are an expression of the Divine.

TRADITIONS OF CHILDHOOD: WESTERN AND INDIAN

In Western antiquity, until perhaps the thirteenth century, adult attitudes toward children were generally dominated by an ideology that had little empathy for the needs of children.[18] This ideology looked upon the child as a nuisance and an unwanted burden, perfunctorily tolerating brutal treatment of children by their parents as well as such associated phenomena as infanticide, the sale of children, and their casual abandonment. It is also demonstrable, however, that there has been a gradual progression in the Western ideology of the child. From the earlier external suppression that permitted physical torture, by the sixteenth and seventeenth centuries the ideological emphasis was decisively shifting towards an internal suppression in which child training and discipline were stressed.

From parental efforts aimed at conquering the child's will, the Western ideology of caretaking progressed further in the nineteenth and twentieth centuries, when the awareness of the sensibilities and needs of children increased appreciably. This movement towards the fostering attitude continues unabated.

The conflict between the rejecting and nurturing attitude towards the child, so marked in the Western history of childhood, is, then, absent in the Indian tradition. As we have seen, the evidence from disparate sources—from medicine to literature, from law to folk songs—is overwhelming that the child in Indian tradition is ideologically considered a valuable and welcome human being to whom the adults are expected to afford their fullest protection, affection, and indulgence. Consider the reflection of this ideology in linguistic usage. In Hindi, for example, what adults do to children is *pālnā poshnā*—protecting-nurturing. They are not "trained," "reared," or "brought up." With its implications of training the child, teaching him to conform to social norms, and "channeling his impulses," the model of *socialization* (which governs contemporary Western caretaking) was a logical next step in a historical evolution from the preceding model of disciplining and conquering a child's will. In its general orientation and focus, such a model is necessarily foreign to the Indian consciousness. In fact, as we saw in our short discussion of *bhakti* songs and poems, the Indian tradition of childhood values precisely those attributes of the child which have not been "socialized." Here it is the child who is considered nearest to a perfect, divine state, and it is the adult who needs to learn the child's mode of experiencing the world. This is not to suggest, however, that the norms and values of adulthood are not conveyed to the child; as we shall see, they are imparted through a clear set of expectations and in a manner that is highly ritualized.

Stages of Indian Childhood

The notion of the human life cycle unfolding in a series of stages, with each stage having its unique "tasks" and moral responsibilities, is an established part of traditional Indian thought, best exemplified in the well-known scheme of *āshrama-dharma*. The four *āshrams* or life stages—student, householder, recluse, and renouncer—as elaborated in the texts, however, focus largely on the period of youth and adulthood and neglect to assign any formal importance to the stages of childhood. We must then turn to the popular understanding of the childhood stages as they are lived in the villages and towns of India and to the rites, the samskaras—the expressive and symbolic performances and ceremonies that focus on the child and mark his transition from one stage to another. An understanding of these stages and the rites marking them is essential to increase our appreciation of the artifacts, objects, and performances to which they have given birth.

The rites of childhood have twin goals. First, they seek to refine and transform the innate nature of the child at birth. Second, the rites aim at a gradual integration of the child into society. The samskāras, in other words, beat time to measured movement that takes the child away from the original mother-infant symbiosis into a full-fledged membership in his community. In different parts of Hindu India and even within the same village there may be variations in the way these rites are performed.[19] Variations within a particular village may be partly due to differences in caste, with the higher castes celebrating more life cycle rites, and partly due to differences in wealth, which determines whether individual rites may be performed on separate occasions or several rites must be combined on one occasion.

The First Stage: Garbha

Since life in Indian thought is presumed to begin with conception, the first stage of the life cycle is *garbha*, the fetal period, and the first rite is *garbhadāna*. It is held immediately after marriage, which provides the appropriate context for conception. The rite is considered obligatory for all householders and highlights the parental wish for offspring, the chief goal of an Indian marriage. The rite also "reminds" the parents and the community of the momentous nature of conception when the soul's "subtle body" enters the conceptus at the moment of fertilization. The qualities of the sperm, the ovum, the *rasa* ("organic sap" or "nutrition"), and the psychic constellation of the soul from its previous incarnation are considered to be the determinants of the embryo's functional and structural growth.

The critical period of fetal development is said to begin in the third month, when the latent "mind" of the fetus becomes conscious or *chetan*. In this stage of *dauhridaya* (literally "bicardiac," with one heart belonging to the fetus and the other to the mother), the unborn child and the mother function psychologically as a unit, mutually influencing each other. The feelings and affects of the fetus—a legacy from its previous birth—are transmitted to the mother through the channels of nutrition. For the future psychological well-being of the child it is imperative that the cravings of the pregnant woman be fully gratified (since they are those of the unborn child) and the unit of pregnant mother and fetus be completely indulged.

The rite marking this period is *godha-bharāna,* which honors the expectant mother. The expectant mother is dressed in a new sari, presented glass bangles, and fed culturally valued foods by the "superior" members of the household, thus reversing the usual order of eating and service. In many parts of the country, this rite is a family affair which does not require an officiating priest. In others, the rite may be accompanied by feasts arranged in gardens outside the house, with much singing of traditional songs, the *sohara*. These both celebrate the occasion and instruct the expectant mother in such matters as the dietary restrictions she must observe during her pregnancy.

The Second Stage: Shishu

Birth begins the second stage of the Indian life cycle of infancy or the *shishu* period, which

95

extends for the first three to four years of the child's life. During this period of prolonged infancy, the Indian child is intensely and intimately attached to his mother. This attachment is an exclusive one, not in the sense of the child being without older and younger siblings close in age who claim, and compete for, the mother's love and care, but in that the Indian child up to the age of four or five directs his demands exclusively toward his mother. This is so in spite of the customary presence in the extended family of many other potential caretakers and substitute mothers. Constantly held, cuddled, crooned and talked to, the Indian infant's experience of his mother is a heady one; his contact with her is of an intensity and duration that differentiate it markedly from the experience of infancy in Western cultures. At the slightest whimper or sign of distress, the infant is picked up and rocked, or given the breast and comforted. Usually, it is the infant's own mother who swiftly moves to pacify him, although in her occasional absence on household matters it may be a sister or an aunt or a grandmother who takes him up to feed, clean, or just soothe him with familiar physical contact. It is by no means uncommon to see an old grandmother pick up a crying child and give him her dried-up breast to suck as she sits there, rocking on her heels and crooning over him.

From the moment of birth, then, and in consonance with the Indian ideology of the child, the infant is greeted and surrounded by direct, sensual body contact, by relentless physical ministrations.[20] An Indian mother is inclined towards total indulgence of her infant's wishes and demands, whether these be related to feeding, cleaning, sleeping, or being kept company. Moreover, she tends to extend this kind of mothering well beyond the time when the "infant" is ready for independent functioning in many areas. Thus, for example, feeding is frequent, at all times of the day and night, and "on demand." And although breast feeding is supplemented with other kinds of food after the first year, the mother continues to give her breast to her child for as long as possible, often up to two or three years: in fact, suckling comes to a gradual end only when there is a strong reason to stop nursing, such as a second pregnancy. And breast contact between mother and infant, we know, is not only conducive to the child's psychological development but is a safeguard against infant mortality.

Similarly without any push from the family, the Indian toddler takes his own time learning to control his bowels, and proceeds at his own pace to master such skills as walking, talking, and dressing himself. As far as the mother's and family's means permit, an infant's wishes are fully gratified and his unfolding capacities and activities accepted, if not always with manifest delight, at least with affectionate tolerance.

The rites that mark this period of infancy are designed to gradually separate the child from the mother and prepare his entry into the wider world of the community. First, there is the *jātakarma* rite, performed just after delivery of the offspring. After the newborn is cleaned, the father comes in to look at the baby's face. The paternal act of looking at a firstborn son, the sacred texts assure him, will absolve him of all his debts to the gods and to his ancestors. The birth of a girl is slightly less meritorious; her gift in marriage brings the father spiritual merit and appreciably increases the store of his good *karma*. Having seen the infant's face, the father goes out and takes a ritual bath. Accompanied by the priests and family elders the father then re-enters the maternity room for the birth ceremonies. He prays for the growth of the infant's talent and intellect, thanks the spot of earth where the birth took place, and praises and thanks the mother for bearing a strong child.

The next samskāra is the naming rite of *nāmakarma*. Depending upon the mother's condition and the auspiciousness of the astrological constellations, this may happen on the tenth, twelfth, fifteenth, or thirty-second postpartum day. The mother and infant emerge from the seclusion of the maternity room into the bustle of an expectant family, as the mother ceremoniously places the baby in the father's lap for the name-giving ceremony.

From the family, the mother and infant unit moves into the wider world in the third or fourth month with the performance of *nishakrāmana,* the child's first outing or "looking at the sun" and "looking at the moon," as the texts poetically describe the infant's ritual introduction to the world and the cosmos. Between the sixth and ninth months, the important rite of *annaprāshana* marks the first time the child is given solid food and thus the onset of a gradual weaning and its psychological counterpart—the process of the child's separation from his mother. In this rite, after prayers to the goddess, a priest offers oblations to the infant's ancestors in his name, thus, in a sense, formally connecting the infant to past generations. Relatives and family friends in the village present the infant with gifts, which minimally include a set of eating utensils—a plate, a bowl, a glass, and perhaps a wooden seat.

The Third Stage: Bālā

If the rites are any guide, the period of infancy is deemed complete by the third year, to be followed by the *bālā* or early childhood stage. Whereas previous rites were common for both male and female infants, now the life cycles of boys and girls begin to diverge. For most females, there are no further rites of childhood; the next principal samskāra in their life cycle will be that of marriage.

For a boy, early childhood begins with the important rite of *mundan* or tonsure. The child is generally taken to the temple of a mother goddess (to the bank of a river in some regions), where his baby hair is shaved and offered to the goddess. In other regions, mundan may be a purely family affair. He is dressed up in new clothes which are miniature replicas of those worn by adult members of his community. The symbolism of death and rebirth—psychologically the death of the mother-infant symbiosis and the birth of the child as a separate individual—is at the heart of the many rituals connected with mundan. Accordingly, in the Bhojpuri region of northern India, before the child's head is shaved and he is dressed in new clothes, the women of the family take the child to the Ganges and ceremonially cross the river in a boat.[21] The symbolism of crossing the river, of death and rebirth, is apparent. Moreover, the folk songs sung at the time of mundan are the sohars, the songs that are also sung at birth. In the popular tradition, it is only after the child's tonsure that he is considered ready for the process of discipline and the family's efforts at socialization.

The Fourth Stage: Kumāra

It is only in the stage of late childhood, *kumāra,* which begins around the age of five to seven years, that the cultural expectations and experiences of boys and girls begin to diverge markedly. For the boy, the world of childhood widens from the intimate cocoon of maternal protection to the unfamiliar masculine network woven by the demands and tensions, the comings and goings, of the men of the family. The most striking feature of his experience is the contrast between an earlier, more or less unchecked benevolent indulgence and the new inflexible standards. As an anthropological account of a Hyderabad village describes the male child's "second birth": "The liberty that he was allowed during this early childhood is increasingly curtailed. Now the accent is on good behavior and regular habits."[22] And a north Indian proverb, with counterparts in other regions of the country, pithily conveys what the boy has to now face: "Treat a son like a *rāja* for the first five years, like a slave for the next ten, and like a friend thereafter."

By contrast, the Indian daughter is not severed from the other women in the household, although she is given new, "grown-up" household tasks and responsibilities, especially in the care of younger children in the family. Her childhood, as compared to her brother's, is shortened in the sense that she takes on domestic responsibilities at an age when her brother is still playing on the streets or, at the most, running small errands.

The difference does not persist in tasks related to the family's occupation. Both boys and girls are initiated at the age of nine or ten into craft skills which they master by the age of fifteen or sixteen, an age at which the children of the farming community are just beginning to be seriously involved in their occupation. In both groups, however, the world of children is not isolated from that of adults, as it is in modern technological societies. Even very young children share the craft or agricultural environment of the adults. An arresting glimpse from a study of children in communities of craftsmen reveals: "When a four-year-old girl in a potters' group cried for her mother's attention, and the mother was ill with fever, the father took her over and distracted her with clay, telling her gently that she should do what he was doing with the ball of clay." Similarly, the young mothers continue their spinning or cutting or block printing with the children around them; sometimes the children go to sleep at the work spot.[23] The child as an inheritor of traditional craft skills is integrated into the family quite differently from a child whose social order emphasizes freedom of opportunity to choose his work, even if the freedom is functionally a limited one and sometimes degenerates into his exploitation as a cheap source of labor.

Discipline in the stage of late childhood becomes a serious affair, with scolding and occasionally light spanking being the main disciplining techniques. Children are rarely praised *openly* for performing assigned tasks or fulfilling adult expectations. This lack of praise does not derive from an absence of parental pride, but rather from the belief that open admiration and praise is risky, since it may well attract the evil eye or otherwise tempt the fates. As numerous studies of Indian childhood have shown, child battering is an extremely rare phenomenon even in the poorest and most deprived groups of society, such as the slums of Bombay.[24] There may be cases of neglect of children, especially in the areas of health care and nutrition, but almost never gross physical abuse. Nothing else can so clearly highlight the continuing strength of the traditional Indian ideology in influencing the contemporary reality of childhood.

Throughout this period, the child is exposed to a whole range of activities which have had as their goal the education of the child into the culture of his birth. Stories of great heroes drawn from the Rāmāyana and Mahābhārata and the Purānas are told, usually by the grandparents, to inculcate virtues the culture regards as praiseworthy. Worldly wisdom is taught through folk tales and the animal stories from the *Panchātāntra*. Festivals, fairs, community congregations, bardic songs, pilgrimages, folk dances and music, visiting theatrical troupes, and wandering saddhus all introduce the child to the larger gamut of life surrounding him, as well as mold his aesthetic sensibilities in a culturally desired fashion.

The rites of this period of childhood, mostly limited to boys of the upper castes, are *vidyārambha* and the *upanayana*. Vidyārambha, performed between the fifth and seventh years, when the child is supposed to be old enough to learn to read and write, is an initiation into learning. Upanayana, on the other hand, marks the culmination, the grand end of childhood. Traditionally performed (depending upon the caste) anywhere between the eighth and twelfth years, upanayana initiates the child's "social birth" into the wider community. As a text puts it, "Till a boy is eight years old he is like one newly born, and only indicates the caste in which he is born. As long as his upanayana ceremony has not been performed the boy incurs no blame as to what is allowed or forbidden![25] The initiation ceremony is elaborate, its preparatory rites designed to drive home the fact of the child's separation from his family and the final break with his mother. In its traditional version, the child is smeared with a yellowish paste and is expected to spend the whole night in a pitch-dark room in absolute silence—a re-creation of the embryonic state—before he emerges the next morning for one of the most moving and poignant ceremonies of this samskāra, the sharing of a meal with his mother, which is supposedly the last time the mother and son will ever eat together. Thus, although as an initiation rite, upanayana contains many rituals symbolizing a hopeful beginning, it neverthe-less also clearly marks the regretted end of a familiar world—the world of childhood.

[1] See D.D. Kosambi, *The Culture and Civilization of Ancient India in Historical Outline* (New Delhi: Vikas, 1970), 16.

[2] Adi Parva, tr. M.M. Dutta, vol. 1 of *The Mahabharata* Calcutta: Oriental Publishing Co. (n.d.) 107-8.

[3] *Ibid.*, 510.

[4] Kālidāsa, *Raghuvamsha*, 3: 45-6 (my translation).

[5] See, for example, M. Cormack, *The Hindu Woman*, (Bombay: Asia Publishing House, 1961) p. 11; S.C. Dube, *Indian Village*, (New York: Harper and Row, 1967) 148-9; T.N. Madan, *Family and Kinship* (Bombay: Asia Publishing House, 1965) 77; L. Minturn and J.T. Hitchcock, "The Rajputs of Khalapur, India," in *Six Cultures: Studies of Child-rearing,* ed. B.B. Whiting (New York: John Wiley, 1963) 307-8. See also, William J. Goode, *World Revolution and Family Patterns,* (New York: The Free Press, 1963) 235-6; and D.G. Mandelbaum, *Society in India,* vol. 1 (Berkeley: University of California Press, 1970) 120. Cases of post-partum depression, for example, are much more commonly reported among mothers who give birth to a daughter than among those who have a son. See M.R. Gaitonde, "Cross-Cultural Study of the Psychiatric Syndromes in Out-Patient Clincs in Bombay, India, and Topeka, Kansas," *International Journal of Social Psychiatry,* 4 (1958):103.

[6] Oscar Lewis, *Village Life in Northern India* (New York: Vintage Books, 1958) 195.

[7] Irawati Karve, *Kinship Organization in India* (Bombay: Asia Publishing House, 1968) 206.

[8] *The Laws of Manu* G. Buhler (Oxford: Clarendon Press, 1886) 114.

[9] *Ibid.*, IV, 179.

[10] *Ibid.*, IV, 282-3.

[11] *Ibid.*, VIII, 299-300: IX, 230.

[12] Richard B. Lyman Jr., "Barbarism and Religion: Late Roman and Early Medieval Childhoood," in *The History of Childhood,* ed. L. de Mause (New York: Harper Torchbooks, 1975) 84.

[13] *Caraka Samhita* (Delhi: Motilal Banarsidass, 1975), Sarira 8:96.

[14] *Susruta Samhita,* Sarira 10:38.

[15] Srinivas Sharma, *Adhunik Hindi Kavya Vatsalya Rasa* quoted in C. Rawat, *Sur Sahitya,* (Mathura: Jawahar Pustakalaya, 1967) 230.

[16] Surdas, *Sursagarsar,* D. Verma (Allahabad: Shitya Bhawan, 1972) 59 (my translation).

[17] Goswami Tulsidas, *Kavitavali,* R.P. Tripathi (Allahabad: Bharati Niketan, n.d.) 3 (my translation).

[18] In this connection, see the various contributions in de Mause's *The History of Childhood,* especially the review essay "The Evolution of Childhood," 1-73.

[19] For a textual description of the contents of the *samskaras* see Raj B. Pandey, *Hindu Samskaras,* (Delhi: Motilal Banarsidass, 1969).

[20] For a more detailed discussion see "Mothers and Infants," chap. 3 in Sudhir Kakar, *The Inner World: A Psychoanalytic Study of Childhood and Society in India* (New York and Delhi: Oxford University Press, 1978).

[21] See R. Sankrantyan and D.K. Upadhyaya, eds. *Hindi Sahitya ka Vrihat Itihas,* vol. 16, part 3 (Kashi: Nagaripracharni Sabha, n.d.) 111.

[22] Dube, *op. cit.,* 149.

[23] S. Anandalakshmi, "Socialization for Competence: A Study of Children in Four Craft Communities" (unpublished manuscript, Lady Irvin College, Delhi).

[24] See D.M. Bassa, "From the Traditional to the Modern: Some Observations on Changes in Indian Child-rearing and Parental Attitudes" in *The Child in his Family: Children and Their Parents in a Changing World,* ed. E.J. Anthony and C. Chiland (New York: J. Wiley, 1978) 333-44, and Champa Aphale, *Growing Up in an Urban Complex* (New Delhi: National, 1976).

[25] P.V. Kare, *History of Dharamsastra,* vol. 2, part 1, (Poona: Bhandarkar Oriental Research Institute, 1933), 180.

Child Care in China

by Bruce Dollar

Societies differ as to how they characteristically raise (socialize) their children. The following selection describes some of the cultural values, beliefs, and institutions of modern China that directly affect the development of its children and the roles of other family members. The institutionalized child care programs in China will be of particular interest to those concerned with the growing use of day care centers in the United States.

The old art of China-watching is giving way to China-witnessing, and one quality of the new China which seems inevitably to impress all recent visitors is the extraordinary vibrancy of Chinese children, from the very youngest to the adolescents, who already tower so noticeably over their grandparents. During my own recent trip within China, my companions and I saw for ourselves the exuberant self-confidence that seems to infuse all Chinese kids, whether they are performing for strangers, participating in a classroom exercise, or playing by themselves.

"Ours is a socialist society; everything is done according to plan." This pronouncement, with which our various Chinese hosts so frequently prefaced their answers to our questions, provides a starting point for understanding how this spirit of exuberance has been achieved. Although Chinese society is largely decentralized to encourage local self-sufficiency and diversification, the whole is knit together by an administrative structure that is more or less uniform from city to city and, somewhat less, from commune (or network of villages) to commune. It is a framework that provides an efficient system of communication and has helped produce a remarkable social cohesion based on commonly held goals and values—which themselves are informed by the teachings of Mao Tse-tung.

The consensus is particularly apparent with respect to the care and training of the young. This is hardly surprising when one considers the enormous stock the Chinese place in producing what they call "revolutionary successors," an apt phrase in a country where revolutionary consciousness has been maintained largely through vivid comparisons with the "bitter past," and where the problem of continuing the revolution into succeeding generations is paramount.

Thus, throughout our visit we constantly encountered—with amazing consistency at various points along a 2,500-mile itinerary—several major ideas about child-rearing in the numerous conversations we had with people in child-related institutions: families, nurseries, kindergartens, and schools. These themes—especially the subordination of personal to social needs, respect for productive labor, altruism, cooperation, and the integration of physical with intellectual labor—together describe the kind of citizen China hopes to produce. The techniques employed to achieve these values are in practice virtually from infancy.

During the years before primary school, which begins at the age of seven, a series of public child care facilities is available to parents who wish to use them. In the cities, where patterns are more uniform, a mother's maternity leave (paid) usually terminates 56 days after birth. Since breastfeeding is the rule in China, the mother may then place her child in the nursing room at her place of work. Most work institutions—factories, hospitals, and government offices, for example—provide this facility for their employees. In a typical arrangement the mother has two half-hour breaks, plus lunch, to visit and nurse her baby during the work day. After work the baby returns home with the mother.

Nursing rooms provide care for infants up to one and a half years old; then they may be sent to one of the various kinds of nurseries. Some of these are attached to the work place or located in the home neighborhood; they may be open only during the work day, or they may be "live-in" nurseries, where children stay overnight and go home on weekends. Kindergartens, usually located in the residential areas, generally care for children from three and a half to seven years old and may also be either part-time or full-time.

In a country in which over 90 percent of all women of working age do work, it might be expected that a similar percentage of children would therefore receive some kind of institutional care. But there are options. The most common is to leave the child in the care of grandparents, who frequently live with the family. Another alternative is to make arrangements with a friend or neighbor. Estimates vary from place to place, but in most cities no more than half the children of nursery school age are in attendance. For kindergarten the figures are higher, especially in the cities, where attendance is over 80 percent.

Since child care is decentralized, different localities often make their own arrangements, which may not conform to the usual patterns. This is particularly true of rural areas, where a lack of resources and the persistence of custom probably account for a lower incidence of public child care facilities. One small village we visited, the Sha Shih Yu Brigade in northeast China, had no permanent facility; only during harvest time, when all hands were needed in the fields, was there organized care for small children. A child care center located in a coalmining area near Tangshan, on the other hand, served 314 children divided into at least five separate age groups, from 56 days to six years old.

How do these institutions work to socialize the children under their care? And what are they like for the kids? In spite of the diversity in organizational structure, the remarkable similarity from place to place, both in the values espoused and the methods used to inculcate them, seems to support a number of generalizations.

One quality that is sure to strike an American observer is the preponderance and style of group activities. A common example is the "cultural performance," usually presented for visitors. Whether they are songs from a revolutionary opera, dances to celebrate a harvest, or a program of folk melodies played on traditional Chinese instruments, these performances are always presented by groups, and it is impossible to pick out a "star."

Although there were exceptions, many early child care facilities we visited seemed rather poorly supplied with the variety of toys and materials that conventional wisdom in the United States says should be on hand to enrich and enliven a child's environment. Although this may have been due to a simple inability to pay for more equipment, the teachers we spoke to did not seem to consider it a shortcoming. Perhaps this is because Chinese children are generally expected to rely on each other for stimulation—at any rate, this seems to be the effect. The situation provides an interesting contrast to that in the United States, where the highly desired "rich environment" often means that kids interact with inanimate materials more than they do with other people.

The small children we saw were not without playthings, however. There was always at least one toy for each child—typically a rubber or plastic doll of a worker, a peasant, or a soldier. Rocking horses were also common, as were military toys and playground equipment that could accommodate many children. But in general the emphasis was on group play. One recent American visitor to a Chinese nursery school reports noticing that the blocks seemed awfully heavy for the small children. "Exactly!" beamed the teachers. "That fosters mutual help."

Chinese teachers actively encourage such group behavior as cooperation, sharing, and altruism. "We praise a child when he shows concern for others' interest," said one kindergarten teacher. "For example, at meal time teachers give out bowls and chopsticks. If a youngster gets a nicer bowl and gives it to someone else, we praise him for it. Or when the children are asked to select a toy and a child gives the best one to a classmate, we praise that, too."

Even in a competitive situation, this teacher said, helping another is more important than winning. "When the children run in a relay race, sometimes one will fall down, especially if he's small. If another child stops to help him get up or to see if he's all right, even though his own team might fall behind, we encourage this." The approach contrasts markedly with methods used in the Soviet Union, another country that stresses the collective in its childrearing practices. There, competition is discouraged between individuals but promoted between groups. Each child is made aware of his importance within his group—say, a row in his classroom—and then competes fiercely for the rewards of a group victory. The Chinese seem genuinely to eschew even this form of competition in favor of straightforward mutual help and cooperation.

But how do teachers deal with improper behavior and matters of discipline? Here is how the question was answered in a conversation with three staff members of a full-time kindergarten in Peking:

Q: What kinds of behavior do you discourage in the children?
A: We criticize those who take toys or other things from others. Or if children beat each other—we criticize that.
Q: Exactly how do you handle such a situation—say, two kids fighting?
A: First, the teacher must understand the reason for the fight. For instance, one might have taken a toy from the other, and the second child hit him. In that case, the teacher will criticize both. This criticism is carried out alone, unless it took place in the class; in that case it will be done in front of the class so that all the children will understand what was wrong. Criticism is to make children understand what was wrong and why.
Q: What kind of punishment do you use?
A: There is no punishment.
Q: Well, what if a child were really intractable? Would you use some mild sanction, such as depriving him of some free play time on the playground?
A: (At this point all three women broke into smiles at our incredulity. Waving their hands back and forth to underscore their words, they said): No, no, nothing like that. We believe in persuasion.

Q: Do other children ever participate in criticism?
A: Generally, no. Unless a third child saw what happened—then he'll be asked to tell.
Q: Let's say the incident was unobserved by any third party and the two kids involved give conflicting versions of what happened. Then how does the teacher act?
A: If the teacher finds a contradiction when both tell what happened, she will try to educate the children. She will note that everyone can make a mistake, including teachers. The mistake that led to the fight is not important, she will say, but telling the truth is very important. At this point the children will probably tell the truth.

This sounded like fine theory, but it provoked some skepticism among those of us who had been teachers. What about teachers who do not have the patience to use such positive techniques? we asked. How do you deal with teachers who don't observe the school's policy? The reply: "We all—teachers and leadership—have the same goal: to cultivate revolutionary successors. So we all work together and help each other. We study our profession together. We have regular criticism and self-criticism sessions, and sometimes we help each other on specific problems."

If we had not already seen many teachers in action here and elsewhere on our trip, we might have been dissatisfied with this answer. But we were constantly struck by the teachers' apparent love for their work in all the early child care institutions we visited. These women, we learned (there were no men), were chosen for their jobs after having shown a particular interest in children, and "sensitivity and love for children" were the criteria most often cited for their recruitment. Credentials were secondary. Since the Cultural Revolution, the amount of training teachers receive has ranged all the way from university graduation to short-term training classes and "learning through practice."

Three of us in the group who were especially interested in child-rearing and education often asked to see child care centers and schools under normal operating conditions. Our guides accommodated these requests by arranging for us to stay behind after the formal tour or to make a low-key visit to a kindergarten, say, without the rest of the group. Some of our most revealing insights occurred during our observation of everyday free playground activities.

One afternoon, for example, at the child care center serving workers of the Fan Ga Chong coal mine area near Tangshan, I spent nearly an hour outside among the four-and-a-half to six-year-olds and their teachers, or "nurses." Here was the one place where I saw what might be called a disruptive child—a little boy who, in the United States, would probably have been labeled hyperkinetic and put on Ritalin. While the other 50 or so children busied themselves with various games—rope jumping, drop the handkerchief, tricycle riding, playing with toys and each other—this boy ran constantly from place to place, trying to be in on everything at once and occasionally interfering with someone else's fun. The nurses, who themselves were taking part in the games, were obviously aware of the boy's actions, but they made no fuss over him. Instead, each time he ran by a nurse, she would reach out, place her hand on the back of his head, and gently guide him away from trouble or toward an activity he might like—usually with a few soothing words. Soon he was off again, and once or twice it was necessary to intervene when he began picking on another child. But always the adults acted cheerfully and patiently, and the boy never became a center of attention. His actions were the closest thing to aggressive or disruptive behavior among children that I saw on the entire trip.

After visiting several classrooms at the Pei Hai Kindergarten, a full-time kindergarten located in a park in Peking, I spent an even longer time on the playground watching free play. Once again I was struck by the way teachers enthusiastically joined in. The children, well over a hundred of them, had formed into a variety of play groups. Some played on slides, a merry-go-round, monkey bars, and swings. Some were organized into class-sized groups for games. Others were in smaller groups, jumping rope or kicking a ball around. There were kids in pairs and kids alone. One gleeful little boy, holding aloft a leafy twig, ran, danced, and twirled with it till he fell down from dizziness. And ranging over the whole playground, sweeping past and through everyone else's games, was a whooping pack of boys chasing a soccer ball, a laughing teacher in the lead.

In one group that especially caught my eye, seven or eight girls were jumping rope, taking turns at the ends of a pink plastic rope and lining up to jump one by one. No teacher was with them. They were very absorbed and used chants and songs to accompany each jumper. Several times while I watched, a minor controversy of some kind would erupt and everything would come to a halt. Maybe it concerned whose turn was next on the rope or how many times one had jumped before missing. Whatever it was, the whole group would come together and heatedly debate their points. With no single girl taking charge, they would quickly work out a settlement that seemed to satisfy everyone and then resume their jumping with all the gusto of before. These little girls were good jumpers, incidentally—so good that after a while they attracted an audience: six little boys found chairs, lined them up to form a small gallery, and proceeded to join in the jumping chants, applauding for each jumper. Great fun for all, highly organized, and by all indications spontaneous and undirected by adults.

In the United States the growing demand for facilities for the care of infants and preschool children has provoked a chorus of urgent questions: Doesn't a baby need a single individual to relate to and identify with as mother? How can a mother be sure that those to whom she entrusts her child will teach the same values she holds? Isn't it the mother's natural role to care for her own children? What is the effect of institutionalized child care on the family?

Obviously, the answers the Chinese have found to these questions are not directly applicable to this country. Yet the insights they provide can be instructive as we seek our own solutions.

There is a strong likelihood that the average child in China will undergo "multiple mothering" of some kind. Even if the mother does not choose to leave her infant in the nursing room where she works, chances are the child will wind up in the care of a neighbor or the grandmother. Offsetting this diversity of "mothers," however, is the near-uniform consensus of values and methods of child-rearing I have described. This consistency seems to go a long way toward providing young children with the kind of security we in the United States might normally associate only with single mothering.

Another aspect of multiple or "shared" mothering, as Ruth Sidel, author of the excellent recent book *Women & Child Care in China,* points out, "is that infants can thrive physically and emotionally if the mother-surrogates are constant, warm, and giving. Babies in China are not subjected to serial mothering; we were repeatedly told that aunties (i.e., nurses) and teachers rarely leave their jobs. And they are warm and loving with the children. The children show none of the lethargy or other intellectual, emotional, or physical problems of institutionalized children. Quite the opposite!"

Everything is planned, and the position of mothers in China is the consequence of a society-wide effort to provide for the economic liberation of women. In keeping with Mao Tse-tung's edict calling for "genuine equality between the sexes," a broad series of programs, including birth control information and prenatal care with maternity leave, in addition to the system of child care facilities, is underway to assume the full participation of women in "building socialism." The objects of unspeakable oppression in prerevolutionary society, Chinese women today have been thoroughly integrated into the labor force, both in factory and commune. And a growing number of them are entering professions—for example, 50 percent of the medical students are now women.

Despite the enormous progress, even the Chinese will concede that full parity with men is not yet a reality. Top governmental, military, and management posts continue to be mostly male preserves. However, women do wield considerable political and administrative power at the local level, where they often run the smallest governmental units, the neighborhood revolutionary committees.

But the key to liberation is still economic independence, which depends on the availability of work. Since 1971 a new source of work for women has appeared: the so-called housewives' factories. These have been organized locally by women who live in housing areas like the Kung Kiang Workers' Residential Area in Shanghai, and whose husbands work in the various nearby factories. As they described it to us, the housewives were looking for ways in which they could contribute productively to the revolution without having to leave the residential area. So they set up their own light industries in workshops near their homes, and by working full- or part-time were able to produce needed commodities, such as flashlight bulbs or men's trousers, while earning extra money for themselves. The entire operation in each case was staffed and run by women.

Since nearly all working-age women in China today work and are no longer economically dependent on their husbands or families, one might well wonder about the effects of these conditions on the family.

By all available evidence the family is thriving in China, and the individual household continues to be the basic social unit. A featured item in every home we visited, as ubiquitous as a portrait of Chairman Mao, was a display of a great many photographs of family members, usually pressed under a piece of glass on top of a bureau or framed on the wall. Our host or hostess would invariably point this out with pride. Signs of active and full participation in family life were everywhere, and all generations were included. A man out with his children is a common sight, as is a child with a grandmother or grandfather.

Parents are obviously revered by children, and so are grandparents. In fact, the complete absence of a "generation gap" is a striking phenomenon to an American. Not only are grandparents well integrated into family life, but old people who have no family or who are disabled live in well-tended "respect for aged" homes and are given important functions that serve the neighborhood.

Far from undermining the family structure, we were repeatedly told, jobs for women and day care for children have made home life easier, having eliminated many former sources of friction and frustration. A major factor here is undoubtedly the mass commitment to working for the betterment of China. Personal gratification seems to derive from each individual's knowledge that he or she makes an important contribution, no matter how small, to the national effort and that the benefits of this contribution, and others like it, will be distributed to all.

Some Discontinuities in the Enculturation of Mistassini Cree Children

by Peter S. Sindell

The establishment of Western schools, especially boarding schools, and curricula in non-Western societies is likely to constitute an extreme type of cultural discontinuity and may do much to force "either-or" choices on their learners (DuBois:102).

Some of the discontinuities which five- or six-year-old Mistassini children experience when they first attend the residential school at La Tuque will be described in this chapter. The world in which these children live before starting school is almost wholly Cree in character. The language spoken at home is Cree, and preschool children have little direct interaction with Euro-Canadians, or "whites." For the small Cree child the most striking figure in the white world is probably the *wabinkiyu,* a form of bogeyman who is thought of as white. When children misbehave parents frequently tell their children that the wabinkiyu is going to take them away.

In the preschool period the children have clear-cut traditional models for identification: parents, grandparents, elder siblings, and other close kin. Most of these kinsmen display behavior and attitudes which conform to traditional Cree values and role expectations.* In addition, these kinsmen reward their children, implicitly and explicitly, for conformity to traditional norms.

When the children enter school they must act according to norms which contradict a great deal of what they have learned before, master a body of knowledge completely foreign to them, and communicate in an incomprehensible language in a strange environment.

In this chapter I shall discuss self-reliance and dependence, the character of interpersonal relations, cooperation and competition, the expression and inhibition of aggression, and role expectations for children. For each topic the traditional milieu and the first year in the school environment will be compared and contrasted.

* This is changing now to a certain extent since some of the older children, who have been to school for many years, act in ways which are not traditional. Therefore, they provide their younger siblings with other models for emulation and identification.

As the children attend school, they form ties with their teachers and counselors and learn more about Euro-Canadian culture. Eventually, older students face situations different from those they faced as small children. Upon reaching adolescence, most students experience a conflict in identity which reflects the cultural discontinuities they experience in school, and in alternating between the urban residential school in winter and the trading post during the summer.

The data upon which the following discussion is based were gathered during fieldwork at Mistassini Post and at the La Tuque Indian Residential School from July 1966, to September 1967. The school is operated by the Anglican Church of Canada for the Indian Affairs Branch. It is located in La Tuque, P.Q., which is 180 miles northeast of Montreal and 300 miles south of Mistassini Post by road. Most Mistassini Cree children between the ages of six and sixteen attend the residential school for ten months of each year while their parents go into the bush to hunt and trap. Other children from Mistassini attend the day school at the Post or attend high school in Sault Ste. Marie, Ontario, while living with white families. Only since 1963, when the La Tuque school opened, have the majority of Mistassini children attended school on a regular basis.

In studying the children, interviews were conducted with the children, their parents, teacher, and counselors before, during, and after school. In addition, a series of behavior-rating forms was utilized with the counselors and teacher and hypotheses about the role of imitation and modeling in acculturation were tested in an experiment. Finally, observational protocols were collected on the children's behavior at the Post and in school. The theoretical framework utilized in the study is that of social learning theory as developed by Bandura and Walters. This theory stresses the importance of such concepts as modeling, imitation, and social reinforcement in the analysis of behavioral and attitudinal change.

The study of the thirteen children who entered school for the first time in September 1966 is that of the first generation of people who will receive extensive formal education. Many of the cultural conflicts discussed below adumbrate those which the children will face as adolescents and adults when they attempt to adapt to changing economic and social conditions in the Waswanipi-Mistassini region.

Self-reliance and Dependence

Before Cree children enter school they experience few limits on their behavior. As infants they are fed on demand. When they grow older they eat when they feel hungry and are free to choose from whatever food is available. Usually something—bannock, dried fish, or dried meat—is readily available. Sleeping too is not rigidly scheduled; and the children simply go to sleep when they are tired.

Further, children are free to explore their natural surroundings, either alone or with siblings or playmates. There are no demarcated territorial boundaries which limit their wanderings at the Post. The number of children in any particular hunting group varies, and therefore, a child may spend much or all of the winter without playmates from his own age group. As a result, children learn to depend upon themselves for amusement. They learn to utilize whatever is available—an old tin stove, a few soft drink bottles, a dead bird, sticks, or stones. Anything the child can reach is a legitimate object for play. If the object is dangerous, parents divert the child's attention or take the object away, but do not reprimand the child. For instance, two- or three-year-old children often handle or play with axes. In general, the only limits placed on a child's behavior relate to specific environmental dangers; for example, children are not allowed to go out in boats alone.

Whereas at home the children have experienced few limits on their freedom of action, at school there are many. In order to cope with the large number of children (277 at the time the study was made), the school requires them to conform to many routines. They must eat three times a day at specified hours, must wake up and go to sleep at set times, and must learn to obey many other seemingly arbitrary rules. For example, children are not allowed in the front foyer of the dormitory and are not allowed to use the front stairway. Their environment is circumscribed also by the boundary of the schoolyard. Occasionally the children leave the school property but only in the company of an adult.

The child is dependent upon others to satisfy almost all of his needs. He must depend on the counselor in his living group ("wing") for clean clothes, soap, toothpaste, and even toilet paper when it runs out. Furthermore, he must line up to receive these supplies at the counselor's convenience. Practically the first English phrase which every child learns is "line up!"

The school, then, reinforces the children into submissive, nonexploratory behavioral patterns. These contravene their previous experiences, which led to self-reliant and exploratory behaviors highly adaptive for life in the bush.

Interpersonal Relations

After a child is weaned he is cared for not only by his mother but increasingly by a wide range of other kin, such as older siblings, young uncles and aunts, and grandparents. Consequently, each child forms close ties with several kinsmen. Fairly frequent shifts in residence and in hunting group composition, early death, and the Cree patterns of adoption, mitigate against the development of extreme dependency on only one or two members of the nuclear family. In fact, it seems likely that some frustration of dependency needs results from the disruption of social relationships noted above. Parents and children interact primarily within networks of close kin. Thus, before they go to school, children gain little experience in interacting with people with whom they do not have close affective ties.

As children enter the school at La Tuque, they interact primarily in the context of large groups: the school class, the wings, and the age groups—Junior Girls (age six to eight) and Junior Boys (age six to ten). The children sleep in rooms with siblings of the same sex, but due to differing schedules on most days they see them only at meals and early in the morning. Since practically all activities are segregated by sex, brothers and sisters have few opportunities to talk to each other. Thus, children's social ties begin to shift from warm affective relations with a small multigenerational kin group comprised of both sexes to shallow contacts with a large peer group of the same sex. Preston notes the implications of this shift for the internalization of social controls (p. 6).

While their peer group expands, the number of adults with whom the children interact shrinks. Each beginning pupil is cared for by only two or three adults: teacher, wing counselor, and Junior counselor. Since each wing counselor is also responsible for an age group, one of the wing counselors is the Junior counselor.

With a large number of children competing for a single adult's attention in any given situation, the children learn to beg for nurturance which they could take for granted at home. Dependent behavior, such as crying and yelling, is reinforced as the children discover its effectiveness in eliciting a response from the adult. At home self-reliance and independence are valued and, therefore, crying is ignored from an early age and children learn not to cry. Children learn in school that the smallest scratch will elicit a great deal of concern because the counselors fear that impetigo will develop. Thus, their early training in silently enduring pain is also contradicted.

109

In summary, the children openly express far more dependence in school than at home, and this dependence is focused on two or three adults rather than upon a multigenerational kin group. At home the children have supportive relationships but these do not involve a high level of overt expression of dependence (Spindler p. 384). Furthermore, the children interact with others far more than they did at home and come to need a high degree of social stimulation.

Cooperation and Competition

Most of the tasks which a child performs at home are done cooperatively and contribute to the welfare of the whole group, usually a nuclear or extended family. Children perform these tasks with siblings, parents or other kin. Cooperation in hunting and in household chores is extremely adaptive since it makes the most efficient use of the group's limited labor resources. Sharing food as well as labor is of major importance in traditional Cree culture. Religious values reinforce this since *mistapeo*, the soul spirit, "is pleased with generosity, kindness and help to others" (Speck p. 44).

Children observe this extensive sharing and cooperation within the kin group and participate directly in it. For example, during the summer, young children often are used to carry gifts of fish, bannock, fowl, and so on, between kin. Observations indicate that the children themselves usually share food and toys readily.

Competition rather than cooperation is the keynote of school life. In class the students are encouraged to compete with each other in answering questions, and those who answer most promptly and correctly gain the teacher's attention and win her approval. Both in school and in the dormitory the children must constantly compete for places in line. Those who are first in line get their food or clothing first or get outside to play soonest. Also, because the dormitory is understaffed, each child must compete with many others to ensure that the counselor attends to his individual needs.

Although the teacher finds it difficult to stimulate many children to respond competitively in class, many older children learn to compete aggressively for food and refuse to share their belongings.

Expression and Inhibition of Aggression

Inhibiting the overt expression of aggression is highly valued in Cree culture and serves to maintain positive affective ties among kinsmen, particularly within the hunting-trapping group. Aggression is defined broadly by the Cree and includes not only fighting but also directly contradicting someone else, refusing a direct request, and raising one's voice inappropriately. (These statements apply particularly to relations between kinsmen.) These forms of behavior are unacceptable except if one is drunk and, thus, considered not responsible for his actions. Fighting when drunk is common and appears to arouse anxiety in children observing this. Laughing at people's mistakes or foibles is not usually defined as aggressive behavior. Gossip, teasing, and the threat of witchcraft are covert means of expressing aggression which are prevalent among the Cree. During enculturation fighting and quarreling are punished.

Punishment seems to be infrequent and usually consists of teasing, ridicule, threats of corporal punishment or reprisals by wabinkiyu, and, occasionally, yelling. But corporal punishment is rare and most often is limited to a light slap with an open hand on top of the head or just above the ear.

In contrast to what they have been taught at home, in school, the children learn to express aggression openly. Counselors and teachers disapprove greatly of the children's constant "tattle taling," which serves to express aggression covertly. On the other hand, overtired and frustrated with the demands of controlling large numbers of children, the adults in the school often yell at the children, speak to them sternly, and, occasionally, swat them. Television and observation of white children are other sources of models for openly aggressive behavior. It is apparent from observing the children that these television models, such as Batman and Tarzan, are very important. Mistassini children also learn to express aggression openly because they are forced to defend themselves against some of the more aggressive children from Dore Lake.

Role Expectations for Children

Cree children learn very early in life the basic components of adult roles through observing their parents and elder siblings. As soon as a child is able to walk he is given small tasks to perform such as carrying a little water or a few pieces of wood. If he does not perform these tasks the child is not punished because Cree parents think he is not old enough to "understand" yet. When the child walks out of the tent for the first time on his own, the "Infants' Rite" is held.

> The essence of the baby's rite is the symbolization of the child's future role as an adult. A boy 'kills,' brings the kill to camp, and distributes the meat; a girl carries in firewood and boughs. (Rogers and Rogers p. 20)

All but one of the thirteen children in the sample participated in this rite.

At about five or six years of age children begin to perform chores regularly and are punished if they do not obey. Among their new chores are caring for smaller siblings and washing dishes; in addition, they begin to carry significant quantities of wood, water, and boughs. Children also begin to contribute food to the family at this age. They pick berries, snare rabbits, hunt birds, and sometimes accompany their parents into the bush to check traps or to get wood, water, or boughs. At approximately the same time as the child begins playing a more responsible role in performing tasks, the parents believe that his ability to conceptualize develops.

Parents conceive of their children as developing gradually into responsible adults. Much of the children's play imitates the activities of their parents, and, thus, rehearses adults' roles. For example, little girls make bannock out of mud, make hammocks and baby sacks for their dolls, and pretend to cook. Little boys hunt birds and butterflies, play with toy boats, and pull cardboard boxes and other objects as if they were pulling toboggans. Little boys and girls sometimes play together in small "play" tents which their parents make for them.

On the other hand, when they go to school, counselors and teachers expect children to live in a world of play unrelated to their future participation in adult society. There are few chores to do and these are peripheral to satisfaction of the basic needs—food, heat, and water—which concerned them at home. Keeping one's room clean and tidy and making one's bed are the principal chores which smaller children are expected to do. Young children are expected to spend most of their time playing and going to school. In school and in the dormitory most play involves large groups of thirty to forty children and consists mainly of organized games such as "Cat and Mouse," "Simon Says," "London Bridge," and relay races. When play is nondirective, children frequently resort to imitative play as they did before coming to school, but sometimes with a new content, for example, playing "Batman," "Spaceghost," or "Counselors."

In discussing the child-rearing practices of some societies like the Cree, Benedict says: "The essential point of such child training is that the child is from infancy continuously conditioned to responsible social participation, while at the same time the tasks that are expected of it are adapted to its capacities" (p. 23-24).

Attending school radically disrupts this development. After only one year of school, parents report that their children "only want to play" and are not interested in performing their chores. Thus, children have already begun to reject their parents' definitions of proper behavior. This kind of intergenerational conflict increases dramatically with each year of school experience. It is exacerbated because the children are in school all winter and thus, fail to learn the technical skills related to hunting and trapping as they mature. This has serious implications for identity conflicts in adolescence since the children are unable to fulfill their parents' expectations. Children who do not attend school are able to assume adult economic roles at about the onset of puberty. For example, boys begin to trap seriously and girls can contribute significantly to the cleaning and preparation of pelts.

Conclusions

Traditional Cree enculturation takes place primarily in the context of multigenerational kin groups and stresses food sharing and cooperative labor, indirect rather than open expression of aggression, and self-reliance. Interpersonal relations within the kin group are supportive, but verbal expression of dependence is discouraged. Children are viewed as "little adults" and contribute labor and food to the kin group commensurate with their level of maturity. Children's self-reliance is placed in the service of the kin group.

During their first year of residential school the beginners experience radical discontinuities in their enculturation. The values, attitudes, and behavioral expectations which motivate the dormitory counselors and teacher in their interaction with the children differ sharply from those of Mistassini Cree parents. In school, children have few tasks and these rarely relate to the welfare of the whole group. Competition and direct expression of aggression are reinforced rather than punished. The children interact primarily in large groups—school class, age group, and wing—and come to need a high rate of social stimulation. Dependence becomes focused on two or three adults, and overt expression of dependence increases since it is effective in eliciting nurturant behavior.

As the data presented in the body of the chapter make clear, during their first year of formal education Mistassini beginners are exposed to great cultural discontinuity. They learn new ways of behaving and thinking and are rewarded for conformity to norms which contradict those which they learned before coming to school. Consequently, after only one year of school they have already begun to change significantly toward acting in ways which are appropriate in Euro-Canadian culture but inappropriate in their own. As they continue their education this process accelerates. After alternating for five or six years between the traditional milieu in the summer and the urban residential school in the winter severe conflicts in identity arise.

In the six years before starting school the children learn behavioral patterns and values which are highly functional for participating as adults in the traditional hunting-trapping life of their parents. Because they must go to school their development into trappers or wives of trappers is arrested. Prolonged residential school experience makes it difficult if not impossible for children to participate effectively in the hunting-trapping life of their parents. Not only do they fail to learn the requisite technical skills, but they acquire new needs and aspirations which cannot be satisfied on the trapline. Yet most Mistassini parents want their children to return to the bush. It remains to be seen how the students will resolve their dilemma.

References

Bandura, Albert, and Richard H. Walters, 1963, *Social Learning and Personality Development*. New York: Holt, Rinehart and Winston, Inc.

Benedict, Ruth, 1954, "Continuities and Discontinuities in Cultural Conditioning." In Margaret Mead and Martha Wolfenstein, eds. *Childhood in Contemporary Cultures*. Chicago: University of Chicago Press.

DuBois, Cora, 1955, "Some Notions on Learning Intercultural Understanding." In G.D. Spindler, ed., *Education and Anthropology*. Stanford, Calif.: Stanford University Press, p. 89-105.

Preston, Richard J., 1966, "Peer Group versus Trapline; Shifting Directions in Cree Socialization." Paper presented at the Annual Meeting of the Pennsylvania Sociological Society, Haverford, Pa., October 15 (mimeographed).

Rogers, Edward S., and Jean H. Rogers, 1963, "The Individual in Mistassini Society from Birth to Death." In *Contributions to Anthropology*, 1960, Part II, pp. 14-36. (Bulletin 190, National Museum of Canada) Ottawa: Roger Duhamel.

Speck, Frank, 1935, *The Savage Hunters of the Labrador Peninsula*. Norman: University of Oklahoma Press.

Spindler, George D., 1963, "Personality, Sociocultural System, and Education among the Menomini," In G.D. Spindler, ed., *Education and Culture*. New York: Holt, Rinehart and Winston, Inc., pp. 351-399.

Free Enterprise and the Ghetto Family

by Jagna Wojcicka Sharff

Jagna Wojcicka Sharff is an urban anthropologist who teaches at City College and Columbia University in New York City. She completed her Ph.D. at Columbia and is writing a book about the project discussed here, entitled Life on Dolittle Street: How Poor People Purchase Immortality.

Street life on Dolittle Street is a sleight of hand. The clumps of six to ten young men who seem to be socializing daily on the corner from early morning until late at night are not there solely for convivial reasons. Nor is the little hole-in-the-wall cigarette store near the corner selling only tobacco cigarettes. Nor is the storefront several tenements down the block just the home of a popular bachelor with lots of friends continuously dropping by. The mechanic next door is not simply repairing cars. And the mothers conversing in small groups and calling out of the windows are not occupied with housework and child care. Nor are the children simply playing. All these places and activities are both what they are and something else, too—and the something else is invariably aimed at adding to the meager resources of the neighborhood, often illegally.

From July 1977 to August 1979, an anthropological team of which I was project director rented a storefront on Dolittle Street, a fictitious name for a well-traveled street that cuts across Manhattan's Lower East Side. The block has provided shelter to successive ethnic groups in the same tenements that now house immigrant Hispanics.

Through earlier research, which included a socioeconomic census of 168 blocks of the neighborhood, we knew a great deal about the area. It suffered from one of the highest fire rates in New York City, and its housing stock ranged from fair to almost uninhabitable. Like some areas of the south Bronx and Brooklyn, more than half the buildings had been abandoned or burned out. The area had one of the highest proportions of households with the lowest incomes in the city and an underemployment rate of about 60 percent. (Underemployment is a concept developed by some economists to provide a measure of worker discouragement, particularly in poverty areas; underemployment encompasses the number of unemployed as well as those who can find only part-time work or jobs at inadequate pay). Finally, about two-thirds of the households in the area had at some point received public assistance.

We also knew that the neighborhood was honeycombed with illegal economic activity and permeated with police undercover operations. Fierce competition between different drug-selling groups and frequent police raids often resulted in violence. There was a high death rate in the neighborhood (among young men in particular), as there is among other poor groups throughout New York City. Several definitive studies show that homicide accounts for more than 20 percent of the deaths among these groups.

Our general perspective followed the approach articulated by anthropologist Marvin Harris in his book *Cultural Materialism*—that human behavior is purposive and adaptive and deserves to be observed and recorded "on the ground." To pursue the strategy Harris had outlined we needed to see how the people of Dolittle Street actually lived their lives. The storefront became our means of integration into the social life of the neighborhood.

We explained our presence as an effort to learn "how people make a living in their neighborhood." We also explained that we were especially interested in the economic and social value of drugs. In turn, we made ourselves available to the residents as advocates, especially in their dealings with the various public agencies that wield so much power over their lives.

It took a great length of time and a great deal of energy before the residents began to tolerate, accept, and finally trust us. But gradually we found our way from the street to the living quarters of the residents. As time passed, we became acquainted with the photograph albums of the households' past. We charted the starlike constellations of their kin, we compiled genealogies, household budgets (very important for our economic analysis), patterns of work and leisure; we participated in the residents' efforts to obtain sufficient food, to keep warm, and to raise their children.

We bore witness to many significant events, some joyful, many grievous. A sudden fire, a raid by the police, a street fair, an accident, a suicide, the birth of a child—all revealed the social and economic alignments that operate under the surface of public life on Dolittle Street.

For example, when a young marijuana dealer was murdered, we sat up with his family, drinking coffee, quietly conversing, while numerous members of the extended kin arrived from as far away as Puerto Rico. We took turns baby tending, cooking, and sleeping on the few available beds. Later we contributed to the neighborhood-wide collection to help the family pay for the funeral expenses. Burial ceremonies on Dolittle Street are a major expense, and the immediate family is expected to bear the financial burden of this rite of passage. (Aside from a modest baptismal party, a proper burial is the only ceremony a resident can look forward to with confidence.) At the public wake in the funeral home we were part of a large throng of mourners—family, neighbors, and the dead boy's friends. It was by participant observation in such events that we began to uncover the networks that bind people together and to understand their behavior.

Most studies of poor people suggest that poverty results from some or all of the following: unwillingness to work, lack of skills, ignorance or apathy about contraceptives—hence large families, hence poverty and the perpetuation in the next generation of poverty-causing qualities through the so-called culture of poverty. Our research suggests the opposite, and our focus here will be on the strategies of survival among the Dolittle residents, especially their cultivation of that ostensible burden of the poor—the large family.

Briefly, we found that poor people are hardworking (no loose generality, as even the sketchy discussion below on the work efforts of the Dolittle people will indicate) and that they quickly develop requisite skills when reasonable work is available. Most significantly, we found that having a large number of children is an immensely useful short-run option pursued by a majority of the households. The large family doesn't keep the poor in poverty, but rather serves as a mechanism for survival.

Essentially, the large-family option involves socializing the children into distinct social roles. We found four—the "street representative," the "young child-reproducer," the "wage earner," and the "scholar/advocate," each of which we will examine later. The aim of this network is to extend the domain of the household and help gather additional resources for the family. Indeed, the children of Dolittle Street can be seen as the "investment portfolio" of the mothers (and sometimes the fathers); a flexible resource for security in both the present and the future, one that will also help establish an economic base so that at least one child can move a step up the economic and social ladder.

The Economic Tightrope of Dolittle Street

Before we examine the social roles into which the young people are guided, we must briefly examine the economic context out of which these roles emerge. If the children can be considered a "strategy for survival," it is in part because the other strategies that are available to the adults have such severe limits.

The figures and facts that follow are based on detailed information about 36 households, consisting of 133 individuals. These households do not form a representative sample in a statistical sense. Yet their activities constitute a fair picture of the difficult and often dangerous economic balancing act that is performed by most of the households on Dolittle Street.

The households have three sources of income: regular work, public assistance, and what some economists call "irregular work"—quasi-legal or illegal activities.

Regular work is quite uncertain. The high rate of underemployment means that the residents can find only sporadic and insecure jobs. Such jobs, when available, are usually in small, undercapitalized, and marginal business ventures. They offer low wages and no opportunity for advancement; they are usually non-unionized and often seasonal. Adding to the crunch in regular job opportunities is the fact that two-thirds of the manufacturing jobs in which Puerto Ricans worked have been lost during the past decade.

For the neighborhood's residents, the income from such jobs varies considerably. Factory workers earn $90 to $120 a week, when they are working. A handyman or janitor earns $40 to $60. A waitress in a restaurant or bar earns $60 to $140. But none of the work is steady.

Regular work is very important for the self-esteem and status of the adult males. The strains imposed by the condition of underemployment can lead to marital instability and worse. For example, over the course of a year, two of the 36 households in our group acquired husband/fathers, while four lost them. Of these four, one man committed suicide, another was murdered, a third was imprisoned, and the fourth, discouraged by his low-wage factory job, quit, and then, after a "grace period" of several months in which he did not find another job, was driven out of the house by his common-law wife.

It is this situation of constant economic and marital insecurity that prompts women with young children to apply for public assistance. The amount of assistance varies from household to household, but the general picture is simple to draw. In 1979, as an example, an average family of four—a mother and three children—received $258 in monthly assistance (called "Pre-Add Allowance"), a sum meant to cover gas, electricity, telephone, clothing, transportation, furnishings, cleaning materials, personal-care items, school supplies, leisure, and so forth. In addition, an average family of four received a limit of $218 a month as its shelter allowance—

a sum that went directly to the landlord, who often charged more than that for a tiny, squalid apartment. And finally, a family of four in our sample received an average of $88 a month in food stamps. The purchasing power of this income is indicated by the fact that at the time of our research the cost of feeding a family of four in New York City, according to the Consumer Price Index, was $352 a month.

To understand the practical value of public assistance in more detail, we worked with our 36 households to itemize their annual budgets and learned that over the course of a year, the households spent an average of 87 percent of their public assistance (Pre-Add, shelter, and food stamps) for a combination of food and rent, which meant that the remaining 13 percent had to pay for utilities, clothing, furniture, transportation, and the rest.

The households used whatever strategies they could devise to close the gap between income and basic expenses. One of them was "doubling up" with unreported common-law husbands, whose contributions from regular work could make a difference between destitution and a very modest standard of living. Young adult children still living at home made similar unreported contributions. But because regular work was so sporadic, even such contributions were often not enough to close the gap. In our households, the annual income derived from regular work ranged from $400 to $3,020, leaving deficits for many of the households in the area of $1,000 to $2,000 a year.

That is the background against which the residents turned to irregular work.

Contrary to popular belief, irregular work does not command large sums. A street vendor of drugs, for example, earns between $25 and $50 a week, a telephone operator for a "numbers" game earns between $75 and $90 a week. (In both cases, larger amounts are turned over to the outside groups running these operations.) Yet these sums are vital to the households, and the residents engaged in irregular work—even the drug-selling street vendors—hand over much of their income to mother and family.

There are three areas of irregular work. The least lucrative and most haphazard is what we call "freelance" work—stealing, mugging, fencing, and the like. Often, young adolescent boys who are not allowed to participate in more organized operations engage in such free-lance activities. Except in relatively smalltime shoplifting, they are not notably successful. They are often caught, arrested, and jailed.

A second source of irregular income is the *bolita*, the illegal lottery. This is the safest of the irregular jobs, but it involves only a small number of participants: a "street collector," a "telephone operator," a "cashier," and a "manager," all of them usually older adults.

The last source of irregular money involves the most people and is the most hazardous— the varied operations of the drug business. Like the *bolita*, the drug business is controlled by groups outside the neighborhood, who skim off the largest portion of the profits. The residents of Dolittle Street work mostly in the more visible, therefore more vulnerable, lower-level retail distribution jobs. For the residents of Dolittle Street, drug selling is a dangerous and low-paying profession that provides necessary income to the area's households.

Perhaps the most lucrative of the lower-echelon jobs is what we call the "drug-o-matic," an operation carried out through a hole in the door of an apartment. The customers, usually strangers to the neighborhood, are often steered to the location by local "touts." They knock on the door, give their order through the hold, pass their money through it, and receive their merchandise in return. The operation resembles automatic bank machines, and the greatest danger comes from competitors, not the police.

Participants in smaller home operations, which include "shooting galleries," run a higher risk of arrest. Shooting galleries are apartments where users can buy heroin and then, for an additional payment (usually $5), "shoot up" and rest in the apartment until ready to leave. There are also several operations that principally sell marijuana: the "drug stand," a small kiosk that also sells regular cigarettes, often by the piece; the "drug store," a storefront where people can buy and smoke marijuana; and "home sales," a kind of Avon-lady marijuana operation, in which women sell small amounts of marijuana to neighbors. Finally, there are street vendors, who have the most vulnerable and dangerous of the drug operation jobs.

This, then, in brief outline, is the harsh and hazardous economic life of the Dolittle neighborhood. But it is only fair to add one more element to the picture—a strategy of survival that conjoins with the economic scramble. Simply put, the residents of Dolittle Street help each other when they can. They are forced to compete for scarce jobs but often share goods and services with one another in regular acts of cooperation. We call this strategy "communal work." A typical example of such communality concerns the children. When the economic situation in one household is unusually low, the women of other households make a point of inviting the children to eat with them. The invitation is never offered in front of the children's mother, because it would embarrass her. Since every household experiences economic low periods, there is a continuous reciprocity in such meal sharing.

The most fascinating communal project we observed on Dolittle Street was that of "crabbing." Several families own crab traps, and during the summer, groups of adults and children set off in the late afternoon several times a week to catch softshell crabs in the waters of Coney Island. The group spends the entire night fishing from the pier. Early in the morning, usually in time for the employed men to get to their jobs, the crabbers return with full buckets. For the rest of the day, the women of the households clean and cook the crabs, and then send generous portions to other families and neighbors via the fire escapes and windows or in packages carried by the children.

The catching and sharing of crabs (the only source of seafood the residents can afford) was perhaps the most joyful community activity in the neighborhood.

In a sense, both the economic struggle and the communal work of the Dolittle residents help to maintain their lives from day to day. But it is through the children that they hope to purchase immortality.

The Young People of Dolittle Street

Much of what the residents of Dolittle Street do to survive is clearly done for the sake of the children. Residents have a telling phrase to describe such efforts: *para el futuro*—for the future.

To the women of Dolittle Street in particular, almost any activity or action is legitimate if it is done for the children—*para el futuro*. So mothers falsely declare themselves as single to the representatives of welfare agencies. They do not see it as a form of cheating, but as a way of assuring their children regular allotments of money, since the insecure, dependent position of the men in the economic market makes the loss of a male a likely possibility. Similarly, the women will sometimes take a job with a "borrowed" Social Security card, especially in cold months, when expenditures are higher. It is, to them, only another effort to provide for their children.

As the children grow, they in turn provide valuable services for the mother and the household. They become, in effect, a human strategy for survival, the essence of which is a network in which the children adopt separate but interlocking roles.

To repeat: We have distilled four basic roles into which the children are socialized by their mothers and kin. Not every household has all four, of course. We are reporting *patterns* found in a majority of the households, patterns that seem to characterize the domestic strategies employed by a large segment of low-income Puerto Ricans in New York City. The roles are: the "street representative," the "young child-reproducer," the "wage earner," and the "scholar/advocate."

The most dangerous of the roles is that of "street representative," which is almost always filled by a young man. The street representative is the family's protector and avenger, and invariably undertakes irregular work, usually associated with the sale of drugs.

A boy who will become his household's street representative is socialized from an early age into this role by older boys and young men. By the age of six, he begins to participate in dangerous, risk-taking activities. As the young boys climb roofs and and fire escapes, walk into the rushing traffic or bike and skate among cars, hitch rides on the backs of vehicles, and otherwise challenge, scuffle, and fight, they are in effect developing the requisite skills of a street representative. As they move into their teens, they join kinship-based male groups in which the older and more experienced members further train them in cooperative "raiding" from the open-air stalls in the neighborhood that sell clothes and food.

Around then, they also often become the physical protectors of their mothers, sisters, and young siblings, and they avenge any wrong done to them. As a defender/avenger, the street representative sees to it that the reputation of the women in his household is protected, and he intervenes in any premature flirtations of his sisters. If a young woman has a *novio* (a fiancé approved by the family, which can happen when the girl is as young as 13), it is the defender's job to tag along on dates as a chaperone.

The learned aggressiveness of the street representative is not easily tolerated by the schools, which, instead of providing alternative skills, usually take active steps to have such students removed. This response encourages the boys to participate more fully in the activities for which their experience has been preparing them: fighting, defending, avenging, raiding, and contributing to their households with earnings from irregular work. Most street representatives begin playing hooky seriously in junior high school. They leave school completely at the age of 16 or 17, by which time they often have had unpleasant encounters with the police, the court system, and the jails.

As a rule, the boys then enter the highly competitive irregular economy, particularly that part of the economy concerned with drugs, and most often they become street vendors. They are on the street corners from mid-morning until well into the night, seven days a week, in all seasons, in all weather. Despite their low earnings ($25 to $50 a week), the job still enables them to contribute to the household's livelihood through work to which they have access and for which they have developed the requisite skills.

Few street representatives live to an old age. Their prospects are suggested by the fact that among our 36 households, six men between the ages of 19 to 30 were killed in drug-related incidents during the two and a half years of research. Because the life of a street representative is so uncertain, at any given time in the cycle of a household, a second young man is usually understudying the role. He is the "street-rep-in-waiting."

The certainty that some boys will not survive to maturity makes it important for households to raise several sons, which is the task the "young child-reproducer" takes over from her mother after the latter's reproductive years are terminated, either by age or tubal ligation. (It has been estimated that 30 percent of adult Puerto Rican women have been sterilized, sometimes against their will.) The young child-reproducer is a girl who is socialized into the traditional feminine role of childbearer. She literally replaces lost household personnel. A 14-year-old girl that we knew, the sister of a young man who had been murdered, gave birth to a baby boy within a year of her brother's death. The baby was named after the dead brother.

The young child-reproducer helps with housekeeping and other facets of child care and contributes her assistance money to the pooled household budget. She usually drops out of school in her early teens. Like the street representative, she is destined to live and to die on Dolittle Street, or its equivalent.

The announcement that a woman is pregnant is greeted with great joy. But the pregnancy of a teenager sometimes brings other reactions, too. When it became known, for example, that a teenager just entering high school was pregnant (she had shown promise in the performing arts), several women told us privately that they had cried all night. "Now her life is going to be wasted, just like mine," they said. But within a few weeks, everyone was enthusiastic again about the prospect of a new child.

In addition to the two above roles, a household usually rears a "wage earner." The wage earner is sometimes a girl, but more usually a boy who has been socialized in a quasi-feminine mode. The macho training applied to the street representative is not applied to him.

We do not understand the dynamics of the process, but from our observations, it is apparent that a sizable minority of children, both boys and girls are encouraged to develop differently from the stereotypical masculine and feminine roles. In the case of boys, we observed a youngster as young as eight years old being spoken of by the adults as a *pato* (colloquial for homosexual) and addressed as "wonder woman" by some of the children. He was an extremely gentle and affectionate person, and offered his cheek to be kissed by everyone. He seemed not to mind the teasing. We believe that the training of passive boys may be adaptive in preparing them to fulfill the requirements of subservient wage laborers.

These boys keep up a steady attendance in school, stay away from street action, help with household chores, and actively participate in their mothers' gossip groups. If they drop out of school, it is only in the last year, and they immediately begin work in wage-labor jobs. Most of their earnings are handed straight over to their mothers. They speak softly and shyly, and move with gentle body movements. Their earnings are essential to their households, and while they themselves might gradually rise out of Dolittle Street, more often a portion of their income is used to sponsor a younger, gifted child, often a girl, to improve her education and thus her career and marital possibilities. This large hope for the future is the "scholar/advocate," usually a girl who has been encouraged to develop assertive skills normally associated with the training of boys. She is the nontraditional female in the sense that the quiet wage earner is the nontraditional male.

The "dominant" girls begin their contribution to the household by accompanying their mothers to welfare institutions and becoming their mother's articulate advocate. These girls usually complete their secondary education, and if the household has the luck to have an employed wage earner, they sometimes go on to college. They do not help with the housework, and if they do have children, they have them later in life and usually limit the size of their family. They are the most likely to obtain secretarial or other pink-collar jobs, the most likely to marry "up," and thus the most likely of any of the children to move up from and out of Dolittle Street, thereby adding to the domain and resources of their households.

In effect, the large family is a kind of social-security system for the present and future of the household. The members of the family are linked in an organic network, to which each contributes according to his or her talent and means, and on which all depend—the risks in the street representative role notwithstanding—for their day-to-day survival.

References

deLone, Richard, *Small Futures: Children, Inequality and the Limits of Liberal Reform*, Harcourt, Brace, Jovanovich, 1979.

Harris, Marvin, *Cultural Materialism: The Struggle for a Science of Culture*, Random House, 1979.

Liebow, Elliott, *Talley's Corner: A Study of Negro Street Corner Men*, Little, Brown, & Co., 1967.

Stack, Carol, *All Our Kin: Strategies for Survival in a Black Community*, Harper & Row, 1975.

Valentine, Bettylou, *Hustling and Other Hard Work: Life Styles in the Ghetto*, Free Press, 1978.

Questions for Discussion:

1.   Outline the main points of difference between the socialization of a Mistassini Cree child and your own using examples from your upbringing.

2.   Outline areas of potential cultural conflict which may be encountered by Cree children in white mainstream schools. How could these conflicts be reduced?

3.   Scholars in the field of education have pointed out the cultural discontinuities ethnic and racial minorities experience in white mainstream schools. Would these resemble the conflicts experienced by the Mistassini? How would they be different?

4.   Outline the main points of difference between the experience of childhood in India and your own. Which Indian patterns would be accepted or rejected in your own culture?

5.   Outline the main differences and similarities between Western and Indian stages of childhood.

6.   Explore the differences and similarities between institutional socialization practices in China and in your own country.

7.   Describe the Chinese concept of "multiple mothering." Could this be applied to situations in the United States?

8.   In her article, Sharff states that "the large family doesn't keep the poor in poverty, but rather serves as a mechanism for survival." Explain what she means in the context of the article.

9.   What other mechanisms of survival does Sharff describe?

B. VALUE ORIENTATIONS

The Persistence of *Ie* in the Light of Japan's Modernization

by Hitoshi Fukue

The year 1945 marked a radical transformation in the history of Japan. Everything prior to it was considered feudalistic, undemocratic and premodern. After the war the country quickly adapted itself to Western democratic forms of society in almost every sphere of life. Rapid economic growth and urbanization have changed the structure of the nation; however, the value systems and cultural characteristics which were present before are still present in the Japanese consciousness and in the social structure.

This paper examines some of the major values and principles of the traditional *ie* system still present in modern Japanese society. First, I would like to clarify what is meant by the *ie* system.

Ie usually has three meanings in the Japanese language: (1) a house as a building, (2) a home, a household, and a family, and (3) a lineal family system (Takeda). The third meaning of *ie* was the most important in traditional Japanese society. *Ie* as a lineal family system transcended the idea of a family as a group of living individuals:

> It [*ie*] was conceived as including the house and property, the resources for carrying on the family occupation, and the graves in which the ancestors were buried, as a unity stretching from the distant past to the present occupying a certain position in the status system of the village or the town. The *ie* in that sense was far more important than the individuals who were at any one time living members of it, and it was seen as natural that the individual personalities of family members should be ignored and sacrificed if necessary for the good of the whole (Fukutake, p. 28).

The lineal family, which was traditionally a male-dominated parent-child relationship, was kept unbroken by the basic principle that the eldest son (or the eldest daughter where there were no sons) brought his bride (or groom) into his (or her) home and the young couple settled down to live in the same household with parents and grandparents. Younger sons in each generation might split off to form their own new *ie*, each of which thereafter continued to perpetuate itself as a "branch family" or as an original "main family," in exactly the same lineal pattern (Fukutake, p. 25).

In this kind of family system, it is not surprising that considerable power was attached to the head of the household, who carried on the line of descent. He usually took charge of the family property, played the central role in rites performed for the ancestors, and directed the labor of family members in the family business. The income of the family business, be it from the farm, store, or workshop, all went into the head of the household's pocket. He in turn provided money for the other members of the household as needed. Given a system which placed such importance on the head of the household, it was natural that the status of the eldest son, destined to be the next head of the household, would also be high and that he would be treated differently from his younger brothers. By contrast, daughters were inessential to their families (Fukutake, pp. 28-30).

Seen from the perspective of social anthropology, Japanese family life presents distinctive characteristics in comparison with those of other societies. Chie Nakane, in her book *Japanese Society,* compares three basic patterns in family life. As demonstrated in the diagram below, in *English* family life the most important room in the house for each member of the family is one's own individual room. Privacy is valued, and one is expected to knock at the door to get permission to enter another's room. One's room is one's castle. In the English family we find a strong consciousness of autonomous individuality. The living room or dining room is a common gathering place for the family to eat, to talk and socialize, and perhaps to discuss personal ideas in a semi-public place. However, individuals always have a room where they can go to collect their thoughts in private.

In the *Indian and Italian* families, members also usually have rooms of their own and feel a corresponding sense of individuality. But the common rooms (living room/dining room) are

English	Indian-Italian	Japanese

 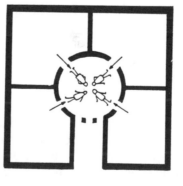  

The above diagram is reprinted with permission of the author.

perceived to be more important than the private rooms. A large amount of time is spent in the common room, and each person, whether young child or an elder, is on an equal footing in conversations. Doors to individuals' private rooms are usually open and anyone may enter without knocking. This type of family life is also relatively responsive to outsiders and tends to flow out into the street.

In the traditional *Japanese* pattern, each household is a distinctly isolated unit of its own, complete with walls and high fence around the house to insure privacy. Yet inside, walls consist of sliding doors made of paper so that privacy is kept to a minimum. The family stays together most of the time and moves from one place to the next, depending on whether it is eating, relaxing, playing or sleeping. As stated ea¡rlier, the head of the household usually has the greatest authority. The rest of the family has to be able to adapt to his needs; otherwise it is not easy to live together under the same roof. Although this pattern tends to create family unity, it widens the gap between the family and outsiders.

This distinctive Japanese family life, which is based on a lineal system of primogeniture and is expressed in the structure of the house, manifests several basic values or characteristics of Japanese culture. These are: rank consciousness, group orientation, emphasis on harmony, and distinction between *uchi* (inside) and *soto* (outside).

1. Rank Consciousness

Rank consciousness arose from the distinct hierarchical order in the traditional household. In the family, children were brought up to perceive clearly their rank in the family hierarchy. This rank consciousness was even extended to the village community where the importance of each household was rated, usually according to the length of its existence in the community. Rank consciousness permeated traditional Japanese society and exists today in interpersonal relations and in business organizations.

In the educational system, for instance, schools are ranked with great care, and each student knows exactly where his school ranks in comparison with the other schools in the community. It is important especially at the college level to gain entrance to a highly ranked institution (Tokyo University is the highest). Many companies and organizations will hire only graduates of the most prestigious schools. This creates what is commonly referred to as "examination hell," in which students compete for admission to them. Similar competition takes place at the precollege level as well and recently entrance exams have even been introduced for prospective kindergarten pupils.

Rank consciousness has a powerful effect on interpersonal relationships as well. A Japanese finds his world clearly divided into three categories: *sempai* (seniors), *Kohai* (juniors), and *doryo* (colleagues) (Nakane, 1970). By contrast, in India and the U.S., lines between these categories may be quite blurred. How one addresses another person is, then, regulated by which category one falls into. For instance, in a male interpersonal relationship, one would have to address Mr. Suzuki as "Suzuki-san," if the latter is the former's senior; as "Suzuki-kun," if junior; and "Suzuki," if simply a colleague. Without knowing these distinctions, one would fail in Japanese interpersonal relationships. How one speaks and behaves are regulated by vertical relationships in Japan, which Nakane calls *tate shakai* (vertical society).

Evidently Japanese feel comfortable and appreciate the stability in vertical human relationships. Once a person understands his place in the hierarchy, he will feel comfortable, because he will always know how to speak and behave in the group. A freshman in college quickly learns to call sophomore students *sempai* and establish a smooth relationship on the basis of the vertical order. (A little confusion may arise when the freshman happens to be older than the sophomore, because age is usually the primary factor in determining one's place in the vertical ladder.)

There is a distinct seniority system which characterizes almost every business organization. In spite of the postwar efforts by Americans to replace the seniority system in Japanese business with a merit system, Japanese companies remained adamantly wedded to the former. They knew that the merit system would cause nothing but conflict and confusion. For the Japanese, the stability produced by the seniority system is much more important than individual merit. This system has eliminated the fear of demotion or discharge from the minds of the employees, which creates deep company loyalty. On the other hand, even though the practice of consensus decision-making allows for the input of junior employees, the seniority system gives older, sometimes incompetent people unmerited freedom and privileges, often at the expense of the younger and more competent. The seniority system has nevertheless maintained a firm hold on Japanese companies, even in the process of modernization.

2. Group Orientation

In the traditional *ie* system, the household itself was considered number one in importance, more so than the concerns of any individual. The family reputation had to be defended at any cost, and the family line which stretched from the distant past to the present, had to be maintained. This group orientation, with its roots in the agrarian society of the past, is manifest in many other facets of the culture, including interpersonal and organizational relationships.

Historically, the predominance of group consciousness over individuality was reinforced by the topographical conditions of the rural community, which necessitated collective enterprise:

> The actual creation of the rice field and laying down of the irrigation system was the first prerequisite. The maintenance of the irrigation system was not something that could be done by an individual household; it inevitably required collective labor by the villagers as a whole group...The communitarian element in agriculture extended itself to other spheres of life: to mutual assistance for weddings and funerals, to cooperative work in house building and repair...people interacted with each other on a basis of real intimacy. It was very important that all decisions concerning the matters of the village should be taken by unanimous agreement. The tight yet solid character of the village community facilitated the typical building block of the Japanese social structure in both rural and urban areas (Fukutake, pp. 33-40).

This particular type of family and the community agricultural life have for centuries produced a deep sense of the group, which is firmly implanted in the minds of the modern Japanese, despite the deterioration of traditional family life and changes in rural social and economic structures.

For this reason, where Americans in interpersonal relationships will emphasize their feelings of independence, the Japanese will do the opposite. As an old Japanese saying goes, the nail that sticks out gets hammered down. Individuality is subordinated by feelings of group consciousness. "Cooperativeness, reasonableness, and understanding of others are the virtues most admired, not personal drive, forcefulness, and individual self-assertion" (Reischauer, p. 135). Americans, therefore, going to Japan are often frustrated by the euphemistic expressions of the Japanese, while the Japanese coming to America often become melancholic by the forceful, direct speech of the Americans.

This emphasis on group loyalty is revealed not only in interpersonal relations, but in the way the Japanese relate to their employers. For the contemporary Japanese, his company is the principal focal point of his life. "A job in Japan is not merely a contractual arrangement for pay, but a means of identification with a larger entity—in other words, a satisfying sense of being part of something big and significant" (Reischauer, p. 131). A company is "my" or "our" company, the primary community to which one belongs and which is all-important in one's life. This is the reason why lifetime employment is normal in Japanese companies. New employees are received by the company as if they were newly-born family members. The company provides employees with housing, hospital benefits, family recreation, gifts on the occasion of marriage, birth and death, and even advice for the education of their children. The company expects employees to give high priority to the goals and interests of the company. The result is that Japanese employees who devote their whole lives to a single company become deeply and emotionally involved with it.

The Japanese affinity for collective behavior may be seen in sightseeing groups made up of school classes, work associates, village organizations, women's societies, and the like. These groups, herded along in orderly rows by a tour guide or bus girl carrying a little flag, have been likened by one commentator to a school of small fish, progressing in orderly fashion in one direction until a pebble dropped into the water stops them and sets them off suddenly in the opposite direction, though again in orderly rows (Reischauer, pp. 134-135). Such blind adherence to the group has been criticized both by Western observers and by the Japanese themselves. It is said that the Japanese lack individual autonomy and originality. It has also been pointed out, however, that this kind of group orientation has made an immeasurable contribution to the process of modernization in Japan by, among other things, helping to mobilize the collective power of the society swiftly and efficiently. Therefore, it would be hard to deny that the rapid modernization of Japan is tied to the collective structure of the traditional *ie* family system.

3. Emphasis on Harmony

The achievement of harmony and the emphasis on it in family life, where children are taught to value it highly, is an integral part of the traditional *ie* system. As early as the seventh century this value played an important role in the political, religious, and personal spheres of Japanese thought.

Prince Shotoku affirmed it in the seventh-century document called the Seventeen Article Constitution:

> Let us cease from wrath, and refrain from angry looks. Nor let us be resentful when others differ from us. For all men have hearts, and each heart has its own leanings. Their right is our wrong, and our right is their wrong. We are not unquestionably sages, nor are they unquestionably fools. Both of us are simply ordinary men. How can anyone lay down a rule by which to distinguish right from wrong? For we are all, one with

another, wise and foolish, like a ring which has no end. Therefore, although others give way to anger, let us on the contrary dread our own faults, and though we alone may be in the right, let us follow the multitude and act like them.

In this moral instruction to the court officials and the public in general, the author of the Constitution placed more importance on a tolerant attitude toward people who held different views than on unflinching commitment to a cause. It meant that to maintain harmonious personal relationships was far more important than proving whether one is right or wrong.

This principle of avoiding personal confrontation in order to maintain smooth personal relationships—however perfunctory adherence to it by many may have been—persisted throughout the long history of Japan. It may be seen, in marked contrast to the West, in the essentially harmonious coexistence of religions in Japan. Religious warfare and dogmatic dissensions are virtually unknown. "No one," says Hajime Nakamura, "has yet taken up a noteworthy controversy between Confucianism and Buddhism, but instead, there are already many who advocate the unity of these religions" (p. 393).

One could say that the Japanese distrust of ideologies which claim ultimate truth has enabled them to mobilize modern workers to focus intensely on the goal of economic growth and prosperity. A cooperative and unifying spirit in human relationships, free from political or religious ideologies, undoubtedly contributes to the generation of dynamic economic activity. Japan's process of modernization, particularly since World War II, has utilized the basic principle of harmony in order to focus all its energy on economic growth.

One could also argue that this kind of cultural ethos has minimized the value of democratic criticism and debate which in Western countries are considered essential to maintain just social organizations. Nakane (p. 35) puts it thus:

> One can easily observe a conversation between a superior and an inferior which is either a one-sided sermon, or the 'I agree completely' style of communication, which does not allow for the statement of opposite views: One would prefer to be silent rather than utter words such as 'no' or 'I disagree.' Japanese fear that such negative statements might hurt the feelings of the superior and that sometimes it could involve the risk of being cast out from the group as an undesirable member.

Group orientation and an emphasis on harmony are naturally linked in Japanese culture as are individualism and an emphasis on justice in Western culture.

4. Distinction of *Uchi* (inside) and *Soto* (outside)

A typical traditional Japanese home was, and still is in many areas, fenced around with high walls of thick bushes or stone which made the house less visible. The individuals of the household unit were closely bound to each other and they formed a tightly knit human nexus. The consciousness of the distinction between *uchi*, meaning "my family," and *soto*, meaning "outsiders," was sharpened by the strong unity of the lineal family system. Whether a person was a blood relative or not was often crucial in the formulation and development of interpersonal relationships. This distinction of *uchi* and *soto* has manifested itself in Japanese psychological exclusivism toward outsiders.

This peculiarly Japanese attitude is expressed in words like *tatemae* and *honne*. *Tatamae* means a principle or policy which a person shows to outsiders and could be interpreted as a person's public image. But *honne* consists of a person's real intentions and real feelings which are usually hidden from outsiders and disclosed only to relatives or insiders. The Japanese differentiate between these two attitudes very clearly and they take it for granted that there are always implicit meanings behind expressed words and attitudes. Therefore one always has to surmise the implicit meanings in expressed words and gestures, which injects a great deal of guesswork into interpersonal relations. The Japanese even have a word, *haragei* (the art of the belly), which means the search for real intentions in personal interactions rather than being satisfied with the surface meaning of words and gestures. How one *appears* outwardly is not so valued as how one *feels* inside.

The distinction of *uchi* and *soto* easily generates an attitude of exclusivism. In a village community, for example, villagers often made a sharp distinction between "our village" and "other villages." Similar distinction was made between "our province" and "other provinces," "our country" and "foreign countries." Today persons from other countries often lament that they are always called *gaijin* (outside person, foreigner) no matter how long they live in the country. The homogeneous construction of the nation and its geographical isolation have reinforced the consciousness of *Nihonjin* (the Japanese) as distinct from foreigners with a far greater intensity than most other societies.

It is also due to *uchi* and *soto* that a Japanese family rarely adopts an orphan or a child with no blood relationship. It sounds remarkable and strange to the Japanese to hear how easily (or so it seems) an American family adopts children, even foreign children, and brings them up as its own.

But the *uchi* and *soto* distinction has provided much for the insiders. As long as one is "inside" a family or an organization, one can expect the full blessings and benefits of it. This exclusivism meets the emotional needs of the individual who seeks security within the group founded on the family *ie* principle. Japan's modernization has been carried out not by changing the *ie* principle but by utilizing it to assure that the material as well as the psychological security of the insiders, whether as members of a family or some other organization, is preserved.

Conclusion

In spite of the unprecedented social transformation of postwar Japan, which brought about urbanization and the deterioration of the traditional *ie* system, its principal values have not disappeared, but rather they are alive in the Japanese consciousness and in Japanese social and economic organizations. Such cultural characteristics as rank consciousness, group orientation, emphasis on harmony, and exclusivism are rooted in the traditional *ie* system and are closely interrelated. They generate a positive impetus toward social order, collective power, solidarity and individual security. These same principles also have a negative side, hindering the development of egalitarianism, individual autonomy, democratic criticism, and philanthropic concerns. It is probable, however, that these *ie* principles will persist in the Japanese psyche for a long time to come.

References

Ben-Dasan, Isaih. *The Japanese and the Jews*. New York and Tokyo: Weatherhill, 1972.

Benedict, Ruth. *The Chrysanthemum and the Sword*. Boston: Houghton Mifflin Co., 1967.

Doi, Takeo. *The Anatomy of Dependence*. New York and Tokyo: Kodansha International Ltd., 1973.

*Fukutake, Tadashi. *The Japanese Social Structure*. Translated by Ronald P. Dore. Tokyo: University of Tokyo Press, 1982.

Lebra, Takie Sugiyama and Lebra, William P., eds. *Japanese Culture and Behavior*. Honolulu: The University Press of Hawaii, 1974.

Nakamura, Hajime. *Ways of Thinking of Eastern Peoples: India-China-Tibet-Japan*. Honolulu: The University Press of Hawaii, 1964.

*Nakane, Chie. *Japanese Society*. Berkeley: University of California Press, 1970.

Nakane, Chie. *Tekio no Joken* [Conditions for Adaptation]. Tokyo: Kodansha, 1972.

*Reischauer, Edwin O. *The Japanese*. Cambridge and London: The Belknap Press of Harvard University Press, 1977.

Suzuki, Takao. *Japanese and the Japanese: Words in Culture*. Tokyo: Kodansha International Ltd., 1978.

Takeda, Choshu. *Nihonjin no Ie to Shukyo* [Japanese *Ie* and Religion]. Tokyo: Hyoronsha, 1976.

*Recommended for further reading.

You've Gotta Have Wa

by Robert Whiting

Wa is the Japanese ideal unity, team play and no individual heroes—a concept that ex-U.S. major-leaguers playing in Japan have had a lot of trouble grasping.

"I don't know what it is they play here," grumbled former California Angel Clyde Wright after his first season as a Tokyo Giant. "All I know is, it ain't baseball." Wright had learned what many expatriates in the Land of the Rising Sun had known for years: baseball, Japanese style, is not the same game that's played in the U.S. Since adopting the sport, the Japanese have changed it around to incorporate the values of samurai discipline, respect for authority and devotion to the group. The result is a uniquely Japanese game, one that offers perhaps the clearest expression among all sports of Japan's national character.

Like the American game, the Nippon version is played with a bat and ball. The same rulebook is also used, but that's where resemblance between the two ends. Training, for example, is nearly a religion in Japan. Baseball players in the U.S. start spring training in March and take no more than five or six weeks to prepare for the season. They spend three to four hours on the field each day and then head for the nearest golf course or swimming pool.

Japanese teams begin training in the freezing cold of mid-January. Each day they're on the field for a numbing eight hours, and then it's off to the dormitory for an evening of strategy sessions and still more workouts indoors. Players run 10 miles every day, and one team, the Taiyo Whales, periodically performs the "Death Climb," 20 sprints up and down the 275 steps of a nearby Shinto shrine.

That's only the beginning. The average Japanese game is more like a board meeting at Mitsubishi than an athletic event. As each new situation arises, there is so much discussion on the field among the manager, coaches and players that most games last three hours.

Unlike their counterparts in the States, losing managers in Japan are seldom fired outright. Instead, they go through an elaborate, time-consuming ritual designed to save face all around. It culminates with a public apology by the deposed skipper, his resignation and, often, an all-expenses-paid trip to the U.S. for him to "study baseball."

131

Such phenomena are the tip of the iceberg. Below the waterline are the concept and practice of group harmony, or *wa*. It is this concept that most dramatically differentiates Japanese baseball from the American game.

The U.S. is a land where the stubborn individualist is honored and where "doing your own thing" is a motto of contemporary society. In Japan, *kojinshugi*, the term for individualism, is almost a dirty word. In place of "doing your own thing," the Japanese have a proverb: "The nail that sticks up shall be hammered down." It is practically a national slogan.

In Japan, holdouts are rare. A player takes what the club gives him and that's that. Demanding more money is *kojinshugi* at its worst, because it shows the player has put his own interests before those of the team. Katsuya Nomura, the Nankai Hawk catcher who has hit 652 home runs in his career, said, upon quietly accepting a miniscule raise after winning yet another of his numerous home-run titles, "If I had asked for more money, the other players would have thought I was greedy."

The U.S. player lives by the rule: "I know what's best for me." In Japan, the only ones who know what's best are the manager and coaches. They have the virtues Orientals most respect going for them—age and experience, hence, knowledge. Their word is law. In the interest of team harmony, they demand that everyone do everything the same way. Superstar Sadaharu Oh must endure the same pregame grind as the lowliest first-year player. At 38 Shinichi Eto, a three-time batting champion and a 10-year All-Star, found that 40 minutes of jogging and wind sprints before each game left him exhausted by game time. He asked to be allowed to train at his own pace. "You've been a great player, Eto-*san*," he was told, "but there are no exceptions in this club. You'll do things according to the rules." Eto lost weight, his batting average dropped, he spent the second half of the season on the bench and then reluctantly announced his retirement. Irrational? Perhaps, but any games lost because Eto was dog-tired were not as important as the example he set.

In the pressure-cooker world of U.S. pro sports, temper outbursts are considered acceptable, and at times even regarded as a salutary show of spirit. Unreleased frustrations, the reasoning goes, might negatively affect a player's concentration. Japanese players are expected to follow Sadaharu Oh's example. "When he strikes out," says an admirer, "he breaks into a smile and trots back to the bench." Oh has been known to be glum during a batting slump, but temper tantrums—along with practical joking, bickering, complaining and other norms of American clubhouse life—are viewed in Japan as unwelcome incursions into the team's collective peace of mind. They offend the finer sensitivities of the Japanese, and as many American players have learned the hard way, Japanese sensitivities *are* finer.

Michio Arito was the captain of the Lotte Orions, a 10-year veteran and the team's longtime batting mainstay. Because of a badly bruised hand he had been able to play only by taking a lot of painkillers, and before a crucial game that would, as it turned out, mean the pennant for the Orions, the manager decided to replace him with a healthier player. When Arito heard he'd been benched, he yelled, threw his glove and slammed his bat against the bench. Next day, at the Orions' victory party, Arito was summoned forth to atone for his sins. After bowing deeply to all, he said, "I am sorry for my childish actions yesterday. I have upset our team spirit and I deeply apologize."

Jim Lefebvre, a former Los Angeles Dodger infielder who spent five years in Japan, can still not quite believe what he saw there. "It's incredible," he says. "These guys are together almost all the time from January to October. They live together, eat together, play baseball together. I've never seen one fight, one argument. In the States, there's always somebody who mouths off and starts trouble."

If you ask a Japanese manager what he considers the most important ingredient of a winning team, he would most likely answer, *wa*. If you ask him how to knock a team's *wa* awry, he'd probably say, "Hire an American."

Former American major-leaguers have been an active part of Japanese baseball for 18 years. The somewhat lower level of play in Japan has given these *gaijin* (outsiders) a temporary reprieve from the athletic scrap heap. And although the Japanese have paid the *gaijin* high salaries, they have not been elated with the overall experience of having them on their teams.

Money is a particular sore point. Foreigners make two or three times as much as Japanese players of similar ability. This, combined with the free Western-style house and the other perks that the *gaijin* seem to view as inalienable rights, sets them too far above their teammates. And more than one American player has brought in an agent to negotiate his contract. That is considered to be in very bad taste. A contract discussion is regarded as a "family affair," with the official team interpreter, despite his obvious bias, acting as a go-between.

Avarice is only part of it, however. Deportment is the rest. Although few Americans hold a Japanese batting or pitching record, many have established standards in the area of bad conduct. For example, the amiable former Dodger Norm Larker set the Japan single-season high for smashed batting helmets, with eight. Joe Stanka, a 6'5", 220-pound behemoth, was ejected from games a record four times in his seven-year stay in Japan. Ken Aspromonte, who later managed the Cleveland Indians, was the first man in the history of Japanese baseball to be fined by his manager for "conduct unbecoming a ballplayer."

Aspromonte pulled off this feat during a sojourn with the Chunichi Dragons of Nagoya back in 1965. Furious after being called out on strikes, Aspromonte stormed back to the bench, kicked over chairs and launched the inevitable attack on the water cooler. He was just doing what comes naturally to many American players, but Dragon Manager Michio Nishizawa did not enjoy the show. He yanked Aspromonte out of the game and suspended him. An incredulous Aspromonte was fined $200 and required to visit Nishizawa's home and issue a formal apology to get back in his manager's good graces.

Other Americans have followed in Aspromonte's footsteps. Ex-Giant Daryl Spencer was one of the more memorable. Like most former major-leaguers, Spencer insisted on following his own training routine, and it was considerably easier than everyone else's. One night, as he was lackadaisically going through his pregame workout, his manager on the Hankyu Braves, Yukio Nishimoto, decided something had to be done.

"You don't look sharp, Spencer-*san*," he said. "You need a rest."

"What do you mean, I need a rest?" Spencer growled. "Who's leading this team in home runs, anyway?"

"I don't think you can hit this pitcher," Nishimoto said.

"I can't hit him? I'm batting .340 against that guy!"

"Not tonight. That's my feeling. You're out."

That was too much for Spencer to take. He was in the dressing room changing into street clothes when he heard his name announced in the starting lineup. Nishimoto had put Spencer down as the third batter, but only because he was planning to "fool" the opposition by inserting a pinch hitter in the first inning.

Now Spencer was smoldering. When the game began and he heard the name of the second batter over the loudspeaker, he decided to get even. Clad in his underwear and shower clogs, he headed for the dugout. Grabbing a bat and smirking in the direction of Nishimoto, he strode out to the on-deck circle to take a few practice swings.

Spencer's entrance delighted the fans, and his picture was in all the papers the next day. Nishimoto was not amused. He ordered Spencer off the field and slapped him with a suspension and a $200 fine. Spencer paid up, later reporting with a wide grin, "It was worth every penny."

In 1972, John Miller became the first American to be released solely for his misconduct. Miller, who played briefly for the Yankees and Dodgers, arrived in Japan in 1970 and soon became the most dangerous batter on the Chunichi Dragons. He was a battler. A U.S. coach once said, "Miller is the kind of guy I'd want on my team. He'll fight you with everything he has. He doesn't know how to quit."

However, Miller wasn't the kind of guy the Japanese wanted. He was seldom on time for practice. If a workout was scheduled for 2 p.m., Miller would arrive at 2:10. This was more serious than it sounds, because his teammates would invariably be raring to go by 1:50.

"He always had some excuse," says a team official. "One day it would be because the traffic was heavy. Another day, he missed the train. He never once said he was sorry."

When reprimanded for being late, Miller's response was most un-Oriental: "Japanese customs are too military. I do good in the games, don't I? What else matters?"

Miller's hot temper sealed his fate as a Dragon. The coup de grace came in the 12th inning of a big game. Miller had been slumping, and he had a bad game. He had been up four times without a hit. The fifth time, with the score tied, he was removed for a pinch hitter.

Miller blew his top. "You didn't have to take me out," he railed at his manager. "I've had it. I don't want to play for you anymore. I don't care if this team wins or not."

To Americans it would have been a fairly routine example of blowing off steam. To the Japanese, however, Miller might just as well have slit his throat. Although he later apologized and finished the year as the team leader in home runs, he was released at the end of the season. A second American on the team, Barton Shirley, who batted 190, was kept. He wasn't a battler.

Willie Kirkland, who had played for the Giants and Indians, was a happy-go-lucky sort who liked to tease his teammates. One day Kirkland was bemusedly watching an aging infielder who had recently been elevated to player-coach straining through a batting drill. "Hey, man, you're a coach now," Kirkland yelled playfully. "You don't have to practice anymore."

The player-coach took Kirkland's jest as a comment on his declining usefulness and he launched a roundhouse right that barely missed. It took half a dozen men to restrain him.

"I was just joking," Kirkland protested. "He was making fun of me," the unappeased coach retorted.

Kirkland left Japan with at least one enemy and considerable doubts about the Japanese sense of humor.

The Japanese didn't find Richie Scheinblum a barrel of laughs, either. A noted clubhouse wit in the U.S., Scheinblum spent his two years as a Hiroshima Carp baiting the umpires. Shane, as he was known on the club's official roster, was frequently agitated by the plate umpire's idea of Scheinblum's strike zone. It was considerably larger than the one Shane had in mind.

Scheinblum searched for a Japanese phrase to convey his sentiments to the men in blue, something that would really get under their collective skins. A Japanese friend came to the rescue, and soon Scheinblum was saying, "You lousy Korean" to arbiters who crossed him.

There is as much love lost between Koreans and Japanese as, say, between William Buckley and Gore Vidal. To the umpires, Scheinblum's taunts were intolerable. To stop him, they imposed a stiff fine each time he uttered the dreaded epithet. When Scheinblum finally departed Japan for the last time, no cries of "Come back, Shane!" were heard—at least, not from the umpires.

It wasn't until Clyde Wright came along that rules of behavior for foreigners were finally codified. Wright, a pitcher of some note with the California Angels, made his first Japanese appearance, with the Yomiuri Giants, in 1976. A self-described "farm boy" from eastern Tennessee, Wright was regarded by those who knew him in America as a tough-as-nails competitor who didn't believe in hiding his feelings.

The Giants are something of a national institution in Japan. They are the oldest team, the winningest (12 pennants in the last 15 years) and by a million miles the most popular. Their games, all of which are nationally televised, get high ratings, and one out of two Japanese will tell you he is a Giant fan.

Their manager, Shigeo Nagashima, is the most beloved sports figure in the land. As a player he won a (Central League) record six batting titles and was personally responsible for the most exciting moment in Japanese baseball history: a game-winning (or *sayonara*) home run in the only professional game Emperor Hirohito has ever attended. Sadaharu Oh plays for the Giants.

The Giants are the self-appointed custodians of national virtue. Popular belief has it that their players are neater, better mannered, more disciplined and more respectful than those of other clubs. Their *wa* is in better tune. In early 1977, when one writer, a former Giant player turned magazine reporter, suggested otherwise in print, he was forever banned from the team clubhouse. Among his blasphemous revelations were: (1) Some Giant players did not like other players on the team; (2) A few players thought Nagashima could be a better manager; (3) Some younger Giants did not especially care for the Saturday night 10 p.m. curfew at the team dormitory; (4) Some Giant wives objected to the season-long "energy-conserving" rule forbidding them to have sexual relations with their husbands. Tame material as far as exposés go, but to the *shoguns* of Yomiuri, the Giant name had been desecrated, and someone had to pay.

Wright also faced the difficulty of being a foreigner on a team that traditionally liked to consider itself pureblooded—Oh's Chinese ancestry and the few closet Koreans on the Giants notwithstanding. Wright was only the second non-Oriental *gaijin* to play for the team, and the sight of a fair-skinned American in a Giant uniform was a bit unsettling to the multitudes. Wright soon gave them reason to be even more unnerved. In the sixth inning of an early season game, with the score tied 1-1, Wright allowed the first two batters to get on base. Nagashima walked out on the field to take him out of the game. Few American managers would have removed him so abruptly. It was Nagashima's feeling, however, that Wright was getting weak, and that was that.

When Wright realized what was happening, he blew a gasket. To the horror of 50,000 fans at Tokyo's Korakuen Stadium and a Saturday night TV audience of millions, he brushed aside Nagashima's request for the ball and stalked off the mound, an angry scowl on his face. Halfway to the bench, he threw the ball against the dugout wall, cursed and disappeared into the clubhouse.

Once inside, he kicked over a trash can, ripped off his uniform, shredded it and flung it into the team bath. Amid a rapid-fire discharge of obscenities, he said something that the official team interpreter was able to understand, "Stupidest damn baseball I've ever seen. If this is the way the Giants treat their foreign ballplayers, I'm going. I've had it."

Nothing like this had ever happened on the Giants. Other teams had problems, but not the proud *Kyojin*. No one had ever shown this much disrespect for Nagashima. Crazy Wright, as he was instantly renamed by the press, became headline news in the sports dailies the next day. Letters, telegrams and phone calls poured into the Yomiuri offices. Outrageous! Inexcusable! Unforgivable! Wright should be sold. Released. Deported. Shot. Drawn and quartered. And not necessarily in that order.

Only Nagashima kept his cool. First, he patiently explained to his American pitcher that what he had done was not "stupid" baseball but simply the Japanese way of playing the game. It's a group effort. Then the manager faced the angry masses. There would be no disciplinary action. He was glad that Wright cared so much about winning. And he wished that some of his Japanese players would show as much fight.

135

Such benevolent words from the prince of Japanese baseball dissipated much of the public's antagonism toward Crazy Wright. It did not, however, pacify the front office. Management was not as eager as Nagashima-*san* to let Western ways penetrate their organization. They issued a set of 10 rules of etiquette that Wright and every other American player the Giants might henceforth deem worthy of their uniform would be obliged to obey.

The Japanese press quickly gave it a name: The *Gaijin* Ten Commandments. This is how they went:

1. Obey all orders issued by the manager.
2. Do not criticize the strategy of the manager.
3. Take good care of your uniform.
4. Do not scream and yell in the dugout or destroy objects in the clubhouse.
5. Do not reveal team secrets to other foreign players.
6. Do not severely tease your teammates.
7. In the event of injury, follow the treatment prescribed by the team.
8. Be on time.
9. Do not return home during the season.
10. Do not disturb the harmony of the team.

Willie Davis, then a practicing Buddhist, thought it would be different for him. Davis was perhaps the best all-round American player ever to come to Japan. He was a 17-year veteran of the major leagues and a former captain of the Los Angeles Dodgers. He had been an All-Star, he could run like a deer and hit and field with a grace and skill that few American big-leaguers, let alone Japanese, possessed. Even at 37, Davis could have continued to play in the U.S.—in fact, he has been a pinch hitter for the Angels this season—but when the chance to go to Japan came in 1977, he took it. Not for the money ($100,000), he insisted, but "for the good of baseball."

Davis was a product of his times, of America's "quest for meaning." While others were exploring the wonders of Transactional Analysis, EST and the like, Davis was a devout member of the *Soka Gakkai,* the Nichiren Buddhist sect that had America chanting. Because Japan was the birthplace of the *Soka Gakkai,* Davis assumed he would be right at home. It was a misguided assumption.

The religion's sacred chant, *namu Myoho renge-kyo,* was an important part of Davis' daily life. He did it faithfully, because it brought him inner peace. When he joined the Dragons, he naturally continued this practice—in the morning, at night, in his room, in the team bath and on the team bus. When not intoning the chant himself, he would play tapes of it on a portable cassette recorder.

Davis reasoned that the chanting would be music to his teammates' ears. Instead, it drove them nuts. They complained: there was no peace and quiet on the team; they couldn't sleep. The incantatory chant that supposedly would bring inner harmony to anyone who regularly intoned it was rapidly eroding the Dragons' collective *wa.*

What particularly annoyed the Japanese players was Davis' locker-room chanting. Before each game, he would pull out his beads, and off he'd go, "*namu Myoho renge-kyo, namu Myoho renge-kyo, namu Myoho renge-kyo.*"

"He'd pray that he'd do well, that the team would win and that nobody would get hurt," his manager, a Japanese-Hawaiian named Wally Yonamine, says, "but it gave the others the feeling they were at a Buddhist funeral."

When the game began, Davis was a ball of fire—at least during the first half of the season. He was by far the most feared Dragon hitter, and on the base paths he displayed a flair the Japanese had never seen before. Nonetheless, the team was in last place. Key players were injured, and the pitching was sub-par. Team *wa* was out of whack, and many Dragons blamed their American Buddhist for it.

It was more than the chanting, which Davis soon modified to please his teammates. There was, for example, the matter of his personal attire. Davis liked his Dragon training suit so much he had a half a dozen made in different colors. He wore them in public, agitating club executives, who felt Davis was tarnishing the team's dignified image.

Davis' biggest liability was his gregariousness. "People didn't understand him," says a team official. "He was loud. He'd get excited. He'd yell a lot and wave his arms. It was all in English and people didn't have the faintest idea what he was saying, but it looked as though he was arguing."

Once he reproached a teammate for not attempting to score on a play that Davis had initiated. "Why didn't you try for home?" Davis shouted. That was the wrong thing to do, because the player was not only the team captain, but also a playing *coach*. In Japan, a player does not yell at a coach, much less question his judgment.

Davis would sometimes practice in stocking feet and he once appeared for a workout with his comely wife, who was wearing hot pants and who jogged with him on the field. "It's so ... so unprofessional," one sportswriter observed. "Davis is destroying our team's spirit in training," grumbled a player. "We can't concentrate on what we're doing."

Several players complained that Davis had special privileges. They referred to him as "Davis, the King," and as "Davis, our precious black *gaijin*."

Yonamine was caught in the middle. "I'd try to tell them not to worry about it," he says. "Forget about how much money a man makes or how little he practices. What he does in the game is all that counts." Few Dragons were willing to accept that piece of American advice.

In August of 1977, when Davis had 25 home runs and a .306 batting average, he broke a wrist in a collision with the outfield fence. It put him out for the year. The Dragons immediately went on a winning streak. During the last two months of the season they had the best record in the league and missed finishing second by a hair.

"It's our pitching," Yanomine insisted. But if you listened to Dragon supporters and students of Japanese baseball, it was all because the team *wa* had been restored.

"I knew Willie as well as anyone," says Lefebvre, a teammate of Davis' on the Dodgers. "He had his quirks, but then we all do. He was named captain, and you're not chosen captain of a team like the Dodgers if you're a troublemaker. If you can't get along with Willie, you don't belong on a baseball team."

The Dragon front office apparently felt that it was Davis who didn't belong on a baseball team—at least not theirs. They traded him, and at the start of the following season the most exciting player ever to wear a Chunichi Dragon uniform was laboring in the backwaters of Fukuoka, contemplating the infinite and subtle mysteries of *wa* in between playing for the lowly Crown Lighter Lions.

Of course, not every American who comes to Japan wreaks havoc on his new team. There have been some, notably Felix Millan, Clete Boyer and George Altman, who did their best to please their Japanese hosts. In turn, the Japanese liked them, describing their demeanor as being *majime*. It means serious, sober, earnest, steady, honest, faithful. They did everything that was asked of them. They kept their mouths shut, their feelings to themselves.

Some, like Boyer, paid a substantial price for the goodwill they engendered. The former Yankee fielding whiz had three reasonably good seasons for the Taiyo Whales, but in his fourth year, when he began to reach the end as a player, he ran smack up against the cultural wall.

Boyer decided that he needed to be used more sparingly, and he asked the club to rest him every third game. "I hit in the first two, but then I get tired," he explained. "I'd do a better job with an extra day off."

The team trainer argued that what Boyer needed was not more rest but more training. Because he was older, the trainer reasoned, Boyer would have to work harder to keep up with the others. The team owner, after considering the probable reaction of the fans to an $80,000-a-year *gaijin* sitting on the bench a third of the time, agreed with the trainer. Boyer reluctantly acquiesced. In an effort to keep his energy level up, he took massive vitamin injections and worked very hard. Still, he finished the season hitting .230 and then retired to coaching. His goodwill, of course, remained intact.

Lefebvre, too, obeyed all the rules, yet he ended up incurring the largest fine in Japanese baseball history. His manager on the Lotte Orions, Masaichi Kaneda, Japan's only 400-game winner and the "God of Pitching," had personally recruited and signed Lefebvre—to a multiyear contract worth $100,000 a year—and had predicted that Lefebvre would win the Triple Crown. Lefebvre hit only .265 with 29 home runs his first season. Hampered by a leg injury, he fared even worse in succeeding years.

Kaneda was so embarrassed that he resorted to open ridicule of his "star" in an effort to regain lost face. Once, after Lefebvre had committed a particularly damaging error, Kaneda apologized to the other players for the American's "poor play." Another time, after a similar misplay, Kaneda temporarily relegated his *gaijin* to a farm team.

Lefebvre tried logic in appealing to Kaneda. "Look, you won 400 games, right?" he said. "That makes you the winningest pitcher in Japanese history, right?"

"Right," Kaneda proudly replied.

"You also lost 250 games, didn't you?"

"Yes."

"Then that also makes you the losingest pitcher in Japanese history."

"Yes, but...."

"But, what? Don't you see? Even the greatest in the game have bad times. Give me a break, will you?"

But Kaneda kept up the pressure. And the unhappy Lefebvre endured it until his fifth season. After being summarily removed from the lineup in the middle of an important game, Lefebvre finally lost control. Walking back to the bench, he threw his glove at the dugout wall, producing a rather loud *whack*.

Kaneda, sitting nearby, assumed that Lefebvre had thrown the glove at him. He sprang to his feet and raised his fists. "You want to fight me?" he yelled. Lefebvre, who saw his playing career rapidly coming to an end anyway, stepped forward to meet the challenge. Coaches intervened, but after the game Kaneda levied a $10,000 fine against his American "trouble-maker" and suspended him.

"It was a big game, and I wanted to stay in it," says Lefebvre, "but what made me even madder was the way Kaneda took me out. He waited until I'd finished my infield warmups, then he came and waved me out. That's embarrassing. But I certainly wasn't trying to throw the glove at him. It missed him by *five* feet."

Kaneda wasn't interested in Lefebvre's version of the incident. If he had misunderstood his *gaijin's* intentions, perhaps others on the team had as well. What would they think if it appeared that the "God of Pitching" tolerated that sort of behavior?

Refused a private audience with Kaneda, Lefebvre took his case to the public. He called a press conference. Yes, he had lost his temper. That he regretted. But, no, he was not guilty as

138

charged. A standard fine of 50,000 yen (about $250) he could understand. But there was no way he would pay the outrageous sum of $10,000. There was no way he *could* pay it. Kaneda was just getting back at him for his failure to win the Triple Crown. Or Kaneda was making him the scapegoat for everything else that was wrong on the team. Or, perhaps, Kaneda was simply taking this opportunity to demonstrate his skills as a *"gaijin* tamer." Whatever the reason, Lefebvre wasn't going to take it all lying down.

When Kaneda heard that he was being openly opposed, he called his own press conference and vowed that Lefebvre would "never, ever again wear the uniform of the Lotte Orions."

Lefebvre was in limbo for weeks, while the coaching staff and management covertly worked to find a solution. At one stage they suggested secretly dropping the fine but making an announcement that Lefebvre had paid it. As long as Kaneda, and his public didn't know the truth, they concluded, Kaneda's ego and image would suffer no damage. Lefebvre refused. He had his own ego and his own image to worry about. He appealed to a highly placed baseball official in the U.S., whom he refuses to identify. The official made a call to Kaneda and the next day the fine was quietly dropped. Lefebvre was allowed to put his uniform back on.

In the 18 years since Don Newcombe and Larry Doby became the first ex-major-leaguers to play in Japan, not a season has passed without a controversial incident involving a *gaijin* player. Last year's "villain," for example, was a former San Diego reserve infielder named John Sipin, who twice during the season took exception to deliveries apparently aimed at his person and engaged the offending pitcher in hand-to-hand combat. After the second melee Sipin was hit with a three-day suspension, fined 100,000 yen($500) and castigated by the press for his "barbaric" behavior. One sports page editorial likened his conduct to that of a *yukuza* (Japanese gangster), while another called Sipin a throwback to the days of the U.S. military occupation when, to hear some Japanese tell it, American GIs regularly roamed the streets beating up on the local citizenry.

"If Sipin doesn't want to get hit by the ball," said one commentator, "he should jump out of the way. There is no place for fighting on the field." In the face of such reasoning, Sipin had no recourse but to acknowledge his sins and promise to mend his ways.

Japanese team officials have understandably grown weary of the perennial conflicts wrought by their foreign imports and in recent years have tried to be more selective in signing Americans. Character investigations have become a standard part of the recruiting process, and more and more managers are going for those quiet, even-tempered types who keep their feelings to themselves and fit into the Japanese system. The 1979 crop of 24 *gaijin* (there is a limit of two per team) is the most agreeable, mildest-mannered group of foreign players ever to play in Japan. It includes Wayne Garrett, Felix Millan, Lee Stanton and Carlos May, as well as a number of unknowns who never quite made it in the majors. There is even an American manager, Don Blasingame. Collectively they are so subdued that one American player's wife says, "This is the best-behaved bunch of ballplayers I've ever been around, either here or in the States. I just can't believe it."

Garrett, a former Met, is so obliging that he agreed to get up at 7:30 and join his teammates in their daily "morning walk." Stanton, late of the Angels and Mariners, amicably allowed the Hanshin Tiger batting coach to change his batting style. May, an ex-White Sox and Yankee, is so low key that some fans can't believe he's American.

Millan, a former Brave and Met, has been the quintessence of propriety. When he arrived last spring for his second year as a Taiyo Whale, he politely refused an offer to let him train as he wished and instead endured all the rigors of a Japanese preseason camp with his teammates. When he was benched on opening day, he sat quietly in the dugout, a shy smile on his face, intently watching the action. When he got his chance to play a week later, he went 4 for 4, won his spot back, and of late has been leading the league with a .354 average.

Davey Hilton, a former Padre, is setting new highs in cross-cultural "understanding." Last year's Central League All-Star second baseman and a hero of the Japan Series, he undertook an off-season weight-training program and arrived in camp this season a proud 20 pounds heavier. He was immediately accused by his suspicious manager of loafing during the winter, reprimanded for being "overweight" and told to reduce. A few days later he developed a sore arm and asked permission to ease up in fielding practice. He was coldly informed that no one got special treatment and was cautioned not to let his American head get too big for his Japanese cap. To top things off, after getting only two hits in his first three games of the season, he was benched and was ordered to take extra batting practice and to alter his batting stance. Through it all Hilton remained calm. "This is Japan," he told himself. "They do things differently here." Predictably, his average began to climb. By mid-season he was over .300, out of the doghouse and on his way to becoming an All-Star again.

Japanese observers are somewhat baffled by this outbreak of civility. One reporter speculated, "It must be the sagging dollar, the recession in the U.S. Americans have it good here, and they're afraid of losing what they have." American players, who pay both Japanese and U.S. income taxes and who wince at such Japanese prices as $50 for a steak dinner, attribute their good manners to other factors: adaptability and a new awareness of cultural differences.

Whatever the reason, the new tranquility is certainly producing results. Americans are having their best year. Twelve of them are batting better than .300, and the affable Chuck Manuel, an ex-Minnesota sub, is leading the Pacific League in home runs, despite having been sidelined for 58 days with a broken jaw.

Of course, a Reggie Jackson might look down his nose at the accomplishments of Manuel and his confreres—given the smaller parks and the slightly inferior level of play in Japan. But with his stormy background, it is doubtful that Jackson-*san*, in spite of his considerable abilities, will ever be invited to come over and prove he can do better.

Questions For Discussion

1.   Fukue's article argues that the traditional *ie* system persists in contemporary Japan and is manifest in the values of rank consciousness, group orientation, harmony, and *uchi/soto*. Give examples of cultural conflict situations which as a result of these values may affect (a) the performance of a Japanese child in an American school and (b) the performance of an American in a Japanese school.

2.   What are the value differences reflected in U.S. and Japanese baseball as described in Whiting's article, "You've Gotta Have *Wa*"?

3.   Is *Wa* a characteristic likely to be imported to the United States? Explain.

C. VERBAL AND NONVERBAL COMMUNICATION

An Introduction to Intercultural Differences and Similarities in Nonverbal Communication
by Suzanne Irujo

Many people believe that the language of gestures is universal. Many people believe that one picture is worth a thousand words, the implication being that what we see is ever so much clearer than what is said. Many people believe that communication means speaking and that misunderstandings only occur with speaking. Many people believe that smiling and frowning and clapping are purely natural expressions. Many people believe that the world is flat. (Condon and Yousef, p. 123)

Some people believe that cultural differences in nonverbal communication are so great that they impede communication even when two people are speaking the same language. Other people believe that human beings are basically the same all over the world—that underneath our differences there are enough universal behaviors to make understanding possible even in the absence of verbal communication.

These two contrary beliefs will be explored in this article. Are some aspects of nonverbal communication universal, or is all nonverbal behavior culturally determined? There is evidence on both sides of the question. For example, Hall documents differences in the use of space and time, LaBarre (1947) presents evidence from anthropological literature showing that gestures and many expressions of emotion vary from culture to culture, and Morris et al. have shown that the meaning of a specific gesture can change from one location to another within the same culture. On the other side, scientists have been presenting evidence for the universality of facial expressions of emotion since the subject was first investigated by Charles Darwin.

This article will present an introduction to the literature on nonverbal behavior from an intercultural perspective. The major areas of nonverbal communication will be surveyed to show where there are cultural differences and where similarities exist. After this brief review (which is not meant to be exhaustive), an attempt will be made to reconcile the disagreement by showing how differing perspectives lead to different conclusions and how the two sides are not really mutually exclusive.

Facial Expressions of Emotion

Evidence for the universality of facial expressions of emotion goes back to Darwin. He believed that certain nonverbal modes of expression, including crying, laughing, blushing, expressions of anger, and others, were innate and universal. The evidence he presented in support of his theory was gathered through observations of infants, descriptions of the insane, informants' decoding of emotions from photographs, observation of paintings and sculpture, questionnaires about other races, and observation of animals. Some of his research methods may be questionable by modern standards; he does, however, present convincing evidence that at least some of the ways in which man expresses emotion are innate.

Darwin's line of research has been continued more recently by several investigators. The ethnologist Eibl-Eibesfeldt (1970, 1972, 1979) initiated a cross-cultural filming program in order to document human expressive behavior. Similarities in smiling, laughing and crying, and patterns of anger, fear, embarrassment and coyness were found by looking at facial expressions of deaf and blind babies. Izard believed that the fundamental emotions are primarily products of evolutionary and hereditary processes and that the face is the site of these fundamental emotions. He found a high degree of agreement in the recognition of facial expressions of emotion across American, European, Oriental and African cultures. Further evidence for the universality of facial expressions of emotion comes from the work of Ekman and Friesen. They had observers in six different countries match a photograph with a word describing an emotion. Their subjects gave the same responses regardless of culture or language.

If facial expressions of emotion are universal, how is it that a Japanese smile may represent embarrassment, sorrow or anger (Miller)? Paul Ekman (1972), in his neurocultural theory of facial expressions, reconciles this seeming contradiction by arguing that the relationship of particular emotions with distinctive facial muscle movements is universal, while the circumstances which elicit a particular emotion may vary from culture to culture. The rules for controlling facial expressions in particular social settings can be different, and emotional arousal may have different consequences. These three factors (elicitors, display rules, and consequences), account for the variance observed between cultures and even within cultures.

Eye Contact

Eye contact and gaze behavior show many cultural variations. The well-known differences between black and white Americans have been documented by LaFrance and Mayo and by K.R. Johnson. Not looking another person in the eye is a recognition of that person's authority for blacks, while whites interpret this as shiftiness and unreliability. When blacks roll their eyes, it is a sign of hostility, impudence and disapproval, often unrecognized as such by whites.

Watson has shown that Arabs, Latin Americans and southern Europeans focus their gaze on their partners during conversation, while East Asians, Indian-Pakistanis and northern

Europeans show a "peripheral gaze" or no gaze at all. Arabs have difficulty carrying on a conversation if they cannot look each other in the eye, as when they are walking side by side down the street, or if one is wearing dark glasses.

Differences in gaze behavior can cause misunderstandings. Latins interpret a direct gaze as having sexual connotations, and a steady stare with raised eyebrows as anger (Nine-Curt). Greeks, who are used to being stared at in public, feel ignored when they go to countries such as England where staring is not considered polite (Argyle).

Kinesics

There may be a few gestures which are universal. Darwin believed that the shoulder shrug was a universal sign of inability to do something, lack of resistance, or lack of fault. Eibl-Eibesfeldt (1970) claims that the eyebrow flash is a universal sign of requesting or accepting social contact. Nodding and shaking the head almost universally means "yes" and "no," although there are some cultural variations, such as the Greek emphatic nod, which is a "No" of annoyance (Eibl-Eibesfeldt, 1979), and the Indian backward wag, which means "Yes."

It would be natural to assume that gestures which are to some degree iconic would be universally understood. Such is not always the case however. Extending the arm with the palm up and waving the fingers would be interpreted as "Come here" by people in some cultures and as "Good-bye" by people in others. Extending the arm with the palm down to indicate height might be understood, but it would be insulting in Colombia if used to refer to a person (Saitz and Cervenka).

Misunderstandings are common when the same gesture has different meanings in different cultures. Gestures associated with the nose usually have negative or distasteful connotations in our society, but a finger-to-the-nose Maori gesture means friendship, and a nose-thumbing gesture used by the Todas signifies respect (Klineberg). The same gesture (making a circle with thumb and forefinger) which means "OK" to a North American can mean money to a Japanese, can signify extreme hostility to an Arab, and be obscene for an Italian.

Gestures such as these, which have specific meanings, are called "emblems." The relationship between an emblem and its meaning in different cultures is as arbitrary and varying as the relationship between a word and its meaning in different languages. Indeed, Morris et al. found that the meanings of certain gestures can vary even within the same culture. Their study showed that, in some cases, a gesture was unknown or had different meanings in neighboring towns. On the other hand, Johnson, Ekman and Friesen found considerable overlap between their inventory of North American emblems and the Colombian gestures described by Saitz and Cervenka. Gestures which do not have specific meanings, but which serve to accompany speech are also culturally defined. Efron showed that gestural differences between immigrant Jews and Italians in New York were lost after assimilation.

Posture

While there is no doubt that human beings universally sit, stand, walk, and lie down, the ways in which they do so appear to be culturally patterned. Hewes (1955, 1957) has documented almost 1,000 different postures and plotted their distribution among various cultures. For example, there is little squatting in northern Europe, but it is widespread in other parts of the world. Choice of posture often depends on such cultural variables as clothing, type of building construction, activity, and sexual customs.

Postures used for specific functions are culturally learned, such as eating lying down as the Romans did, or sleeping hunched over on one's knees as the Tibetans do (Key). Certain cultures seem to have acquired stereotyped forms of posture and movement; Germans are "stiff" and North Americans are "bouncy." Postures or ways of walking may also have specific meanings; to a Puerto Rican, the stomach protruding toward another means "Touch me" or "Hug me" (Nine-Curt). American blacks have a way of signifying contempt while walking away from another person (K.R. Johnson), which white Americans seldom recognize.

Haptics

Cultures vary widely in the amount of touching which is common. Africans, Arabs and Hispanics touch a great deal in interpersonal relationships, whereas in Britain, Japan and the U.S., there is very little touching (Argyle). Jourard (1966) observed 180 touches between Puerto Ricans in a one-hour observation in a coffee house; by contrast, there were only two touches between North American pairs in the same amount of time, and none between English pairs.

In addition to varying amounts of touching, there are differences in who touches whom where. A study by Jourard and Rubin was replicated in Japan by Elzinger to compare bodily accessibility of Japanese and Americans. There was more physical contact among Americans than Japanese, and Americans had more contact with friends of the opposite sex. Females were relatively accessible in both countries, but Japanese females were touched more by their mothers, and American females more by their fathers. Barnlund also used Jourard's Body Accessibility Questionnaire to compare nonverbal self-disclosure of Japanese and American men and women aged 18 to 24. His results are similar to Elzinger's; Americans reported nearly twice as much physical contact as Japanese, most of it being with opposite-sex friends. The physical accessibility of the Japanese was much more limited, especially with their fathers. Barnlund also compared males and females in both cultures and concluded that cultural differences were stronger than sexual differences.

Children are conditioned by their culture to accept varying degrees of tactile contact (Frank). Departures from the norm to which one is accustomed cause embarrassment and discomfort.

Proxemics

Differences in the use of space often create perplexing problems because participants are unaware of what it is that is causing the problem. Most North Americans do not realize that the distance they choose for a particular interaction depends upon its nature; Hall has documented the distances which Americans choose for intimate, personal, social-consultative and public interactions. However, these distances vary in other cultures. For example, what is intimate distance in the United States is personal distance in Latin America (Nine-Curt). The result is that Anglos see Latins as being too close, too pushy, or too sexy, and Latins see Anglos as being aloof, cold, or uninterested. Even within Latin America, there are variations in the use of space. Shuter found that people in Costa Rica interacted more closely than those in Panama, who in turn interacted more closely than those in Colombia.

Caution must be exercised in interpreting research of this type, however, because situational variables must also be taken into account. Little found that in general, Greeks, Americans, Italians, Swedes and Scots preferred increasing distances for interaction, but that the relationship of the participants changed the preferred distance. Sex and age of the interactants make a difference (Baxter), as does social class. Aiello and Jones concluded that black and Puerto Rican children had closer interaction distances than white children, but further research by Scherer showed that this effect might be more a function of social class than of culture or race.

Environment

In all parts of the world, people create shelters for protection from the physical environment. To some degree, the characteristics of houses in various cultures are determined by climate. However, home and community design are also related to cultural factors (Altman and Chemers). The way a village is laid out can reflect religious beliefs, as in the case of the Oglala Sioux, whose circular conception of the world was reflected in round tepees set in a circle. Walls can reflect the value of privacy; the Japanese have thick sturdy walls around their homes to keep the rest of the world out, but the thin movable walls inside the house reveal the fact that privacy within the family is not important. In some cases, cultural factors override physical factors and result in homes which are not well adapted to the physical environment. In India, many homes are oriented to the east for religious reasons, even if that means that the entrance to the home faces up a steep hill (Rapoport).

Interior design is also a reflection of culture. Placement of furniture and other objects can serve to inhibit or facilitate communication. Condon and Yousef show how different styles of homes reveal cultural values and patterns of communication. Hazard demonstrated how the designs of courtrooms in various cultures reflect the relative importance of judge, jury and prosecutor.

The created environment is a reflection of culture, but people are also shaped by their creations. Bochner points out that for many traditional societies, a change to Western-style housing also involves changes in values and behavior.

Paralinguistics

Vocal qualities, vocalizations, and the use of silence are some of the areas in which paralinguistic phenomena affect nonverbal communication. Of course, the suprasegmental elements of language (stress, pitch, etc.) can affect communication. Intonation patterns are often the last element of a first language to disappear in learning a second, and they can cause misinterpretations. East Indians working in England are often misjudged because their different intonation patterns are interpreted as rudeness by native speakers of English (Gumperz). Voice modifications are used differently in different cultures; blacks use falsetto in situations of great emotion and in storytelling and joking (Key). This contrasts with the use of falsetto by white males to mimic women or homosexuals. Modifications of language elements also have different meanings in different societies. According to Key, labialization is a sign of tenderness in Hungarian, palatalization is an expressive device among Czech children, muscle constriction is a feature of male speech among the Amahuaca, and devoicing is used as a sign of respect or mourning in many areas of the world. Language and non-language sounds also vary in meaning. A hiss in Japan is a sign of approval rather than rejection or contempt, and the alveolar click (tsk), which means "for shame" to most North Americans, means "no" to a Greek or Arab (Key). Foreign students in the United States have difficulty decoding utterances containing glottal stops: uh uh; uh huh; ah ah; oh oh. Finally, the use of silence varies around the world. Key mentions such examples as an Arab's use of silence to establish privacy, Peruvian and Brazilian Indians' silence when a guest enters, and the African Gbeya's obligatory silence while eating. In Japan, silence is used to avoid expressing disagreement and to respond to a threatening situation (Barnlund).

Other Behaviors

Americans do not normally use olfactory behavior as a source of information because our culture expects natural odors to be covered up with deodorants and perfumes. Strong perspiration or breath odor evokes a negative response. In other cultures, the sense of smell takes on more importance. For an Arab, smelling a friend is an element of personal involvement (Knapp).

The presentational aspect of nonverbal behavior includes clothing, artifacts and appearance. Clothing is important in dance, as in the display of the tartan kilt in the Highland Fling and the sleeve movements of Asian dance, and in communication, as in American Indian blanket gestures and the nonverbal language of the toga in Ethiopia (Key). Artifacts are important in themselves, as in the rich gestural fan language of the Spanish and Chinese, and as they are part of other gestures — cigarettes, wine glasses, etc. (Key). Here again, differences can cause embarrassment; public use of a toothpick is acceptable in Europe but not in the United States. Personal appearance may also be important or have communication value in religious ceremonies, in mourning, or in sending various messages about oneself. However, appearance only has meaning within a particular cultural and social setting (Argyle).

Conclusion

This brief review has included only a few examples of the many cultural differences which exist in nonverbal behavior. Can these differences be reconciled with the idea that there is something universal about our ways of expressing ourselves? Eibl-Eibesfeldt and LaBarre will not resolve their differences by criticizing each other for being "naive and unscholarly" (Eibl-Eibesfeldt 1972, p. 311) or for indulging in "speculative nonsense" (LaBarre 1964, p. 194).

Part of the contradiction comes from different ways of looking at culture. An emic approach to the study of culture takes a participant perspective and looks at the culture from inside itself (Harris). Comparisons and evaluations are made only on the basis of criteria which come from within the system itself and thus are relevant only in terms of internal functions. Comparisons between one culture and another cannot be made from an emic perspective, so differences remain apparent. The emic approach is the one most often used by anthropologists. Psychologists, on the other hand, will more often use an etic approach to the study of culture. The constructs used to categorize and classify the culture system come from outside it and are derived from theories which are external to the phenomena being studied (Harris). This makes it possible to compare various cultures and to look for universals.

It should also be remembered that the claim of universality has been made only for facial expressions of emotion; it is generally agreed that gestures and most other aspects of nonverbal communication are culturally determined. In addition, the proponents of universality recognize that a universal facial expression may be changed by a culturally-learned display rule (Ekman) or that an inborn pattern may have a learned meaning (Eibl-Eibesfeldt 1972).

It is not really necessary to resolve the conflict between the universalists and the particularists. Most people would agree that both nature and nurture influence human behavior. The controversy between heredity and environment is not one in which an either/or choice must be made.

Nonverbal behavior contains both universal patterns and culture-specific meanings. There is little doubt that differences in nonverbal behavior can contribute to miscommunication, misunderstanding, incomprehension, and embarrassment. This would be attested to by anybody who has lived or traveled in another country. However, the negative influence of these differences can be reduced. Interference in nonverbal communication occurs when people attach their own meanings to the nonverbal behavior of others. Knowledge of the fact that differences exist will help avoid this kind of interference and make it easier to learn new meanings for familiar behavior patterns. This openness to new meanings, plus the use of those universal behavior patterns which do exist, can serve to promote better intercultural understanding.

References

Aiello, John R. and Stanley E. Jones. 1971. "Field study of the proxemic behavior of young children in three subcultural groups." *Journal of Personality and Social Psychology* 19:351-356.

Altman, Irwin and Martin M. Chemers. 1980. "Cultural aspects of environment-behavior relations." In Harry C. Triandis and Richard W. Brislin, eds. *Handbook of Cross-Cultural Psychology*, Vol. 5: Social Psychology. Boston: Allyn and Bacon, Inc. pp. 335-393.

Argyle, Michael. 1972. "Non-verbal communication in human social interaction." In Hinde, R.A. ed. *Non-Verbal Communication*. Cambridge: Harvard University Press.

*Argyle, Michael. 1975. *Bodily Communication*. New York: International Universities Press, Inc.

Barnlund, Dean C. 1975. *Public and Private Self in Japan and the United States*. Tokyo: The Simul Press, Inc.

Baxter, J.C. 1970. "Interpersonal spacing in natural settings." *Sociometry* 33:444-456.

Bochner, S. 1975. "The house form as a cornerstone of culture." In R. Brislin, ed. *Topics in Culture Learning*, Vol. 3. Honolulu: East-West Center. pp. 9-20.

*Condon, John C. and Fathi S. Yousef. 1975. *An Introduction to Intercultural Communication*. Indianapolis: The Bobbs-Merrill Co., Inc.

Darwin, Charles. 1872. *The Expression of the Emotions in Man and Animals*. London: John Murray. Reprinted Chicago: University of Chicago Press, 1965.

Efron, David. 1941. *Gesture and Environment*. New York: King's Crown Press. Reprinted as *Gesture, Race and Culture*. The Hague: Mouton, 1972.

Eibl-Eibesfeldt, I. 1970. "The expressive behavior of the deaf and blind born." In von Cranach, M. and Vine, I., eds. *Non-verbal Behavior and Expressive Movements*. London: Academic Press.

Eibl-Eibesfeldt, I. 1972. "Similarities and differences between cultures in expressive movements." In Hinde, R.A., ed. *Non-Verbal Communication.* Cambridge: University Press.

Eibl-Eibesfeldt, I. 1979. "Universals in human expressive behavior." In Wolfgang, Aaron, ed. *Nonverbal Behavior: Applications and Cultural Implications.* New York: Academic Press.

Ekman, Paul. 1972. "Universals and cultural differences in facial expressions of emotion." In Cole, James K., ed. *Nebraska Symposium on Motivation, 1971.* Lincoln: University of Nebraska Press.

Ekman, Paul and W.V. Friesen. 1971. "Constants across cultures in the face and emotion." *Journal of Personality and Social Psychology* 17:124-129.

Elzinger, R.H. 1975. "Nonverbal communication: Body accessibility among Japanese." *Psychologia* 18:205-211.

Frank, Lawrence K. 1957. "Tactile communication." *Genetic Psychology Monographs* 56:209-225.

Gumperz, John J. 1982. *Discourse Strategies.* New York: Cambridge University Press.

Hall, Edward T. 1966. *The Hidden Dimension.* New York: Doubleday and Co.

*Harper, R.G., A.M. Wiens and J.D. Matarazzo, eds. 1978. *Non Verbal Communication: The State of the Art.* New York: John Wiley and Sons.

Harris, M. 1968. *The Rise of Anthropological Theory.* New York: Crowell.

Hazard, J.N. 1962. "Furniture arrangement as a symbol of judicial roles." *A Review of General Semantics* 19:181-188.

Hewes, G. 1955. "World distribution of certain postural habits." *American Anthropologist* 52:231-244.

Hewes, G. 1957. "The anthropology of posture." *Scientific American* 196:123-132.

Izard, Carroll E. 1971. *The Face of Emotion.* New York: Appleton-Century-Crofts.

Johnson, H.G., P. Ekman and W.V. Friesen. 1975. "Communicative body movements: American emblems." *Semiotica* 15:335-353.

Johnson, K.R. 1971. "Black kinesics: Some nonverbal communication patterns in the black culture." *Florida Foreign Language Reporter* 9 (Spring-Fall): 17-20, 57.

Jourard, S.M. 1966. "An exploratory study of body-accessibility." *British Journal of Social and Clinical Psychology* 15:278-282.

Jourard, S.M. and J.E. Rubin. 1968. "Self-disclosure and touching: A study of two modes of interpersonal encounter and their interrelation." *Journal of Humanistic Psychology* 8:39-48.

*Key, Mary Ritchie. 1975. *Paralanguage and Kinesics.* Metuchen, NJ: The Scarecrow Press.

Klineberg, Otto. 1935. *Race Differences.* New York: Harper and Bros.

*Knapp, Mark L. 1978. *Nonverbal Communication in Human Interaction.* New York: Holt, Rinehart and Winston.

LaBarre, Weston. 1947. "The cultural basis of emotions and gestures." *Journal of Personality* 16:49-68.

*LaBarre, Weston. 1964. "Paralinguistics, kinesics and cultural anthropology." In Sebeok, T.A., A.S. Hayes and M.C. Bateson, eds. *Approaches to Semiotics.* The Hague: Mouton.

LaFrance, Marianne and Clara Mayo. 1976. "Racial differences in gaze behavior during conversations: Two systematic observational studies." *Journal of Personality and Social Psychology* 33:547-552.

Little, K.B. 1968. "Cultural variations in social schemata." *Journal of Personality and Social Psychology* 10:107.

Miller, Roy A. 1967. *The Japanese Language.* Chicago: University of Chicago Press.

*Morain, Genelle G. 1978. *Kinesics and Cross-Cultural Understanding*. Arlington, VA: The Center for Applied Linguistics.

Morris, D., P. Collett, P. Marsh and M. O'Shaughnessy. 1979. *Gestures, Their Origins and Distribution*. New York: Stein and Day.

Nine-Curt, Carmen Judith. 1976. *Non-Verbal Communication in Puerto Rico*. Cambridge: National Assessment and Dissemination Center for Bilingual/Bicultural Education.

*Ramsey, Sheila J. 1979. "Nonverbal behavior: An intercultural perspective." In Molefi, K.A., E. Newmark and C.A. Blake, eds. *Handbook of Intercultural Communication*. Beverly Hills, CA: Sage Publishing Co.

Rapoport, A. 1969. *House Form and Culture*. Englewood Cliffs, NJ: Prentice-Hall.

Saitz, R.L. and E.J. Cervenka. 1962. *Handbook of Gestures*. Reissued as *Handbook of Gestures: Colombia and the United States*. The Hague: Mouton.

*Samovar, L.A. and R.E. Porter, eds. 1976. *Intercultural Communication: A Reader*. Belmont, CA: Wadsworth Publishing Co., Inc.

Scherer, S.E. 1974. "Proxemic behavior of primary school children as a function of their socioeconomic class and subculture." *Journal of Personality and Social Psychology* 29:800-805.

Shuter, S.E. 1974. "Proxemics and tactility in Latin America." *Journal of Communication* 26:3:46-52.

Watson, O.M. 1970. *Proxemic Behavior: A Cross-Cultural Study*. The Hague: Mouton.

*Wolfgang, Aaron, ed. 1979. *Nonverbal Behavior: Application and Cultural Implications*. New York: Academic Press.

* Recommended for further reading.

Communicative Competence: A Historical and Cultural Perspective

by Paula Menyuk and Diane Menyuk

Most societies consider communication behavior to be the hallmark of intelligence. All societies have criteria for categorizing the communication within that society as being on a continuum from good to bad. However, societies differ in what they consider to be good or bad communication. For example, in some societies high verbal output is considered to be a sign of immaturity while in others the inverse is true (Hymes, 1979).

In this paper we will discuss the differing views of what communication behavior should be. Then we will present data on conflicts between groups in the United States in their view of what is good communicative behavior. These differences, we will argue, lead to differences in what is defined as intelligent and non-intelligent behavior. Finally we will discuss the impact of these views on the education of children in the United States at the present and, prospectively, in the future.

History of Views of Communicative Behavior

The nineteenth century in the West saw the crystallization of certain notions concerning the nature of cultural differences, notions which are observable still in contemporary attitudes. One of the concepts that most influenced the development of these notions was that of evolution. Humanity was, in the schema of such seminal scholars as Durkheim, Marx, and Spencer, pictured as having moved via a series of fixed stages from a state of "primitiveness" to one of "civilization." A qualitative judgment was frequently (though by no means always) attached to this passage—which was regarded as inevitable and unvarying.

The work of many nineteenth-century anthropologists extrapolated from this concept a theoretical paradigm with which to describe and classify extant cultures. Such scholars as Tylor, Morgan, and Frazier saw the cultures they studied as currently at some specific stage of development. Morgan's typology, for instance, consisted of the categories "savagery," "barbarism," and "civilization." There were numerous concomitant theories (reminiscent of some of those heard today) regarding the "developmental potential" of societies whose cultures were

151

considered to belong to one of the "lower" evolutionary stages. Although many of the most eminent figures in the field argued strenuously for the notion of inevitable and ubiquitous progress (though occurring at different rates in different societies), the typologies which they created—consisting of stepped categories with an accompanying list of "cultural characteristics"—doubtless contributed to the solidification within both the academic and popular minds of the idea that a group of people can be defined as a "race," statically and indissolubly articulated by an inherent set of specific features.

These "specific features" included elements from a variety of cultural subsystems, both material and cognitive, e.g. economy, social structure, religion and language. Perceived as a "bundle of attributes," such characteristics were taken to form a natural totality—a "racial heritage." Thus judgments passed upon one aspect of a society's way of life generally informed perception of the whole. This is quite clear in the instance of Western evaluations of "primitive societies" wherein a "simple and crude" technology was felt to indicate a similarly elementary and coarse mentality, social life, religion, and so forth. One prominent theme among certain nineteenth-century anthropologists was the notion that there existed:

> an observable connection between the distinctive characteristics of a language and the mentality of the race who created it (Henson, p.7)

and

> as certain races were primitive, so the languages which they spoke were similarly simple and underdeveloped (Henson, p.9).

To these scholars Indo-European languages represented civilized thought and culture. "Primitive languages," which were assessed using grammatical, semantic and phonetic categories derived from European languages, were judged impoverished according to the extent to which they were felt to deviate from the European standard. Three major charges were leveled against the linguistic systems of simple societies: (1) they were incapable of any but the most basic abstractions and generalizations; (2) they were unable to attain any real degree of precision because of severely limited vocabularies and the extreme latitude they permitted in pronunciation and (3) they changed with great rapidity because of their lack of formalization (Henson, pp. 9-15):

> From 20 to 40 years is probably a liberal allotment for the average life of a very low savage language (Payne, 1899, in Henson p. 11).

The notion that a language may be granted a special status through a process of formalization is an ancient and rather potent one in Western thought. Historians of the science of linguistics trace the emergence of their discipline back to the efforts of the Greeks to conventionalize and codify Greek. This trend continued into the Roman period and reached something of an apex in the Middle Ages, during which great efforts were made to study and preserve Latin (seen as the "language of learning") in a state of formalized linguistic *correctness*. Latin, which grew increasingly detached from the business of everyday life, somehow became simultaneously linguistically sanctified—regarded by many as a language qualitatively different from and qualitatively *better* than all others (Robins, pp. 7-70). This notion that there exists some natural conjunction between the *formalization* of a language and its *quality*—which is then frequently linked to rigor of thought or ability to conceptualize—is well embedded in Western consciousness.

A further reinforcement to common beliefs regarding the existence of a fundamental link between language and mind and the relative quality of different languages, came in the growth of modern European nationalism. Language was identified with the "genius" of a people and the link between a nation and its language grew more urgent:

> A people without a language is only half a nation. A nation should guard
> its language more than its territories (Davies, 1845, in Fishman, p. 48).

As such ideologies developed, the contrastive, evaluative aspect of linguistic nationalism also intensified. Thus in the mid-nineteenth century German nationalist sentiment drew forth comments such as this:

> He who teaches his children to learn the French language, or permits
> them to learn it, is delirious; he who persists in doing this sins against the
> Holy Ghost; he who allows his daughter to study French is about as good
> as he who teaches his daughters the virtues of prostitution (Jahn in
> Fishman, p. 53).

The French for their part, particularly the philosophers of the eighteenth century, saw language as an essential factor in man's development of consciousness. They posited that as man had evolved from a primitive to a civilized state, so his language had become an increasingly efficient tool for the production of ideas and abstractions. Certain of these philosophers divided all languages into two categories: (1) transpositive, those with no word order, and (2) analogous, those with a fixed word order. The philosophers adjudged languages which they considered "analogous" to be superior to those of the "transpositive" variety because they believed that thought possessed a *natural* order and that the quality of a language was dependent upon how closely its order paralleled that of spontaneous cognition (Juliard, pp. 43-52). It was hardly surprising that French was seen as

> the most perfect of modern languages and perhaps of all languages…it
> follows most closely the natural order of things and their relationships,
> the objects of our thoughts, and it is the most faithful expression of the
> truest ideas (Bonald in Fishman, pp. 63-64).

These eighteenth-century philosophers based much of their theorizing regarding language on the concept of progress—the past, present, and future as the continuous moving forward of civilization. This understanding of history formed the underpinning for much nineteenth-century thinking on the evolution of social formations. In a scheme proposed by Condorcet, language and social life are depicted as having mutually transformed one another over time, transcending continually the inadequacies of their previous incarnations as they climbed inexorably through time toward the civilized heights of eighteenth-century European thought and language.

Such attitudes of mind inform much thinking which has occurred on the nature of the differences between various languages. Lack of formalization and unfamiliar semantic, grammatical, and phonetic systems have frequently been interpreted to indicate a "primitive" cognitive capacity.

This attitude toward language is by no means a purely Western phenomenon. It can be observed in the epithets which the Aztecs of Mexico applied to peoples who could not speak

Nahua (the Aztec language), epithets such as "popoluca" (unintelligible) or "totonac" (rustic) (Wolf, p. 41). It surfaces in arguments made by Indians pressing for the adoption of Tamil or Bengali—rather than the frequently favored Hindi—as the official Indian language. It is claimed that the former are inherently superior to the latter because of their long literary histories (Apte, p. 148). It can be seen once again in the attitude assumed by various villages of the linguistically diverse island of Papua New Guinea toward one another's dialects:

> Speakers will insist that their own variety is the best, that it is the easiest and clearest to understand, that it is in fact understood by people for miles around, that it is easiest to learn, and so on. Other varieties are judged to be some kind of corruption or aberration from the speaker's own, and imitations occasion much mirth on the part of any local audience (Sankoff, p. 289).

These perceptions emerge in large part from the sense of naturalness which any speaker feels for his native language, indeed for his entire cultural repertoire. Such attitudes extend not simply to the language itself, but also to the way in which it is used. It has grown increasingly clear since Dell Hymes' seminal essay of 1962 on the ethnography of speaking that learning and using a language involves more than becoming capable of generating grammatical utterances which are meaningful. In order to be considered intelligent and competent by members of a given culture and to avoid embarrassing or even disastrous miscommunications, a speaker must learn to use a language correctly in terms of the social restraints (Gumperz, p. 251) which are placed upon it. There exists a huge range of behaviors—including such things as what subjects one may discuss and with whom, the way in which one frames a statement, question or argument, the protocol of turn-taking, when one should not talk, and so forth—which are integral to the communicative function language serves. Together such behaviors constitute a linguistic minefield replete with opportunities for verbal misfires, misfires every bit as extreme as those produced by the tourist with the proverbially incorrect phrasebook.

The mistakes which result from not knowing how to use a language correctly convey to listeners semantic messages which are more than simply inaccurate. They send, in addition, messages which misinform the listener about personal attributes of the speaker—his intelligence, attitudes, level of sensitivity, emotional state, etc. Statements such as "Only an idiot would have said something like that in front of my mother," "He's so rude; he's constantly interrupting," or "He can't think straight—he never gets to the point," are indications of such judgments at work. In fact, however, the criteria according to which a piece of linguistic behavior will be judged polite, aggressive, convincing, stupid, belligerent, insincere, and so forth, will vary enormously between cultures.

One standard often used for evaluating the intelligence and sensitivity of a given speaker is that of knowing when to talk and how much to say. The often posed question—which also serves as a rebuke—"Don't you know when to keep quiet?" reminds us of the importance of understanding the proper use of silence. The notion of when silence is proper and with what frequency one may lapse into it, however, is a matter extremely specific to any given culture.

Kenneth Basso, who has done fieldwork among the Western Apache, has examined the role of silence within Apache society, where discourse is considered to be filled with "strange" silences. Basso lists a number of instances in which verbal communication is kept to a minimum. These include: (1) when meeting strangers (introductions are often omitted and silences can continue for hours or even days), (2) when in the initial stages of courting, (3) when getting "cussed out" (being the focus of another's anger, whether it is justified or not, and (4) when with people who are sad, particularly following a bereavement (pp. 69-79). Many of these situations are ones which, within the context of a number of other societies, would call for a good deal of verbal interaction. Failure to comment appropriately, and at the correct length, would be taken as a sign of strangeness, stupidity, or rudeness.

The placing of value upon silence is by no means unusual—it occurs within all societies. What *does* vary quite widely from one society to another is rather the notion of what constitutes appropriate context and intensity. In contrasting American and Danish styles of conversation, for instance, Karl Reisman remarks that whereas Americans tend to feel a need to fill in the "gaps" (the very word is revealing) which appear in conversation—believing that gaps indicate a lack of rapport—the Danish assume the reverse and seem to prize such periods of silence:

> I used to have some Danish in-laws and once while we were visiting them an American friend announced that he was arriving for a visit. We welcomed him, but as we knew that he was particularly prone to fill gaps in conversations we suggested quite strongly…that he let silences sit for awhile before talking. Although the rule is quite simple, it is usually quite difficult for people to change their cues, habits, or what have you in these matters. My in-laws were quite glad to see him…yet by the end of the first evening these kindly Danes could stand his presence no longer—simply because [to them] an evening without silence was emotionally intolerable (p. 112).

In rather sharp contrast to this Danish attitude, one may consider the style of verbal interaction favored by the occupants of the West Indian island of Antigua. In the context of Antiguan society, the ability to engage creatively and loudly in verbal battles, to leap in and out of conversations continuously, to dramatize oneself—and to appreciate the dramatizations of others—are all regarded as necessary conversational skills and as indications of a speaker's intelligence and social attainments. During the course of a given conversation several individuals will speak simultaneously and interruptions are constant. Repetition, cursing and boasting are in many contexts positively valued with the result that interactions frequently appear to outsiders to be almost anarchic (Reisman, pp. 110-124). To members of the Antiguan culture, however, such behaviors are part of a general and accepted style of interpersonal relationships:

> Questions on why people can fall asleep or shift subject in the middle of a sentence are usually answered in terms of the person's feelings— 'That's what he feels to do'—and the strong value put on not constraining one's feelings by artificial structures. A very beautiful and subtle attention to the feelings of others is a marked feature of West Indian tact (Reisman, p. 115).

The patterns of verbal interaction which are absorbed by speakers through a process of enculturation frequently lead individuals to pass judgment upon one another based upon inappropriate criteria. The paradigm of argument favored by Chinese speakers is adjudged by those whose native language is English to lack clarity, precision and forcefulness, and to further an image of "oriental deviousness," because Chinese speakers prefer to lead up bit by bit to a final conclusion, whereas English speakers like to start off with a clear statement of the topic. For their part the Chinese evaluate the English bit-by-bit approach as pushy, rude and narrow-minded and as contributing to an image of "occidental crudity" (Young, pp. 72-84).

Such judgments often end in a frustrated condemnation of the other's intellectual abilities and emotional sensitivity. Clearly the importance of achieving an understanding of the socially constructed patterning of linguistic behavior cannot be overestimated in furthering attempts to avoid arriving at such unfortunate and unwarranted conclusions.

Different Views of Communicative Competence in the United States

For many decades the view in the United States and in some other Western societies concerning the deaf was that unless and until deaf individuals achieved oral language competence they were not only linguistically deprived but also intellectually deprived. It wasn't until the past decade that researchers began to look at the native language of the deaf, American sign language in this country, and discovered that this language was a "true" language in the sense that it was rule-governed and that these rules could be used to convey different intents. Further, on standard tests of intelligence used in the U.S., it was shown that deaf individuals were similar to hearing individuals in some of the cognitive tasks tested, delayed in others and ahead in still others (Vernon). Experience (including the experience of hearing) appeared to be the most crucial factor in determining whether or not the deaf individuals were on a par with, behind or in advance of hearing individuals relative to particular tasks.

Attitudes toward the deaf might appear to be an extraordinary example of linguistic and cultural bias, except that similar attitudes toward children with different dialects or language backgrounds can also be found. For a long time, many researchers in educational and developmental psychology believed that children who were delayed in the acquisition of mainstream American English because of coming from a different language background (the second language learner) were also delayed in intellectual development. They held, in addition, that children who had acquired a dialect different from the mainstream dialect were intellectually different as well. In this latter case intellectual difference was attributed to "cultural deprivation" rather than simply dialect difference, but the two factors were often equated.

Such a confounding of factors can frequently be found in the discussion of findings in studies examining the language processing of "bilingual" and "dialect different" children. For example, in a study of monolingual English and bilingual English-German and English-French children, Braun and Klassen (p. 1,867) conclude (1) that monolingual children's level of language was more sophisticated than that of their bilingual age peers, (2) that bilinguals had a greater tendency to make errors in their speech and (3) that teaching bilinguals to be monolingual "could have a salutary effect on language development...especially those who are exposed to a meager quantity of adult speech in their home and community activities." These statements hopelessly confuse knowledge of English with knowledge of language and curiously suggest that some bilingual speakers are "exposed to a meager quantity of adult speech."

Other kinds of statements have been made about children acquiring a dialect different from standard English. In most instances these statements refer to low-income status black children who have been found to perform more poorly on language tests (of standard English) as well as on some standard intelligence tests. For example, Bereiter, et al., found that the language of these children lacked logical relations. They used expressions such as "They mine" and "Nobody can't do that." With this same population of children it was found that they did not perform as well as middle-class white children on standard intelligence tests—in particular, on sub-tests of vocabulary, verbal analogies and other tests requiring verbal logic. It seems clear that their use of standard English is being confounded with the ability to think logically. Inversely, the use of a dialect of English is confounded with thinking illogically.

Issues related to language knowledge, language use, and intelligence emerged in a book published in 1970, edited by F. Williams and entitled *Language and Poverty*. As early as then, controversies on the topic are evident. For example, Bernstein in comparing two children, one from a working-class family and the other from a middle-class family states: "It is not that working-class children do not have in their lexical repertoire the vocabulary used by middle-class children. Nor is it the case that the children differ in the tacit understanding of the linguistic rule system" (Williams, p. 27). Bernstein argues that it is not language knowledge but, rather, language use that differentiates the children. The working-class child uses language that is context-bound and the middle-class child makes his meaning clear regardless of context.

Engelmann, in the same publication, takes an opposite view. He states: "Too frequently, a four-year-old child of poverty does not understand the meaning of such words as 'long,' 'full,' 'animal,' 'red,' 'under,' 'first'..." (p. 201) and thus indicates that there *is* a vocabulary deficit. Blank states: "Man sees himself, in comparison with other animals, as unique in his mental development, and, in particular, in his capacity for achieving high levels of symbolic activity" (p. 64). She sees the learning disorders of "disadvantaged" children as representing a weakness in man's greatest strength—symbolic activity. However, Labov, in the same volume argues for the logic of so-called non-standard English using data from conversations with standard and non-standard language users. He concludes that not only is the language per se of the non-standard English speaker logical but, also, that this speaker uses his language to hypothesize, solve problems, engage in theory testing, etc.; that is, to engage in symbolic activity. The factors that play a role in whether or not such language is elicited are all the variables which exist within the context in which the language behavior is being observed. These variables include topic, participants' familiarity with each other, affiliations among participants, and the physical parameters of the situation.

The above juxtaposition of statements is somewhat unfair in that they were removed from their contexts. However, the confounding of language knowledge, language use and intelligent behavior is clear. Some researchers in the 1970s, for example, appeared to confuse vocabulary availability with concept development, and limited use of language in certain contexts with inability to engage in symbolic activity. Researchers in the 1980s are, apparently, continuing to confuse these factors. For example, Hall and Kaye compared the performance of black and white low- and middle-income boys, aged 6 to 9, on a series of tasks. They found that middle-class and white children did better than black and lower-class children on I.Q. tests (Ravens and P.P.V.T.) but showed few differences in recall tasks and *inconsistent* differences in learning and transfer tasks. Again, level of "standard" behavior could be equated with intelligent behavior. This way of thinking could (and has in the past) led to the conclusion that children whose language knowledge and language use were different from the standard are somehow deficient.

An alternative conclusion is not only possible but has over the past few years become acceptable to some developmental psychologists, psycholinguists and educators. In this view, difference is not seen as a deficit, but, rather as a reflection of varying ways in which cultures rear their children. The realizations that have led to changes in the interpretation of comparative developmental findings are exemplified in the conclusions of a study of black infants (Friedman and DeBoer). The researchers found, using standard intelligence tests (those measuring early motor and then verbal behavior) that there was a decline in the black infants' performance after the first 12 to 18 months. They suggest that the decline may be caused (1) by divergence in abilities and competences stressed in social and cultural settings, (2) by language differences, *especially* social differences in normative expectations of adult-child relations in reference to speaking and being spoken to, and (3) by differences in what tests actually evaluate; that is, one I.Q. test may have a different meaning in terms of functional behavior as compared to another, although both are, by label, measuring the "same" ability. These conclusions suggest that the depressed performance of some groups of children may not be caused by diminished knowledge of the language or a diminished intelligence but, rather, by a difference in experience.

Educational Implications

The acceptance of the above notion has led to important changes in theoretical views of the relation between language, cognition and culture. It has also resulted in an interesting series of experiments and, perhaps, to a difference in how the educational process is thought to take place. We will briefly discuss each of these changes in the remaining pages of this article.

As is pointed out by Dasen, a controversy appears to exist between those theorists who, apparently, characterize cognitive development as a sequence of stages that all children go through and those who believe that cognitive abilities (or competences) exist in every normal human being, but that the unfolding of these abilities takes different forms because of the experiences of the individual.

An example of the differences in these points of view can be found in the interpretation given to findings related to the "level of thinking" of people who fail formal operational tasks. Formal operational thinking is characterized by Piaget as being the most mature level of thinking. Failure in performing formal operational tasks might indicate that those who fail are arrested at a more "primitive" level of thinking than those who carry them out. However, as Piaget himself suggested, such thinking might be limited to one particular area of expertise. Others have argued that our view of what a valid expression of formal operational thinking is might be biased by our own cultural experiences. Thus, the hunting of the Kalahari Bushmen might not immediately be seen as an expression of such thinking, but it does require reasoning based on hypothesis testing ("hypothetico-deductive reasoning"), a prerequisite of formal operational thinking (Flavell, p. 117).

This latter view leads to the second position stated above that all levels of thinking are developed in all normal individuals but take *particular* expression depending on culture. In both the cognitive development and language development literature a third position is possible and that is: development can be characterized as a universal sequence that takes expression in varying ways, depending on particular cultural and linguistic experiences *and* a sequence that is culturally and linguistically specific. This third position implies that there are differences in experience that can make a difference in the development of knowledge. What determines how people hunt (i.e. what instruments are used in what manner) and the rules which govern language use are examples. It is these kinds of areas of development which, because of their dependency on particular experience with language (i.e. explanation and example), may be most amenable to change by schooling (Cole and Andrade). An example from language development follows.

Much recent research in language development and the classroom has been concerned with how children from different cultural backgrounds engage in narrative communication. One such study (Michaels) examined and compared "sharing time" behavior of black children from low SES (socioeconomic status) families and white children from middle SES families. The narrative styles of the two groups of children differed, and these differences were characterized by the researchers in the following way: the black children's narrative style was topic-associated while the white children's was topic-centered. The black children led into the topic with a fairly long introduction and tended to refer back to it only occasionally. The white children, on the other hand, stated the topic at the outset and referred back to it frequently. The teacher gave a low evaluation to the black children's narratives and, indeed, referred one of the children to the school psychologist for testing.

This example indicates not only that different cultures and languages mark important communication categories in different ways, but also that differences in experience can also make a difference in the development of knowledge. This difference is brought about not by any intrinsic difference in competence, but, rather, by an outsider's attitude toward an individual's performance and by the criteria by which the outsider judges whether it is competent or not. Clearly then, a teacher's attitude toward a student's competence can have an effect on what and how well that student learns.

These kinds of communication behaviors can be characterized as thinking in complexes (topic-associated) and thinking in hierarchies (topic-centered), terms used by Vygotsky to identify the behaviors he observed in concept development. Thinking in complexes, according to Vygotsky, is an earlier stage of concept development than thinking in hierarchies. In these terms, the narrative verbal behavior of the black children might be characterized as being an indication of a delay in cognitive development or as some disorder in the thinking process. This, apparently, was the judgment made by the teacher about one of the children in the above example. However, current research in both linguistic and non-linguistic development is more and more directed toward determining group and individual differences with a view to understanding them as differences rather than categorizing them as normal or deficient. In addition, the research indicates that education per se can have significant impact on how these groups and individuals express their thinking. Thus, educators who maintain that difference from the norm is a deficiency are engaged in a self-defeating exercise that does not allow for change when clearly change is possible.

In this review of some aspects of language, cognition and culture, it is our hope that the reader has been led to the logical conclusion that differences in how languages and cultures identify competences are indications that these competences in fact exist. Given this conclusion, educators can view their task as one of providing children the experiential opportunity to exercise these competences in new areas, rather than as having to eliminate their "deficiencies."

Bibliography

Apte, M.L. 1976. "Multilingualism in India and its socio-political implications: an overview." In W.M. O'Barr and J.F. O'Barr (Eds.) *Language and Politics*. The Hague: Mouton.

Basso, K. H. 1972. 'To give up on words: silence in western Apache culture.' In P.P. Giglioli (Ed.) *Language and Social Context*. Middlesex, England: Penguin Books, Ltd.

Bereiter, C., S. Engelmann, J. Osborn and P.A. Reidford. 1966. "An academically oriented pre-school for culturally deprived children." In F. Hechinger (Ed.) *Pre-school Education Today*. New York: Doubleday.

Braun, C. and B. Klassen. 1971. "A transformational analysis or oral syntactic structuring of children representing varying ethnolinguistic communities." *Child Development*, 42, pp. 1859-1871.

Cole, M. and Andrade, D. 1982. "The influence of schooling on concept formation: some preliminary inclusions." *The Quarterly Newsletter of the Laboratory of Human Cognition*, 4, pp. 9-26.

Dasen, P.R. 1980. "Psychological differentiation and operational development: a cross-cultural link." *The Quarterly Newsletter of the Laboratory of Comparative Human Cognition*, University of California at San Diego, 3, pp. 81-86.

Fishman, Joshua, A. 1972. *Language and Nationalism: Two Integrative Essays*. Rowley, Massachusetts: Newbury House Publishers.

Flavell, J. 1977. *Cognitive Development*. Englewood Cliffs, New Jersey: Prentice Hall, Inc.

Friedman, D.G. and M. DeBoer. 1979. "Biological and cultural differences in early child development." *Annual Review of Anthropology*, 8, pp. 579-600.

Gumperz, J. 1974. "Linguistic and social interaction in two communities." In B.G. Blount (Ed.) *Language, Culture and Society*. Cambridge, Massachusetts: Winthrop Publishers, Inc.

Hall, V.C. and D.B. Kaye. 1980. "Early patterns of cognitive development." Monograph SRCD, 45, Serial No. 184.

Henson, Hilary. 1974. *British Social Anthropologists and Language*. Oxford: Clarendon Press.

Hymes, D. 1979. "Sapir, competence, voices." In C.J. Fillmore, D. Kempler and W. S-Y. Weng. *Individual Differences in Language Ability and Language Behavior* (pp. 33-46). New York: Academic Press.

Hymes, D. 1962. "The ethnography of speaking." In T. Gladwin and W.C. Sturtevant (Eds.) *Anthropology and Human Behavior*.

Juliard, P. 1970. *Philosophies of Language in Eighteenth-Century France*. The Hague: Mouton.

Michaels, S. 1981. "'Sharing time': children's narrative styles and differential access to literacy." *Language in Society*, 10, pp. 49-76.

Reisman, K. 1974. "Contrapuntal conversations in an Antiguan village." In R. Bauman and J. Sherzer (Eds.) *Exploration in the Ethnography of Speaking*. Cambridge: Cambridge University Press.

Robins, R.H. 1967. *A Short History of Linguistics*. Bloomington and London: Indiana University Press.

Sankoff, G. 1976. "Political power and linguistic inequality in Papua New Guinea." In W.M. O'Barr and J.F. O'Barr (Eds.) *Language and Politics*. The Hague: Mouton.

Vernon, M. 1967. "Relationships of language to the thinking process." *Archives of General Psychiatry*, 16, pp. 325-333.

Vygotsky, L. 1972. *Thought and Language*. Cambridge: M.I.T. Press.

Williams, F. (Ed.) 1970. *Language and Poverty*. Chicago: Markham Publishing Company.

Wolf, E.R. 1959. *Sons of the Shaking Earth*. Chicago: University of Chicago Press.

Young, L. 1982. "Inscrutibility revisited." In J. Gumperz (Ed.) *Language and Social Identity*. Cambridge: Cambridge University Press.

What No Bedtime Story Mean.
Narrative Skills
at Home and School
by Shirley Brice Heath

In the preface to *S/Z*, Roland Barthes' work on ways in which readers read, Richard Howard writes: "We require an education in literature...in order to discover that *what we have assumed*—with the complicity of our teachers—*was nature is in fact culture, that what was given is no more than a way of taking*" (emphasis added; Howard 1974, ix). This statement reminds us that the *culture* children learn as they grow up is, in fact, "ways of taking" meaning from the environment around them. The means of making sense from books and relating their contents to knowledge about the real world is but one "way of taking" that is often interpreted as "natural" rather than learned. The quote also reminds us that teachers (and researchers alike) have not recognized that ways of taking from books are as much a part of learned behavior as are ways of eating, sitting, playing games, and building houses. As school-oriented parents and their children interact in the preschool years, adults give their children, through modeling and specific instruction, ways of taking from books which seem natural in school and in numerous institutional settings such as banks, post offices, businesses, or government offices. These *mainstream* ways exist in societies around the world that rely on formal educational systems to prepare children for participation in settings involving literacy. In some communities these ways of schools and institutions are very similar to the ways learned at home; in other communities the ways of school are merely an overlay on the home-taught ways and may be in conflict with them.[1]

Yet little is actually known about what goes on in story-reading and other literacy-related interactions between adults and preschoolers in communities around the world. Specifically, though there are numerous diary accounts and experimental studies of the preschool reading experiences of mainstream middle-class children, we know little about the specific literacy features of the environment upon which the school expects to draw. Just how does what is frequently termed "the literate tradition" envelop the child in knowledge about interrelationships between oral and written language, between knowing something and knowing ways of labeling and displaying it? We have even less information about the variety of ways children from *non-mainstream* homes learn about reading, writing, and using oral language to display knowledge in their preschool environment. The general view has been that whatever it is that mainstream school-oriented homes have, these other homes do not have it; thus these children are not from the literate tradition and are not likely to succeed in school.

A key concept for the empirical study of ways of taking meaning from written sources across communities is that of *literacy events:* occasions in which written language is integral to the nature of participants' interactions and their interpretive processes and strategies. Familiar literacy events for mainstream preschoolers are bedtime stories, reading cereal boxes, stop signs, and television ads, and interpreting instructions for commercial games and toys. In such literacy events, participants follow socially established rules for verbalizing what they know from and about the written material. Each community has rules for socially interacting and sharing knowledge in literacy events.

This paper briefly summarizes the ways of taking from printed stories families teach their preschoolers in a cluster of mainstream school-oriented neighborhoods of a city in the Southeastern region of the United States. We then describe two quite different ways of taking used in the homes of two English-speaking communities in the same region that do not follow the school-expected patterns of bookreading and reinforcement of these patterns in oral storytelling. Two assumptions underlie this paper and are treated in detail in the ethnography of these communities (Heath 1983): (1) each community's ways of taking from the printed word and using this knowledge are interdependent with the ways children learn to talk in their social interactions with caregivers and (2) there is little or no validity to the time-honored dichotomy of "the literate tradition" and "the oral tradition." This paper suggests a frame of reference for both the community patterns and the paths of development children in different communities follow in their literacy orientations.

Mainstream School-Oriented Bookreading

Children growing up in mainstream communities are expected to develop habits and values which attest to their membership in a "literate society." Children learn certain customs, beliefs, and skills in early enculturation experiences with written materials: the bedtime story is a major literacy event which helps set patterns of behavior that recur repeatedly through the life of mainstream children and adults.

In both popular and scholarly literature, the "bedtime story" is widely accepted as a given—a natural way for parents to interact with their child at bedtime. Commercial publishing houses, television advertising, and children's magazines make much of this familiar ritual, and many of their sales pitches are based on the assumption that in spite of the intrusion of television into many patterns of interaction between parents and children, this ritual remains. Few parents are fully conscious of what bedtime storyreading means as preparation for the kinds of learning and displays of knowledge expected in school. Ninio and Bruner, in their longitudinal study of one mainstream middle-class mother-infant dyad in joint picture-book reading, strongly suggest a universal role for bookreading in the achievement of labeling by children.

In a series of "reading cycles," mother and child alternate turns in a dialogue: the mother directs the child's attention to the book and/or asks what-questions and/or labels items on the page. The items to which the what-questions are directed and labels given are two-dimensional representations of three-dimensional objects, so that the child has to resolve the conflict between perceiving these as two-dimensional objects and as representations of a three-dimensional visual setting. The child does so "by assigning a privileged, autonomous status to pictures as visual objects" (1978: 5). The arbitrariness of the picture, its decontextualization, and its existence as something which cannot be grasped and manipulated like its "real" counterparts is learned through the routines of structured interactional dialogue in which mother and child take turns playing a labeling game. In a "scaffolding" dialogue (cf. Cazden), the mother points and asks "What is 'x'?" and the child vocalizes and/or gives a nonverbal signal of attention. The mother then provides verbal feedback and a label. Before the age of two, the child is socialized into the "initiation-reply-evaluation sequences" repeatedly described as the central structural feature of classroom lessons (e.g., Sinclair and Coulthard; Griffin and Humphry; Mehan). Teachers ask their students questions which have answers prespecified in the mind of the teacher. Students respond, and teachers provide feedback, usually in the form of an evaluation. Training in ways of responding to this pattern begins very early in the labeling activities of mainstream parents and children.

Maintown Ways

This patterning of "incipient literacy" (Scollon and Scollon) is similar in many ways to that of the families of fifteen primary-level school teachers in Maintown, a cluster of middle-class neighborhoods in a city of the Piedmont Carolinas. These families (all of whom identify themselves as "typical," "middle-class," or "mainstream,") had preschool children, and the mother in each family was either teaching in local public schools at the time of the study (early 1970s), or had taught in the academic year preceding participation in the study. Through a research dyad approach, using teacher-mothers as researchers with the ethnographer, the teacher-mothers audio-recorded their children's interactions in their primary network—mothers, fathers, grandparents, maids, siblings, and frequent visitors to the home. Children were expected to learn the following rules in literacy events in these nuclear households:

> 1 As early as six months of age, children *give attention to books and information derived from books*. Their rooms contain bookcases and are decorated with murals, bedspreads, mobiles, and stuffed animals which represent characters found in books. Even when these characters have their origin in television programs, adults also provide books which either repeat or extend the characters' activities on television.

> 2 Children, from the age of six months, *acknowledge questions about books*. Adults expand nonverbal responses and vocalizations from infants into fully formed grammatical sentences. When children begin to verbalize about the contents of books, adults extend their questions from simple requests for labels (What's that? Who's that?) to ask about the attributes of these items (What does the doggie say? What color is the ball?)

> 3 From the time they start to talk, children *respond to conversational allusions to the content of the books; they act as question-answerers who have a knowledge of books*. For example, a fuzzy black dog on the street is likened by an adult to Blackie in a child's book: "Look, there's a Blackie. Do you think *he's* looking for a boy?" Adults strive to maintain with children a running commentary on any event or object which can

be book-related, thus modeling for them the extension of familiar items and events from books to new situational contexts.

4 Beyond two years of age, children *use their knowledge of what books do to legitimate their departures from "truth."* Adults encourage and reward "book talk," even when it is not directly relevant to an ongoing conversation. Children are allowed to suspend reality, to tell stories which are not true, to ascribe fiction-like features to everyday objects.

5 Preschool children *accept book and book-related activities as entertainment.* When preschoolers are "captive audiences" (e.g., waiting in a doctor's office, putting a toy together, or preparing for bed), adults reach for books. If there are no books present, they talk about other objects as though they were pictures in books. For example, adults point to items and ask children to name, describe, and compare them to familiar objects in their environment. Adults often ask children to state their likes or dislikes, their view of events, and so forth, at the end of the captive audience period. These affective questions often take place while the next activity is already underway (e.g., moving toward the doctor's office, putting the new toy away, or being tucked into bed), and adults do not insist on answers.

6 Preschoolers *announce their own factual and fictive narratives* unless they are given in response to direct adult elicitation. Adults judge as most acceptable those narratives which open by orienting the listener to setting and main character. Narratives which are fictional are usually marked by formulaic openings, a particular prosody, or the borrowing of episodes in story books.

7 When children are about three years old, adults discourage the highly interactive participative role in bookreading children have hitherto played and children *listen and wait as an audience.* No longer does either adult or child repeatedly break into the story with questions and comments. Instead, children must listen, store what they hear, and on cue from the adult, answer a question. Thus, children begin to formulate "practice" questions as they wait for the break and the expected formulaic-type questions from the adult. It is at this stage that children often choose to "read" to adults rather than to be read to.

A pervasive pattern of all these features is the authority which books and book-related activities have in the lives of both the preschoolers and members of their primary network. Any initiation of a literacy event by a preschooler makes an interruption, an untruth, a diverting of attention from the matter at hand (whether it be an uneaten plate of food, a messy room, or an avoidance of going to bed) acceptable. Adults jump at openings their children give them for pursuing talk about books and reading.

In this study, writing was found to be somewhat less acceptable as an "anytime activity," since adults have rigid rules about times, places, and materials for writing. The only restrictions on bookreading concern taking good care of books: they should not be wet, torn, drawn on, or lost. In their talk to children about books, and in their explanations of why they buy children's books, adults link school success to "learning to love books," "learning what books can do for you," and "learning to entertain yourself and to work independently." Many of the adults also openly expressed a fascination with children's books "nowadays." They generally judged them as more diverse, wide-ranging, challenging, and exciting than books they had as children.

The mainstream pattern. A close look at the way bedtime story routines in Maintown taught children how to take meaning from books raises a heavy sense of the familiar in all of us who have acquired mainstream habits and values. Throughout a lifetime, any school-successful individual moves through the same processes described above thousands of times. Reading for comprehension involves an internal replaying of the same types of questions adults ask children of bedtime stories. We seek *what explanations,* asking what the topic is, establishing it as predictable and recognizing it in new situational contexts by classifying and categorizing it in our mind with other phenomena. The what-explanation is replayed in learning to pick out topic sentences, write outlines, and answer standardized tests which ask for the correct titles to stories, and so on. In learning to read in school, children move through a sequence of skills designed to teach what-explanations. There is a tight linear order of instruction which recapitulates the bedtime story pattern of breaking down the story into small bits of information and teaching children to handle sets of related skills in isolated sequential hierarchies.

In each individual reading episode in the primary years of schooling, children must move through what-explanations before they can provide *reason-explanations* or *affective commentaries.* Questions about why a particular event occurred or why a specific action was right or wrong come at the end of primary-level reading lessons, just as they come at the end of bedtime stories. Throughout the primary grade levels, what-explanations predominate, reason-explanations come with increasing frequency in the upper grades, and affective comments most often come in the extra-credit portions of the reading workbook or at the end of the list of suggested activities in textbooks across grade levels. This sequence characterizes the total school career. High school freshmen who are judged poor in compositional and reading skills spend most of their time on what-explanations and practice in advanced versions of bedtime story questions and answers. They are given little or no chance to use reason-giving explanations or assessments of the actions of stories. Reason-explanations result in configurational rather than hierarchical skills, are not predictable, and thus do not present content with a high degree of redundancy. Reason-giving explanations tend to rely on detailed knowledge of a specific domain. This detail is often unpredictable to teachers and is not as highly valued as is knowledge which covers a particular area of knowledge with less detail, but offers opportunity for extending the knowledge to larger and related concerns. For example, a primary-level student whose father owns a turkey farm may respond with reason-explanations to a story about a turkey. His knowledge is intensive and covers details perhaps not known to the teacher and not judged as relevant to the story. The knowledge is unpredictable and questions about it do not continue to repeat the common core of content knowledge of the story. Thus such configured knowledge is encouraged only for the "extras" of reading—an extra-credit oral report or a creative picture and story about turkeys. This kind of knowledge is allowed to be used once the hierarchical what-explanations have been mastered and displayed in a particular situation and, in the course of one's academic career, only when one has shown full mastery of the hierarchical skills and subsets of related skills which underlie what-explanations. Thus, reliable and successful participation in the ways of taking from books that teachers view as natural must, in the usual school way of doing things, precede other ways of taking from books.

These various ways of taking are sometimes referred to as "cognitive styles" or "learning styles." It is generally accepted in the research literature that they are influenced by early socialization experiences and correlated with such features of the society in which the child is reared as social organization, reliance on authority, male-female roles, and so on. These styles are often seen as two contrasting types, most frequently termed "field independent-field dependent" (Witkin et al.) or "analytic-relational" (Kagan, Siegel, and Moss; Cohen 1968, 1969, 1971). The analytic field-independent style is generally presented as that which correlates positively with high achievement and general academic and social success in school. Several studies discuss ways in which the style is played out in school—in preferred ways of responding to pictures and written text and selecting from among a choice of answers to test items.

Yet, we know little about how behaviors associated with either of the dichotomized cognitive styles (field-dependent/relational and field-independent/analytic) were learned in early patterns of socialization. To be sure, there are vast individual differences which may cause an individual to behave so as to be categorized as having one or the other of these learning styles. But much of the literature on learning styles suggests a preference for one or the other is learned in the social group in which the child is reared and in connection with other ways of behaving found in that culture. But how is a child socialized into an analytic field-independent style? What kinds of interactions does he enter into with his parents and the stimuli of his environment which contribute to the development of such a style of learning? How do these interactions mold selective attention practices such as "sensitivity to parts of objects," "awareness of obscure, abstract, nonobvious features," and identification of "abstractions based on the features of items" (Cohen 1969: 844-45)? Since the predominant stimuli used in school to judge the presence and extent of these selective attention practices are written materials, it is clear that the literacy orientation of preschool children is central to these questions.

The foregoing descriptions of how Maintown parents socialize their children into a literacy orientation fit closely those provided by Scollon and Scollon for their own child Rachel. Through similar practices, Rachel was "literate before she learned to read" (1979: 6). She knew, before the age of two, how to focus on a book and not on herself. Even when she told a story about herself, she moved herself out of the text and saw herself as author, as someone different from the central character of her story. She learned to pay close attention to the parts of objects, to name them, and to provide a running commentary on features of her environment. She learned to manipulate the contexts of items, her own activities, and language to achieve book-like, decontextualized, repeatable effects (such as puns). Many references in her talk were from written sources; others were modeled on stories and questions about these stories. The substance of her knowledge, as well as her ways of framing knowledge orally, derived from her familiarity with books and bookreading. No doubt, this development began by labeling in the dialogue cycles of reading (Ninio and Bruner), and it will continue for Rachel in her preschool years along many of the same patterns described by Cochran-Smith for a mainstream nursery school. There the teacher and students negotiated story-reading through the scaffolding of teachers' questions and running commentaries which replayed the structure and sequence of story-reading learned in their mainstream homes.

Close analyses of how mainstream school-oriented children come to learn to take from books at home suggest that such children learn not only how to take meaning from books, but also how to talk about it. In doing the latter, they repeatedly practice routines which parallel those of classroom interaction. By the time they enter school, they have had continuous experience as information-givers; they have learned how to perform in those interactions which surround literate sources throughout school. They have had years of practice in interaction situations that are the heart of reading—both learning to read and reading to learn in school.

They have developed habits of performing which enable them to run through the hierarchy of preferred knowledge about a literate source and the appropriate sequence of skills to be displayed in showing knowledge of a subject. They have developed ways of decontextualizing and surrounding with explanatory prose the knowledge gained from selective attention to objects.

They have learned to listen, waiting for the appropriate cue which signals it is their turn to show off this knowledge. They have learned the rules for getting certain services from parents (or teachers) in the reading interaction (Merritt 1979). In nursery school, they continue to practice these interaction patterns in a group rather than in a dyadic situation. There they learn additional signals and behaviors necessary for getting a turn in a group and responding to a central reader and to a set of centrally defined reading tasks. In short, most of their waking hours during the preschool years have enculturated them into (1) all those habits associated with what-explanations, (2) selective attention to items of the written text, *and* (3) appropriate interactional styles for orally displaying all the know-how of their literate orientation to the environment. This learning has been finely tuned and its habits are highly interdependent. Patterns of behaviors learned in one setting or at one stage reappear again and again as these children learn to use oral and written language in literacy events and to bring their knowledge to bear in school-acceptable ways.

Alternative Patterns of Literacy Events

But what corresponds to the mainstream pattern of learning in communities that do not have this finely tuned, consistent, repetitive, and continuous pattern of training? Are there ways of behaving which achieve other social and cognitive aims in other sociocultural groups?

The data below are summarized from an ethnography of two communities—Roadville and Trackton—located only a few miles from Maintown's neighborhoods in the Piedmont Carolinas. Roadville is a white working-class community of families steeped for four generations in the life of the textile mill. Trackton is a working-class black community whose older generations have been brought up on the land, either farming their own land or working for other landowners. However, in the past decade, they have found work in the textile mills. Children of both communities are unsuccessful in school; yet both communities place a high value on success in school, believing earnestly in the personal and vocational rewards school can bring and urging their children "to get ahead" by doing well in school. Both Roadville and Trackton are literate communities in the sense that the residents of each are able to read printed and written materials in their daily lives, and on occasion they produce written messages as part of the total pattern of communication in the community. In both communities, children go to school with certain expectancies of print and, in Trackton especially, children have a keen sense that reading is something one does to learn something one needs to know (Heath 1980). In both groups, residents turn from spoken to written uses of language and vice versa as the occasion demands, and the two modes of expression seem to supplement and reinforce each other. Nonetheless there are radical differences between the two communities in the ways in which children and adults interact in the preschool years; each of the two communities also differs from Maintown. Roadville and Trackton view children's learning of language from two radically different perspectives: in Trackton, children "learn to talk," in Roadville, adults "teach them how to talk."

Roadville

In Roadville, babies are brought home from the hospital to rooms decorated with colorful, mechanical, musical, and literacy-based stimuli. The walls are decorated with pictures based on nursery rhymes, and from an early age, children are held and prompted to "see" the wall decorations. Adults recite nursery rhymes as they twirl the mobile made of nursery-rhyme characters. The items of the child's environment promote exploration of colors, shapes, and textures: a stuffed ball with sections of fabrics of different colors and textures is in the crib; stuffed animals vary in texture, size, and shape. Neighbors, friends from church, and relatives come to visit and talk to the baby, and about him to those who will listen. The baby is fictionalized in the talk to him: "But this baby wants to go to sleep, doesn't he? Yes, see those little eyes gettin' heavy." As the child grows older, adults pounce on word-like sounds and turn them into "words," repeating the "words," and expanding them into well-formed sentences. Before they can talk, children are introduced to visitors and prompted to provide all the expected politeness formulas, such as "Bye-bye," "Thank you," and so forth. As soon as they can talk, children are reminded about these formulas, and book or television characters known to be "polite" are involved as reinforcement.

In each Roadville home, preschoolers first have cloth books, featuring a single object on each page. They later acquire books which provide sounds, smells, and different textures or opportunities for practicing small motor skills (closing zippers, buttoning buttons, etc.). A typical collection for a two-year-old consisted of a dozen or so books—eight featured either the alphabet or numbers, others were books of nursery rhymes, simplified Bible stories, or "real-life" stories about boys and girls (usually taking care of their pets or exploring a particular feature of their environment). Books based on Sesame Street characters were favorite gifts for three- and four-year-olds.

Reading and reading-related activities occur most frequently before naps or at bedtime in the evening. Occasionally an adult or older child will read to a fussy child while the mother prepares dinner or changes a bed. On weekends, fathers sometimes read with their children for brief periods of time, but they generally prefer to play games or play with the children's toys in their interactions. The following episode illustrates the language and social interactional aspects of these bedtime events; the episode takes place between Wendy (two years three months old at the time of this episode) and Aunt Sue who is putting her to bed.

> [Aunt Sue (AS) picks up book, while Wendy (W) crawls about the floor, ostensibly looking for something]
>
> W: uh uh
> AS: Wendy, we're gonna read, uh, read this story, come on, hop up here on this bed.
> [Wendy climbs up on the bed, sits on top of the pillow, and picks up her teddy bear]
> [Aunt Sue opens book, points to puppy]
> AS: Do you remember what this book is about? See the puppy? What does the puppy do?
> [Wendy plays with the bear, glancing occasionally at pages of the book, as Aunt Sue turns. Wendy seems to be waiting for something in the book]

AS: See the puppy?
      [Aunt Sue points to the puppy in the book and looks at Wendy to
      see if she is watching]
W: uh huh, yea, yes ma'am
AS: Puppy sees the ant, he's a li'l
      [Wendy drops the bear and turns to the book]
      fellow. Can you see that ant? Puppy has a little ball.
W: ant bite puppy
      [Wendy points to ant, pushing hard on the book]
AS: No, the ant won't bite the puppy, the [turns page] puppy wants to
      play with the ant, see?
      [Wendy tries to turn the page back; AS won't let her, and Wendy
      starts to squirm and fuss]
AS: Look here, here's someone else, the puppy
      [Wendy climbs down off the bed and gets another book]
W: read this one
AS: Okay, you get back up here now. [Wendy gets back on bed]
AS: This book is your ABC book. See the A, look, here, on your spread,
      there's an A. You find the A. [The second book is a cloth book, old
      and tattered, and long a favorite of Wendy's. It features an apple
      on the cover, and its front page has an ABC block and ball. Through
      the book, there is a single item on each page, with a large
      representation of the first letter of the word commonly used to
      name the item. As AS turns the page, Wendy begins to crawl about
      on her quilt, which shows ABC blocks interspersed with balls and
      apples. Wendy points to each of the As on the blanket and begins
      talking to herself. AS reads the book, looks up, and sees Wendy
      pointing to the As in her quilt.]
AS: That's an A, can you find the A on your blanket?
W: there it is, this one, there's the hole too. [pokes her finger through
      a place where the threads have broken in the quilting]
AS: [AS points to ball in book] Stop that, find the ball, see, here's
      another ball.

This episode characterizes the early orientation of Roadville children to the written word. Bookreading time focuses on letters of the alphabet, numbers, names of basic items pictured in books, and simplified retellings of stories in the words of the adult. If the content or story plot seems too complicated for the child, the adult tells the story in short, simple sentences, frequently laced with requests that the child give what-explanations.

Wendy's favorite books are those with which she can participate: that is, those to which she can answer, provide labels, point to items, give animal sounds, and "read" the material back to anyone who will listen to her. She memorizes the passages and often knows when to turn the pages to show that she is "reading." She holds the book in her lap, starts at the beginning, and often reads the title, "Puppy."

Adults and children use the title of the book or phrases such as "the book about a puppy" to refer to reading material. When Wendy acquires a new book, adults introduce the book with phrases such as "This is a book about a duck, a little yellow duck. See the duck. Duck goes quack quack." On introducing a book, adults sometimes ask the child to recall when they have seen a real specimen such as that one treated in the book: "Remember the duck on the College lake?" The child often shows no sign of linking the yellow fluffy duck in the book with the large brown and grey mallards on the lake, and the adult makes no efforts to explain that two such disparate-looking objects go by the same name.

As Wendy grows older, she wants to "talk" during the long stories and the Bible stories, and she wants to carry out the participation she so enjoyed with the alphabet books. However, by the time she reaches three and a half, Wendy is restrained from such wide-ranging participation. When she interrupts, she is told:

> Wendy, stop that, you be quiet when someone is reading to you. You
> listen; now sit still and be quiet.

Often Wendy immediately gets down and runs away into the next room saying "no, no." When this happens, her father goes to get her, pats her bottom, and puts her down hard on the sofa beside him. "Now you're gonna learn to listen." During the third and fourth years, this pattern occurs more and more frequently; only when Wendy can capture an aunt who does not visit often does she bring out the old books and participate with them. Otherwise, parents, Aunt Sue, and other adults insist that she be read a story and that she "listen" quietly.

When Wendy and her parents watch television, eat cereal, visit the grocery store, or go to church, adults point out and talk about many types of written material. On the way to the grocery, Wendy (at three years eight months) sits in the backseat, and when her mother stops at a corner, Wendy says "Stop." Her mother says "Yes, that's a stop sign." Wendy has, however, misread a yield sign as *stop*. Her mother offers no explanation of what the actual message on the sign is, yet when she comes to the sign, she stops to yield to an oncoming car. Her mother, when asked why she had not given Wendy the word "yield," said it was too hard. Wendy would not understand, and "it's not a word we use like *stop*."

Wendy recognized animal cracker boxes as early as 10 months, and later, as her mother began buying other varieties, Wendy would see the box in the grocery store and yell "Cook cook." Her mother would say, "Yes, those are cookies. Does Wendy want a cookie?" One day Wendy saw a new type of cracker box, and screeched "Cook cook." Her father opened the box and gave Wendy a cracker and waited for her reaction. She started the "cookie," then took it to her mother, saying "You eat." The mother joined in the game and said "Don't you want your *cookie*?" Wendy said "No cookie. You eat." "But Wendy, it's a cookie box, see?" and her mother pointed to the "C" of *crackers* on the box. Wendy paid no attention and ran off into another room.

In Roadville's literacy events, the rules for cooperative discourse around print are repeatedly practiced, coached, and rewarded in the preschool years. Adults in Roadville believe that instilling in children the proper use of words and understanding of the meaning of the written word are important for both their educational and religious success. Adults repeat aspects of the learning of literacy events they have known as children. In the words of one Roadville parent: "It was then that I began to learn ... when my daddy kept insisting I *read* it, *say* it right. It was then that I *did* right, in his view."

The path of development for such performance can be described in three overlapping stages. In the first, children are introduced to discrete bits and pieces of books—separate items, letters of the alphabet, shapes, colors, and commonly represented items in books for children (apple, baby, ball, etc.). The latter are usually decontextualized, not pictured in their ordinary contexts, and they are represented in two-dimensional flat line drawings. During this stage, children must participate as predictable information-givers and respond to questions that ask for specific and discrete bits of information about the written matter. In these literacy events, specific features of the two-dimensional items in books which are different from their "real" counterparts are not pointed out. A ball in a book is flat; a duck in a book is yellow and fluffy; trucks, cars, dogs, and trees talk in books. No mention is made of the fact that such features do not fit these objects in reality. Children are not encouraged to move their understanding of books into other situational contexts or to apply it in their general knowledge of the world about them.

In the second stage, adults demand an acceptance of the power of print to entertain, inform, and instruct. When Wendy could no longer participate by contributing her knowledge at any point in the literacy event, she learned to recognize bookreading as a performance. The adult exhibited the book to Wendy: she was to be entertained, to learn from the information conveyed in the material, and to remember the book's content for the sequential followup questioning, as opposed to ongoing cooperative participatory questions.

In the third stage, Wendy was introduced to preschool workbooks which provided story information and was asked questions or provided exercises and games based on the content of the stories or pictures. Follow-the-number coloring books and preschool "push-out and paste" workbooks on shapes, colors, and letters of the alphabet reinforced repeatedly that the written word could be taken apart into small pieces and one item linked to another by following rules. She had practice in the linear, sequential nature of books: begin at the beginning, stay in the lines for coloring, draw straight lines to link one item to another, write your answers on lines, keep your letters straight, match the cutout letter to diagrams of letter shapes.

The differences between Roadville and Maintown are substantial. Roadville adults do not extend either the content or the habits of literacy events beyond bookreading. They do not, upon seeing an item or event in the real world, remind children of a similar event in a book and launch a running commentary on similarities and differences. When a game is played or a chore done, adults do not use literate sources. Mothers cook without written recipes most of the time; if they use a recipe from a written source, they do so usually only after confirmation and alteration by friends who have tried the recipe. Directions to games are read, but not carefully followed, and they are not talked about in a series of questions and answers which try to establish their meaning. Instead, in the putting together of toys or the playing of games, the abilities or preferences of one party prevail. For example, if an adult knows how to put a toy together, he does so; he does not talk about the process, refer to the written material and "translate" for the child, or try to sequence steps so the child can do it.[2] Adults do not talk about the steps and procedures of *how* to do things; if a father wants his preschooler to learn to hold a miniature bat or throw a ball, he says "Do it this way." He does not break up "this way" into such steps as "Put your fingers around here," "Keep your thumb in this position," "Never hold it above this line." Over and over again, adults do a task and children observe and try it, being reinforced only by commands such as "Do it like this," "Watch that thumb."

Adults at tasks do not provide a running verbal commentary on what they are doing. They do not draw the attention of the child to specific features of the sequences of skills or the attributes of items. They do not ask questions of the child, except questions which are directive or scolding in nature, ("Did you bring the ball?" "Didn't you hear what I said?"). Many of their commands contain idioms which are not explained: "Put it up," or "Put that away now" (meaning to put it in the place where it usually belongs), or "Loosen up," said to a four-year-old boy trying to learn to bat a ball. Explanations which move beyond the listing of names of items and their features are rarely offered by adults. Children do not ask questions of the type "But I don't understand. What is that?" They appear willing to keep trying, and if there is ambiguity in a set of commands, they ask a question such as "You want me to do this?"

(demonstrating their current efforts), or they try to find a way of diverting attention from the task at hand.

Both boys and girls during their preschool years are included in many adult activities, ranging from going to church to fishing and camping. They spend a lot of time observing and asking for turns to try specific tasks, such as putting a worm on the hook or cutting cookies. Sometimes adults say "No, you're not old enough." But if they agree to the child's attempt at the task, they watch and give directives and evaluations: "That's right, don't twist the cutter." "Turn like this." "Don't try to scrape it up now, let me do that." Talk about the task does not segment its skills and identify them, nor does it link the particular task or item at hand to other tasks. Reason-explanations such as "If you twist the cutter, the cookies will be rough on the edge," are rarely given, or asked for.

Neither Roadville adults nor children shift the context of items in their talk. They do not tell stories which fictionalize themselves or familiar events. They reject Sunday School materials which attempt to translate Biblical events into a modern-day setting. In Roadville, a story must be invited or announced by someone other than the storyteller, and only certain community members are designated good storytellers. A story is recognized by the group as a story about one and all. It is a true story, an actual event which occurred to either the storyteller or to someone else present. The marked behavior of the storyteller and audience alike is seen as exemplifying the weaknesses of all and the need for persistence in overcoming such weaknesses. The sources of stories are personal experience. They are tales of transgressions which make the point of reiterating the expected norms of behavior of man, woman, fisherman, worker, and Christian. They are true to the facts of the event.

Roadville parents provide their children with books; they read to them and ask questions about the books' contents. They choose books which emphasize nursery rhymes, alphabet learning, animals, and simplified Bible stories, and they require their children to repeat from these books and to answer formulaic questions about their contents. Roadville adults also ask questions about oral stories which have a point relevant to some marked behavior of a child. They use proverbs and summary statements to remind their children of stories and to call on them for simple comparisons of the stories' contents to their own situations. Roadville parents coach children in their telling of a story, forcing them to tell about an incident as it has been pre-composed or pre-scripted in the head of the adult. Thus, in Roadville, children come to know a story as either an accounting from a book, or a factual account of a real event in which some type of marked behavior occurred and there is a lesson to be learned. Any fictionalized account of a real event is viewed as a *lie*; reality is better than fiction. Roadville's church and community life admit no story other than that which meets the definition internal to the group. Thus children cannot decontextualize their knowledge or fictionalize events known to them and shift them about into other frames.

When these children go to school they perform well in the initial stages of each of the three early grades. They often know portions of the alphabet, some colors and numbers, can recognize their names, and tell someone their address and their parents' names. They will sit still and listen to a story, and they know how to answer questions asking for what-explanations. They do well in reading workbook exercises which ask for identification of specific portions of words, items from the story, or the linking of two items, letters, or parts of words on the same page. When the teacher reaches the end of story-reading or the reading circle and asks questions such as "What did you like about the story?", relatively few Roadville children answer. If asked questions such as "What would you have done if you had been Billy [a story's main character]?", Roadville children most frequently say "I don't know" or shrug their shoulders.

Near the end of each year, and increasingly as they move through the early primary grades, Roadville children can handle successfully the initial stages of lessons. But when they move ahead to extra-credit items or to activities considered more advanced and requiring more independence, they are stumped. They turn frequently to teachers asking "Do you want me to do this? What do I do here?" If asked to write a creative story or tell it into a tape recorder, they retell stories from books; they do not create their own. They rarely provide emotional or personal commentary on their accounting of real events or book stories. They are rarely able to take knowledge learned in one context and shift it to another; they do not compare two items or events and point out similarities and differences. They find it difficult either to hold one feature of an event constant and shift all others or to hold all features constant but one. For example, they are puzzled by questions such as "What would have happened if Billy had not told the policemen what happened?" They do not know how to move events or items out of a given frame. To a question such as "What habits of the Hopi Indians might they be able to take with them when they move to a city?", they provide lists of features of life of the Hopi on the reservation. They do not take these items, consider their appropriateness in an urban setting, and evaluate the hypothetical outcome. In general, they find this type of question impossible to answer, and they do not know how to ask teachers to help them take apart the questions to figure out the answers. Thus their initial successes in reading, being good students, following orders, and adhering to school norms of participating in lessons begin to fall away rapidly about the time they enter the fourth grade. As the importance and frequency of questions and reading habits with which they are familiar decline in the higher grades, they have no way of keeping up or of seeking help in learning what it is they do not even know they don't know.

Trackton

Babies in Trackton come home from the hospital to an environment which is almost entirely human. There are no cribs, car beds, or car seats, and only an occasional high chair or infant seat. Infants are held during their waking hours, occasionally while they sleep, and they usually sleep in the bed with parents until they are about two years of age. They are held, their faces fondled, their cheeks pinched, and they eat and sleep in the midst of human talk and noise from the television, stereo, and radio. Encapsuled in an almost totally human world, they are in the midst of constant human communication, verbal and nonverbal. They literally feel the body signals of shifts in emotion of those who hold them almost continuously; they are talked about and kept in the midst of talk about topics that range over any subject. As children make cooing or babbling sounds, adults refer to this as "noise," and no attempt is made to interpret these sounds as words or communicative attempts on the part of the baby. Adults believe they should not have to depend on their babies to tell them what they need or when they are uncomfortable; adults know, children only "come to know."

When a child can crawl and move about on his own, he plays with the household objects deemed safe for him—pot lids, spoons, plastic food containers. Only at Christmastime are there special toys for very young children; these are usually trucks, balls, doll babies, or plastic cars, but rarely blocks, puzzles, or books. As children become completely mobile, they demand ride toys or electronic and mechanical toys they see on television. They never request nor do they receive manipulative toys, such as puzzles, blocks, take-apart toys or literacy-based items, such as books or letter games.

Adults read newspapers, mail, calendars, circulars (political and civic events-related), school materials sent home to parents, brochures advertising new cars, television sets, or other products, and the Bible and other church-related materials. There are no reading materials especially for children (with the exception of children's Sunday School materials), and adults do not sit and read to children. Since children are usually left to sleep whenever and wherever they fall asleep, there is no bedtime or naptime as such. At night, they are put to bed when adults go to bed or whenever the person holding them gets tired. Thus, going to bed is not framed in any special routine. Sometimes in a play activity during the day, an older sibling will read to a younger child, but the latter soon loses interest and squirms away to play. Older children often try to "play school" with younger children, reading to them from books and trying to ask questions about what they have read. Adults look on these efforts with amusement and do not try to convince the small child to sit still and listen.

Signs from very young children of attention to the nonverbal behaviors of others are rewarded by extra fondling, laughter, and cuddling from adults. For example, when an infant shows signs of recognizing a family member's voice on the phone by bouncing up and down in the arms of the adult who is talking on the phone, adults comment on this to others present and kiss and nudge the child. Yet when children utter sounds or combinations of sounds which could be interpreted as words, adults pay no attention. Often by the time they are twelve months old, children approximate words or phrases of adults' speech; adults respond by laughing or giving special attention to the child and crediting him with "sounding like" the person being imitated. When children learn to walk and imitate the walk of members of the community, they are rewarded by comments on their activities: "He walks just like Toby when he's tuckered out."

Children between the ages of twelve and twenty-four months often imitate the tune or "general Gestalt" (Peters) of complete utterances they hear around them. They pick up and repeat chunks (usually the ends) of phrasal and clausal utterances of speakers around them. They seem to remember fragments of speech and repeat these without active production. In this first stage of language learning, the repetition stage, they imitate the intonation contours and general shaping of the utterances they repeat. Lem (one year two months old) in the following example illustrates this pattern.

Mother:	[talking to neighbor on porch while Lem plays with a truck on the porch nearby] But they won't callback, won't happen=
Lem:	=call back
Neighbor:	Sam's going over there Saturday, he'll pick up a form=
Lem:	=pick up on, pick up on [Lem here appears to have heard *form* as *on*]

The adults pay no attention to Lem's "talk," and their talk, in fact, often overlaps his repetitions.

In the second stage, repetition with variation, Trackton children manipulate pieces of conversation they pick up. They incorporate chunks of language from others into their own ongoing dialogue, applying productive rules, inserting new nouns and verbs for those used in the adults' chunks. They also play with rhyming patterns and varying intonation contours.

Mother:	She went to the doctor again.
Lem (at two years two months):	
	[in a sing-song fashion] went to de doctor, tractor, dis my tractor, doctor on a tractor, went to de doctor.

Lem creates a monologue, incorporating the conversation about him into his own talk as he plays. Adults pay no attention to his chatter unless it gets so noisy as to interfere with their talk.

In the third stage, participation, children begin to enter the ongoing conversation about them. They do so by attracting the adult's attention with a tug on the arm or pant leg, and they help make themselves understood by providing nonverbal reinforcements to help recreate a scene they want the listener to remember. For example, if adults are talking, and a child interrupts with seemingly unintelligible utterances, the child will make gestures, extra sounds, or act out some outstanding features of the scene he is trying to get the adult to remember. Children try to create a context, a scene, for the understanding of their utterance.

This third stage illustrates a pattern in the children's response to their environment and their ways of letting others know their knowledge of the environment. Once they are in the third stage, their communicative efforts are accepted by community members, and adults respond directly to the child, instead of talking to others about the child's activities as they have done in the past. Children continue to practice for conversational participation by playing, when alone, both parts of dialogues, imitating gestures as well as intonation patterns of adults. By two and a half years all children in the community can imitate the walk and talk of others in the community or frequent visitors such as the man who comes around to read the gas meters. They can feign anger, sadness, fussing, remorse, silliness, or any of a wide range of expressive behaviors. They often use the same chunks of language for varying effects, depending on nonverbal support to give the language different meanings or cast it in a different key (Hymes 1974). Girls between three and four years of age take part in extraordinarily complex stepping and clapping patterns and simple repetitions of hand clap games played by older girls. From the time they are old enough to stand alone, they are encouraged in their participation by siblings and older children in the community. These games require anticipation and recognition of cues for upcoming behaviors, and the young girls learn to watch for these cues and to come in with the appropriate words and movements at the right time.

Preschool children are not asked for what-explanations of their environment. Instead, they are asked a preponderance of analogical questions which call for non-specific comparisons of one item, event, or person with another: "What's that like?" Other types of questions ask for specific information known to the child but not the adults: "Where'd you get that from?" "What do you want?" "How come you did that?" (Heath 1982). Adults explain their use of these types of questions by expressing their sense of children: they are "comers," coming into their learning by experiencing what knowing about things means. As one parent of a two-year-old boy put it: "Ain't no use me tellin' 'im: 'Learn this, learn that, what's this, what's that?' He just gotta learn, gotta know; he see one thing one place one time he know how it go, see sump'n like it again, maybe it be the same, maybe it won't." Children are expected to learn how to know when the form belies the meaning, to know contexts of items, and to use their understanding of these contexts to draw parallels between items and events. Parents do not believe they have a tutoring role in this learning; they provide the experiences on which the child draws and reward signs of their successfully coming to know.

Trackton children's early stories illustrate how they respond to adult views of them as "comers." The children learn to tell stories by drawing heavily on their abilities to render a context, to set a stage, and to call on the audience's power to join in the imaginative creation of a story. Between the ages of two and four years, the children, in a monologue-like fashion, tell stories about things in their lives, events they see and hear, and situations in which they have been involved. They produce these spontaneously during play with other children or in the presence of adults. Sometimes they make an effort to attract the attention of listeners before they begin the story, but often they do not. Lem, playing off the edge of the porch, when he was about two and a half years of age, heard a bell in the distance. He stopped, looked at Nellie and Benjy, his older siblings, who were nearby and said:

Way
Far
Now
It a church bell
Ringin'
Dey singin'
Ringin'
You hear it?
I hear it
Far
Now.

Lem had been taken to church the previous Sunday and had been much impressed by the church bell. He had sat on his mother's lap and joined in the singing, rocking to and fro on her lap, and clapping his hands. His story, which is like a poem in its imagery and line-like prosody, is in response to the current stimulus of a distant bell. As he tells the story, he sways back and forth.

This story, somewhat longer than those usually reported from other social groups for children as young as Lem,[3] has some features which have come to characterize fully-developed narratives or stories. It recapitulates in its verbal outline the sequence of events being recalled by the storyteller. At church, the bell rang while the people sang. In the line "It a church bell," Lem provides his story's topic, and a brief summary of what is to come. This line serves a function similar to the formulae often used by older children to open a story: "This is a story about (a church bell)." Lem gives only the slightest hint of story setting or orientation to the listener; where and when the story took place are capsuled in "Way, Far." Preschoolers in Trackton almost never hear "Once upon a time there was a _____" stories, and they rarely provide definitive orientations for their stories. They seem to assume listeners "know" the situation in which the narrative takes place. Similarly, preschoolers in Trackton do not close off their stories with formulaic endings. Lem poetically balances his opening and closing in an inclusion, beginning "Way, Far, Now." and ending "Far, Now." The effect is one of closure, but there is no clearcut announcement of closure. Throughout the presentation of action and result of action in their stories, Trackton preschoolers invite the audience to respond or evaluate the story's actions. Lem asks "You hear it?" which may refer either to the current stimulus or to yesterday's bell, since Lem does not productively use past tense endings for any verbs at this stage in his language development.

Preschool storytellers have several ways of inviting audience evaluation and interest. They may themselves express an emotional response to the story's actions; they may have another character or narrator in the story do so often using alliterative language play; or they may detail actions and results through direct discourse or sound effects and gestures. All these methods of calling attention to the story and its telling distinguish the speech event as a story, an occasion for audience and storyteller to interact pleasantly and not simply to hear an ordinary recounting of events or actions.

Trackton children must be aggressive in inserting their stories into an ongoing stream of discourse. Storytelling is highly competitive. Everyone in a conversation may want to tell a story, so only the most aggressive wins out. The content ranges widely, and there is "truth" only in the universals of human experience. Fact is often hard to find, though it is usually the seed of the story. Trackton stories often have no point—no obvious beginning or ending; they go on as long as the audience enjoys and tolerates the storyteller's entertainment.

Trackton adults do not separate out the elements of the environment around their children to tune their attentions selectively. They do not simplify their language, focus on single-word utterances by young children, label items or features of objects in either books or the environment at large. Instead, children are continuously contextualized, presented with almost continuous communication. From this ongoing, multiple-channeled stream of stimuli, they must themselves select, practice, and determine rules of production and structuring. For language, they do so by first repeating, catching chunks of sounds and intonation contours and by practicing these without specific reinforcement or evaluation. But practice material and models are continuously available. Next the children seem to begin to sort out the productive rules for speech and practice what they hear about them with variation. Finally, they work their way into conversations, hooking their meanings for listeners into a familiar context by recreating scenes through gestures, special sound effects, etc. These characteristics continue in their story-poems and their participation in jump-rope rhymes. Because adults do not select out, name, and describe features of the environment for the young, children must perceive situations, determine how units of the situations are related to each other, recognize these relations in other situations, and reason through what it will take to show their correlation of one situation with another. The children can answer questions such as "What's that like?" ["It's like Doug's car"] but they can rarely name the specific feature or features which make two items or events alike. For example, in the case of saying a car seen on the street is "like Doug's car," a child may be basing the analogy on the fact that this car has a flat tire and Doug's also had one last week. But the child does not name (and is not asked to name) what is alike between the two cars.

Children seem to develop connections between situations or items not by specification of labels and features in the situations, but by configuration links. Recognition of similar general shapes or patterns of links seen in one situation and connected to another seem to be the means by which children set scenes in their nonverbal representations of individuals and later in their verbal chunking, then segmentation and production of rules for putting together isolated units. They do not decontextualize; instead they heavily contextualize nonverbal and verbal language. They fictionalize their "true stories," but they do so by asking the audience to identify with the story through making parallels from their own experiences. When adults read, they often do so in a group. One person, reading aloud, for example, from a brochure on a new car decodes the text, displays illustrations and photographs, and listeners relate the text's meaning to their experiences asking questions and expressing opinions. Finally, the group as a whole synthesizes the written text and the negotiated oral discourse to construct a meaning for the brochure (Heath 1985).

When Trackton children go to school, they face unfamiliar types of questions which ask for what-explanations. They are asked as individuals to identify items by name and to label features such as shape, color, size, number. The stimuli to which they are to give these responses are two-dimensional flat representations which are often highly stylized and bear little resemblance to the "real" items. Trackton children generally score in the lowest percentile range on the Metropolitan Reading Readiness tests. They do not sit at their desks and complete reading workbook pages; neither do they tolerate questions about reading materials which are structured along the usual lesson format. Their contributions are in the form of "I had a duck at my house one time," "Why'd he do that?" or they imitate the sound effects teachers may produce in stories they read to the children. By the end of the first three primary grades, their general language arts scores have been consistently low, except for those few who have begun to adapt to and adopt some of the behaviors they have had to learn in school. But the majority not only fail to learn the content of lessons, they also do not adopt the social interactional rules for school literacy events. Print in isolation bears little authority in their world. The kinds of questions asked of reading books are unfamiliar. The children's abilities to link metaphorically two events or situations and to recreate scenes are not tapped in the school; in fact, *these abilities often cause difficulties,* because they enable children to see parallels teachers did not intend, and indeed, may not recognize until the children point them out (Heath 1978).

By the end of the lessons or by the time in their total school career when reason-explanations and affective statements call for the creative comparison of two or more situations, it is too late for many Trackton children. They have not picked up along the way the composition and comprehension skills they need to translate their analogical skills into a channel teachers can accept. They seem not to know how to take meaning from reading; they do not observe the rules of linearity in writing, and their expression of themselves on paper is very limited. Orally taped stories are often much better, but these rarely count as much as written compositions. Thus, Trackton children continue to collect very low or failing grades, and many decide by the end of the sixth grade to stop trying and turn their attention to the heavy peer socialization which usually begins in these years.

From Community to Classroom

A recent review of trends in research on learning pointed out that "learning to read through using and learning from language has been less systematically studied than the decoding process" (Glaser 1979: 7). Put another way, how children learn to use language to read to learn has been less systematically studied than decoding skills. Learning how to take meaning from writing before one learns to read involves repeated practice in using and learning from language through appropriate participation in literacy events such as exhibitor-questioner and spectator-respondent dyads (Scollon and Scollon 1979) or group negotiation of the meaning of a written text. Children have to learn to select, hold, and retrieve content from books and other written or printed texts in accordance with their community's rules or "ways of taking," and the children's learning follows community paths of language socialization. In each society, certain kinds of childhood participation in literacy events may precede others, as the developmental sequence builds toward the whole complex of home and community behaviors characteristic of the society. The ways of taking employed in the school may in turn build directly on the preschool development, may require substantial adaptation on the part of the children, or may even run directly counter to aspects of the community's pattern.

At home. In *Maintown* homes, the construction of knowledge in the earliest preschool years depends in large part on labeling procedures and what-explanations. Maintown families, like other mainstream families, continue this kind of classification and knowledge construction throughout the child's environment and into the school years, calling it into play in response to new items in the environment and in running commentaries on old items as they compare to new ones. This pattern of linking old and new knowledge is reinforced in narrative tales which fictionalize the teller's events or recapitulate a story from a book. Thus for these children the bedtime story is simply an early link in a long chain of interrelated patterns of taking meaning from the environment. Moreover, along this chain, the focus is on the individual as respondent and cooperative negotiator of meaning from books. In particular, children learn that written language may represent not only descriptions of real events, but decontextualized logical propositions, and the occurrence of this kind of information in print or in writing legitimates a response in which one brings to the interpretation of written text selected knowledge from the real world. Moreover, readers must recognize how certain types of questions assert the priority of meanings in the written word over reality. The "real" comes into play only after prescribed decontextualized meanings; affective responses and reason-explanations follow conventional presuppositions which stand behind what-explanations.

Roadville also provides labels, features, and what-explanations, and prescribes listening and performing behaviors for preschoolers. However, Roadville adults do not carry on or sustain in continually overlapping and interdependent fashion the linking of ways of taking meaning from books to ways of relating that knowledge to other aspects of the environment. They do not encourage decontextualization; in fact, they proscribe it in their own stories about themselves and their requirements of stories from children. They do not themselves make analytic statements or assert universal truths, except those related to their religious faith. They lace their stories with synthetic (nonanalytic) statements which express, describe, and synthesize actual real-life materials. Things do not have to follow logically so long as they fit the past experience of individuals in the community. Thus children learn to look for a specific moral in stories and to expect that story to fit their facts of reality explicitly. When they themselves recount an event, they do the same, constructing the story of a real event according to coaching by adults who want to construct the story as they saw it.

Trackton is like neither Maintown nor Roadville. There are no bedtime stories; in fact, there are few occasions for reading to or with children specifically. Instead, during the time these activities would take place in mainstream and Roadville homes, Trackton children are enveloped in different kinds of social interactions. They are held, fed, talked about, and rewarded for nonverbal, and later verbal, renderings of events they witness. Trackton adults value and respond favorably when children show they have come to know how to use language to show correspondence in function, style, configuration, and positioning between two different things or situations. Analogical questions are asked of Trackton children, although the implicit questions of structure and function these embody are never made explicit. Children do not have labels or names of attributes of items and events pointed out for them, and they are asked for reason-explanations not what-explanations. Individuals express their personal responses and recreate corresponding situations with often only a minimal adherence to the germ of truth of a story. Children come to recognize similarities of patterning, though they do not name lines, points, or items which are similar between two items or situations. They are familiar with group literacy events in which several community members orally negotiate the meaning of a written text.

At school. In the early reading stages, and in later requirements for reading to learn at more advanced stages, children from the three communities respond differently, because they have learned different methods and degrees of taking from books. In comparison to Maintown children, the habits Roadville children learned in bookreading and toy-related episodes have not continued for them through other activities and types of reinforcement in their environment. They have had less exposure to both the content of books and ways of learning from books than have mainstream children. Thus their need in schools is not necessarily for an intensification of presentation of labels, a slowing down of the sequence of introducing what-explanations in connection with bookreading. Instead they need *extension of these habits to other domains* and to opportunities for practicing habits such as producing running commentaries, creating exhibitor/questioner and spectator/respondent roles. Perhaps most important, Roadville children need to have articulated for them *distinctions in discourse strategies and structures.*

Narratives of real events have certain strategies and structures; imaginary tales, flights of fantasy, and affective expressions have others. Their community's view of narrative discourse style is very narrow and demands a passive role in both creation of and response to the account of events. Moreover, these children have *to be reintroduced to a participant frame of reference to a book*. Though initially they were participants in bookreading, they have been trained into passive roles since the age of three years, and they must learn once again to be active information-givers, taking from books and linking that knowledge to other aspects of their environment.

Trackton students present an additional set of alternatives for procedures in the early primary grades. Since they usually have few of the expected "natural" skills of taking meaning from books, they must not only learn these, but also *retain their analogical reasoning practices* for use in some of the later stages of learning to read. They must *learn to adapt the creativity in language, metaphor, fictionalization, recreation of scenes and exploration of functions and settings of items they bring to school*. These children already use narrative skills highly rewarded in the upper primary grades. They distinguish a fictionalized story from a real-life narrative. They know that telling a story can be in many ways related to play; it suspends reality, and frames an old event in a new context, it calls on audience participation to recognize the setting and participants. They must now *learn as individuals to recount factual events in a straightforward way* and *recognize appropriate occasions for reason-explanations and affective expressions*. Trackton children seem to have skipped learning to label, list features, and give what-explanations. Thus they need to *have the mainstream or school habits presented in familiar activities with explanations related to their own habits of taking meaning* from the environment. Such "simple," "natural" things as distinctions between two-dimensional and three-dimensional objects may need to be explained to help Trackton children learn the stylization and decontextualization which characterizes books.

To lay out in more specific detail how Roadville and Trackton's ways of knowing can be used along with those of mainstreamers goes beyond the scope of this paper. However, it must be admitted that a range of alternatives to ways of learning and displaying knowledge characterizes all highly school-successful adults in the advanced stages of their careers. Knowing more about how these alternatives are learned at early ages in different sociocultural conditions can help the school to provide opportunities for *all* students to avail themselves of these alternatives early in their school careers. For example, mainstream children can benefit from early exposure to Trackton's creative, highly analogical styles of telling stories and giving explanations, and they can add the Roadville true story, with strict chronicity and explicit moral, to their repertoire of narrative types.

In conclusion, if we want to understand the place of literacy in human societies and ways children acquire the literacy orientations of their communities, we must recognize two postulates of literacy and language development:

> 1 Strict dichotomization between oral and literate traditions is a construct of researchers, not an accurate portrayal of reality across cultures.
> 2 A unilinear model of development in the acquisition of language structures and uses cannot adequately account for culturally diverse ways of acquiring knowledge or developing cognitive styles.

Roadville and Trackton tell us that the mainstream type of literacy orientation is not the only type even among Western societies. They also tell us that the mainstream ways of acquiring communicative competence do not offer a universally applicable model of development. They offer proof of Hymes' assertion a decade ago that "it is impossible to generalize validly about 'oral' vs. 'literate' cultures as uniform types" (Hymes 1973: 54).

Yet in spite of such warnings and analyses of the uses and functions of writing in the specific proposals for comparative development and organization of cultural systems (cf. Basso: 432), the majority of research on literacy has focused on differences in class, amount of education, and level of civilization among groups having different literacy characteristics.

"We need, in short, a great deal of ethnography" (Hymes 1973: 57) to provide descriptions of the ways different social groups "take" knowledge from the environment. For written sources, these ways of taking may be analyzed in terms of *types of literacy events*, such as group negotiation of meaning from written texts, individual "looking things up" in reference books, writing family records in Bibles, and the dozens of other types of occasions when books or other written materials are integral to interpretation in an interaction. These must in turn be analyzed in terms of the specific *features of literacy events*, such as labeling, what-explanations, affective comments, reason-explanations, and many other possibilities. Literacy events must also be interpreted in relation to the *larger sociocultural patterns* which they may exemplify or reflect. For example, ethnography must describe literacy events in their sociocultural contexts, so we may come to understand how such patterns as time and space usage, caregiving roles, and age and sex segregation are interdependent with the types and features of literacy events a community develops. It is only on the basis of such thoroughgoing ethnography that further progress is possible toward understanding cross-cultural patterns of oral and written language uses and paths of development of communicative competence.

References

Basso, K. (1974). The ethnography of writing. In R. Bauman & J. Sherzer (eds.), *Explorations in the ethnography of speaking*. New York: Cambridge University Press.

Cazden, C. B. (1979). Peekaboo as an instructional model: Discourse development at home and at school. *Papers and Reports in Child Language Development* 17: 1-29.

Chanan, G., & Gilchrist, L. (1974). *What school is for*. New York: Praeger.

Childs, C. P., & Greenfield, P. M. (1980). Informal modes of learning and teaching. In N. Warren (ed.), *Advances in cross-cultural psychology*, vol. 2. London: Academic Press.

Cochran-Smith, M. (1981). The making of a reader. Ph.D. dissertation. University of Pennsylvania.

Cohen, R. (1968). The relation between socio-conceptual styles and orientation to school requirements. *Sociology of Education* 41: 201-20.

————. (1969). Conceptual styles, culture conflict, and nonverbal tests of intelligence. *American Anthropologist* 71 (5): 828-56.

————. (1971). The influence of conceptual rule-sets on measures of learning ability. In C. L. Brace, G. Gamble, & J. Bond (eds.), *Race and intelligence*. (Anthropological Studies, No. 8, American Anthropological Association). 41-57.

Glaser, R. (1979). Trends and research questions in psychological research on learning and schooling. *Educational Researcher* 8 (10): 6-13.

Goody, E. (1979). Towards a theory of questions. In E. N. Goody (ed.), *Questions and politeness: Strategies in social interaction*. Cambridge University Press.

Griffin, P., & Humphrey, F. (1978). Task and talk. In *The study of children's functional language and education in the early years*. Final report to the Carnegie Corporation of New York. Arlington, Va.: Center for Applied Linguistics.

Heath, S. (1978). *Teacher talk: Language in the classroom*. (Language in Education 9.) Arlington, Va.: Center for Applied Linguistics.

————. (1980). The functions and uses of literacy. *Journal of Communication* 30 (1): 123-33.

————. (1982). Questioning at home and school: A comparative study. In G. Spindler (ed.), *Doing ethnography: Educational anthropology in action*. New York: Holt, Rinehart & Winston.

————. (1983). *Ways with words*. New York: Cambridge University Press.

————. (1985). Protean shapes: Ever-shifting oral and literate traditions. In D. Tannen & M. S. Troike (eds.), *Perspectives on Silence*. Norwood, N. J.: Ablex.

Howard, R. (1974). A note on S/Z. In R. Barthes, *Introduction to S/Z*. Trans. Richard Miller. New York: Hill and Wang.

Hymes, D. H. (1973). On the origins and foundations of inequality among speakers. In E. Haugen & M. Bloomfield (eds.), *Language as a human problem*. New York: W. W. Norton & Co.

————. (1974). Models of the interaction of language and social life. In J. J. Gumperz & D. Hymes (eds.), *Directions in sociolinguistics*. New York: Holt, Rinehart and Winston.

Kagan, J., Siegel, I., & Moss, H. (1963). Psychological significance of styles of conceptualization. In J. Wright & J. Kagan (eds.), *Basic cognitive processes in children*. (Monographs of the society for research in child development.) 28 (2): 73-112.

Mehan, H. (1979). *Learning lessons*. Cambridge, Mass.: Harvard University Press.

Merritt, M. (1979). Service-like events during individual work time and their contribution to the nature of the rules for communication. NIE Report EP 78-0436.

Ninio, A., & Bruner, J. (1978). The achievement and antecedents of labelling. *Journal of Child Language* 5: 1-15.

Payne, C., & Bennett, C. (1977). "Middle class aura" in public schools. *The Teacher Educator* 13 (1): 16-26.

Peters, A. (1977). Language learning strategies. *Language* 53: 560-73.

Scollon, R., & Scollon, S. (1979). The literate two-year old: The fictionalization of self. *Working Papers in Sociolinguistics.* Austin, Tex: Southwest Regional Laboratory.

Sinclair, J. M., & Coulthard, R. M. (1975). *Toward an analysis of discourse.* New York: Oxford University Press.

Sutton-Smith, B. (1981). *The folkstories of children.* Philadelphia: University of Pennsylvania Press.

Umiker-Sebeok, J. D. (1979). Preschool children's intraconversational narratives. *Journal of Child Language* 6 (1): 91-110.

Witkin, H., Paterson, F., Goodenough, R., & Birnbaum, J. (1966). Cognitive patterning in mildly retarded boys. *Child Development* 37 (2): 301-16.

First presented at the Terman Conference on Teaching at Stanford University, 1980, this paper has benefitted from the cooperation with M. Cochran-Smith of the University of Pennsylvania. She shares an appreciation of the relevance of Roland Barthes' work for studies of the socialization of young children into literacy; her research (1981) on the story-reading practices of a mainstream school-oriented nursery school provides a much needed detailed account of early school orientation to literacy.

[1] Terms such as *mainstream* or *middle-class* cultures or social groups are frequently used in both popular and scholarly writings without careful definition. Moreover, numerous studies of behavioral phenomena (for example, mother-child interactions in language learning) either do not specify that the subjects being described are drawn from mainstream groups or do not recognize the importance of this limitation. As a result, findings from this group are often regarded as universal. For a discussion of this problem, see Chanan and Gilchrist 1974, Payne and Bennett 1977. In general, the literature characterizes this group as school-oriented, aspiring toward upward mobility through formal institutions, and providing enculturation which positively values routines of promptness, linearity (in habits ranging from furniture arrangement to entrance into a movie theatre), and evaluative and judgmental responses to behaviors which deviate from their norms.

In the United States, mainstream families tend to locate in neighborhoods and suburbs around cities. Their social interactions center not in their immediate neighborhoods, but around voluntary associations across the city. Thus a cluster of mainstream families (and not a community — which usually implies a specific geographic territory as the locus of a majority of social interactions) is the unit of comparison used here with the Trackton and Roadville communities.

[2] Behind this discussion are findings from cross-cultural psychologists who have studied the links between verbalization of task and demonstration of skills in a hierarchical sequence, e.g., Childs and Greenfield 1980; see Goody 1979 on the use of questions in learning tasks unrelated to a familiarity with books.

[3] Cf. Umiker-Sebeok's (1979) description of stories of mainstream middle-class children, ages 3-5, and Sutton-Smith 1981.

Man at the
Mercy of Language
by Peter Farb

Every human being is creative both in putting together novel statements and in employing them in various speech situations. Yet no one is free to employ his innate capacity in any way he wishes. Indeed, freedom of speech does not exist anywhere, for every community on earth forbids the use of certain sounds, words, and sentences in various speech situations. In the American speech community, for example, the habitual liar faces social sanctions—and criminal punishment should he lie under oath. Speakers are not allowed to misrepresent what they are selling, to defame other people in public, to maliciously shout "Fire!" in a crowded movie theater, or to utter obscenities on the telephone. In addition, less obvious constraints upon freedom of speech may exist. They may be the structures of languages themselves—and they may restrict the speaker as rigidly as do the community's social sanctions.

Every moment of the day the world bombards the human speaker with information and experiences. It clamors for his attention, claws at his senses, intrudes into his thoughts. Only a very small portion of this total experience is language—yet the speaker must use this small portion to report on all the experiences that exist or ever existed in the totality of the world since time began. Try to think about the stars, a grasshopper, love or hate, pain, anything at all—and it must be done in terms of language. There is no other way; thinking is language spoken to oneself. Until language has made sense of experience, that experience is meaningless.

This inseparableness of everything in the world from language has intrigued modern thinkers, most notably Ludwig Wittgenstein, of Cambridge University, who was possibly this century's most influential philosopher. He stated the problem very directly: "The limits of my language mean the limits of my world." Wittgenstein offered pessimistic answers to questions about the ability of language to reveal the world. He claimed that language limited his capacity to express certain ideas and opinions; nevertheless, he did manage to say a great deal about topics he felt were inexpressible. By the time of his death in 1951, Wittgenstein had arrived at a more positive view of language. If its limits—that is, the precise point at which sense becomes nonsense—could somehow be defined, then speakers would not attempt to express the inexpressible. Therefore, said Wittgenstein, do not put too great a burden upon language. Learn its limitations and try to accommodate yourself to them, for language offers all the reality you can ever hope to know.

For tens, and perhaps hundreds, of thousands of years, people regarded language as a holy instrument that let them look out upon the world in wonder and fear and joy. "In the beginning was the Word" is the reassuring first line of the Gospel According to St. John. Only in the last few decades have people suspected that their window on the world has a glass that gives a distorted view. Language no longer is certain to open up new sights to the imagination; rather, it is thought by some to obscure the vision of reality. The French philosopher Jean-Paul Sartre, who has often written about what he calls today's "crisis of language," has stated: "Things are divorced from their names. They are there, grotesque, headstrong, gigantic, and it seems ridiculous to … say anything at all about them: I am in the midst of things, nameless things." Indeed, in this century many of the foundation "things" of civilization—God, truth, fact, humanity, freedom, good and evil—have become nameless and have lost their traditional reference points. An entire generation has grown up that distrusts language's ability to express a true picture of reality and relies upon the empty intercalations of *like, you know, I mean*. The world has grown inarticulate at the very time that an unprecedented number of words flood the media. The output has burgeoned, but speakers have retreated into the worn paths of stock phrases. A statistical study of telephone speech showed that a vocabulary of only 737 words was used in 96 per cent of such conversations. Apparently people speak more, yet say less.

Exaggerated anxieties about language's ability to express reality result in the pathology of "logophobia" (literally, "fear of words"). Logophobia has found popular expression in recent decades in the movement known as General Semantics. Two books with this point of view have had a wide readership—Stuart Chase's *Tyranny of Words* and S.I. Hayakawa's *Language in Action*—and both derive their ideas largely from the writings of a Polish count. Alfred Korzybski (1879-1950) was an engineer, an officer in the Russian army, an official at the League of Nations, and a researcher into mental illness after he migrated to the United States. The key element in his theory about language was: "The map does not represent all of the territory." That is, no matter how much detail a cartographer puts into a drawing of a map, it can never represent all of the ridges, slopes, valleys, and hillocks in a territory. Korzybski similarly believed that language can no more say everything about an event than the map can show everything in a territory. *The grass is green* cannot be a true utterance because it is incomplete. What kind of grass? Where is it growing? What shade of green is meant?

Korzybski felt that speakers could nevertheless emancipate themselves from the tyranny of language by changing their orientation. They must imitate mathematics as a way to state precise relationships between things; they must avoid abstractions; they must be wary of the troublesome word *is* because it often implies an identification that does not exist in reality. Freedom from language's distortions would be achieved by rigorously rating all statements to determine whether speakers could back them up. And no longer would general words that expressed categories be acceptable. A *cow* would not be just a cow, but a particular kind of animal, with certain characteristics, named "Elsie" or "Bossie."

Almost all linguists reject Korzybski's theories on the basis of their logophobia and their inadequate solutions. Nevertheless, he did isolate a logical contradiction: Language is supposed to communicate experience, yet by its very nature it is incapable of doing so. A moment's thought reveals how ill-equipped language is to render a true account of an experience. Picture an autumn scene with a single leaf close up: its color scarlet and edged with burnished gold, the spaces between the veins eaten out by insects in a filigree pattern, the edges gracefully curled, the different textures of the upper and lower surfaces, the intense light of Indian summer falling on the leaf. And this leaf which I have scarcely begun to describe is only one out of the countless millions that surround a stroller in the autumn woods, each unique in its color and shape, the way it catches the light and flutters in the breeze.

How can language possibly render such an experience? The obvious fact is that it cannot—and few people would want it to, for such detail would bog down language in a morass of trivial observations. People do not demand that language describe an entire experience, even if it could. No one confuses speech about a leaf with a real leaf any more than people confuse a painting of a leaf with a leaf. The function of language is not to duplicate reality, but to recall it, comment upon it, and make predictions about it. A much more significant limitation upon language is that each language can comment upon experience only in its own way. Some languages of interior New Guinea, for example, are severely hampered in conveying even leaf color because they lack a convenient terminology to describe colors other than black and white.

Since human beings are born with the same senses and approximately the same degree of intelligence, they should be able to report equally well whatever they experience. But different languages make such equality difficult to achieve. Imagine two forest rangers, one a white speaker of Standard English and the other an Indian speaker of Navaho, riding together on inspection in Arizona. They notice a broken wire fence. When they return to their station, the English-speaking ranger reports *A fence is broken*. He is satisfied that he has perceived the situation well and has reported it conscientiously. The Navaho, though, would consider such a report vague and perhaps even meaningless. His report of the same experience would be much different in Navaho—simply because his language demands it of him.

First of all, a Navaho speaker must clarify whether the "fence" is animate or inanimate; after all, the "fence" might refer to the slang for a receiver of stolen goods or to a fence lizard. The verb the Navaho speaker selects from several alternatives will indicate that the fence was long, thin, and constructed of many strands, thereby presumably wire (the English-speaking ranger's report failed to mention whether the fence was wood, wire, or chain link). The Navaho language then demands that a speaker report with precision upon the act of breaking; the Indian ranger must choose between two different verbs that tell whether the fence was broken by a human act or by some nonhuman agency such as a windstorm. Finally, the verb must indicate the present status of the fence, whether it is stationary or is, perhaps, being whipped by the wind. The Navaho's report would translate something like this: "A fence (which belongs to a particular category of inanimate things, constructed of long and thin material composed of many strands) is (moved to a position, after which it is now at rest) broken (by nonhumans, in a certain way)." The Navaho's report takes about as long to utter as the English-speaking ranger's, but it makes numerous distinctions that it never occurred to the white ranger to make, simply because the English language does not oblige him to make them.

Each language encourages its speakers to tell certain things and to ignore other things. *The women bake a cake* is an acceptable English sentence. Speakers of many other languages, though, would regard it as inadequate and would demand more specific information, such as whether exactly two women or more than two women did the baking, and whether the women are nearby or distant. Some languages would force their speakers to select a word for "cake" that tells whether the cake is round or rectangular and whether or not the cake is visible to the listener at the time of speaking. Many languages are not as concerned as English that the tense of the verb tell whether the cake was baked in the past, is being baked now, or will be baked in the future—although some languages make even finer distinctions of tense than English does. Several American Indian languages of the Pacific Northwest divide the English past tense into recent past, remote past, and mythological past.

The way people talk about the color spectrum, and even perceive it, varies from one speech community to another, although all human eyes see the same colors because colors have their own reality in the physical world. Color consists of visible wavelengths which blend imperceptibly into one another. No sharp breaks in the spectrum separate one color from another, such as orange from red. But when speakers in most European communities look at a rainbow, they imagine they see six sharp bands of color: red, orange, yellow, green, blue, and purple. Chopping the continuous spectrum of the rainbow into color categories in this way is an arbitrary division made by European speech communities. People elsewhere in the world, who speak languages unrelated to European ones, have their own ways of partitioning the color spectrum. The Shona of Rhodesia and the Bassa of Liberia, for example, have fewer color categories than speakers of European languages, and they also break up the spectrum at different points, as the diagrams show:

Figure One

English

/ red / orange / yellow / green / blue / purple /

Shona

/ cipsuka / cicena / citema / cipsuka /

Bassa

/ ziza / hui /

The Shona speaker divides the spectrum into three portions, which he pronounces approximately as *cipsuka, cicena,* and *citema* (*cipsuka* appears twice because it refers to colors at both the red end and the purple end of the spectrum). Of course, the Shona speaker is able to perceive and to describe other colors—in the same way that a speaker of English knows that *light orangish yellow* is a variant of yellow—but the Shona's basic divisions represent the portions of the spectrum for which his language has convenient labels.

Charts obtainable at paint stores provide samples of hundreds of colors to help homeowners select the exact ones they want. An English speaker who glances quickly at one of these charts recognizes certain colors and can name them immediately as *yellow, green,* and so forth. Other colors require a moment of hesitation before the speaker finally decides that a particular hue falls into the category of, let us say, *green* rather than *yellow.* Still other colors demand not only considerable thought but also a hyphenated compromise, such as *greenish-yellow.* Finally, the English speaker finds himself totally unable to name many colors by any of the categories available to him; he is forced to make up his own term or to use a comparison, such as *It looks like the color of swamp water.* The ease with which verbal labels can be attached to colors is known as "codability." The color that a speaker of English unhesitatingly describes as *green* has high codability for him, and it also evokes a quick response from speakers of his language, who immediately know what hues fall into that category. Similarly, when a Shona says *citema,* a high-codability color, other members of his speech community immediately know that he refers to "greenish-blue." In contrast, the color that a speaker describes as *like swamp water* has low codability, which means that other speakers cannot be certain exactly what color is intended.

Some linguists have found in color codability a fruitful way to experiment with the relationships between thought and language. In one such experiment, people who served as test subjects were shown a large selection of plastic squares, each colored differently. Usually, when someone sees a color, his mind stores it for a mere few moments and he can identify the color again only if he sees it almost immediately. If a delay occurs, the stored image is no longer a reliable guide because it has become faint and distorted. Yet when the squares were hidden from sight even for several minutes, the test subjects could pick out again certain colors—the high-codability ones for which the English language has convenient labels like *red, blue, yellow*, and so on. Subjects were able to remember the high-codability colors because they had simply attached common English-language words to them. In other words, they stored colors in their minds not as colors but as verbal labels for them. Even though the images had completely faded from their memories after a few moments, the subjects still remembered the verbal labels they had given the colors—and they were therefore able to identify the plastic square again. The human being's ability to encode experience in this way is not limited to color. Similar experiments have been performed with other experiences, such as the recognition of facial expressions, and the results have been the same.

Experiments like these have shown that at least one aspect of human thought—memory—is strongly influenced by language. That is not the same thing, however, as proving that man is at the mercy of his language. The convenient labels that a speech community gives to certain colors are a great aid in remembering them, but the absence of such labels does not prohibit a community from talking about the low codability colors. When people develop a need for an expanded color vocabulary—as have artists, decorators, and fashion designers—they simply invent one. Witness the recent plethora of colors for decorating the home: *riviera blue, alpine green, lime frost, birch gray*, and so forth.

Nevertheless, the colors that a speaker "sees" often depend very much upon the language he speaks, because each language offers its own high-codability color terms. Recently, two anthropologists at the University of California, Brent Berlin and Paul Kay, have attempted to show that speech communities follow an evolutionary path in the basic color terms they offer their speakers. For example, several New Guinea tribes have in their vocabularies only two basic color words, which translate roughly as "black" (or "dark") and "white" (or "light"). A greater number of languages in widely separated areas of the world possess three color terms—and the startling fact is that they usually retain words for "black" and "white" and add the same third color, "red." The languages that have four color terms retain "black," "white," and "red"—and almost always add either "green" or "yellow." Languages with five color terms add the "green" or the "yellow" that was missed at the fourth level, with the result that nearly all such languages have words for "black" (or "dark"), "white" (or "light"), "red," "green," and "yellow," and for no other colors. Languages with six terms add a word for "blue," and those with seven terms add a word for "brown."

The completely unanticipated inference of this study is that the languages of the world, regardless of their grammars, follow an evolutionary sequence, at least so far as color terms go. A language usually does not have a word that means "brown" unless it already has the six earlier color words. A language rarely has "blue" in its vocabulary unless it already has words for both "green" and "yellow." (English, and most western European languages, Russian, Japanese, and several others add four additional color terms—"gray," "pink," "orange," and "purple"—but these languages do not do so until they already offer the seven previous color terms.) Berlin and Kay believe that a language, at any given point in time, can be assigned to only one stage of basic color terms and apparently must have passed through the prior stages in the appropriate sequence. Such regularity on the part of unrelated languages in adding color terms is astonishing, and no one has as yet offered a suitable explanation for it.

Berlin and Kay have also correlated this sequence with the general complexity of the cultures in which the languages are spoken. Languages with only the two color terms "black" and "white" are spoken in cultures at a very simple level of technology—and the only languages known to have all eleven terms are spoken in cultures with a long history of complexity. Between these two extremes are the languages of such people as the Tiv of Africa with three terms, the Homeric Greeks and Ibo of Africa with four terms, the Bushmen of Africa and the Eskimos of North America with five, and the Mandarin Chinese as well as the Hausa and Nupe of Africa with six. Of course, it is understandable that cultures have more need to talk about different colors as they grow more complex. Small bands of New Guinea hunters need to evaluate the darkness of shadows which might conceal enemies or animal prey; complex European cultures need additional terms to talk about color-coded electrical circuits. Even since Berlin and Kay put forth in 1969 their startling analysis of the basic color terms in ninety-eight languages, their findings have been under attack, primarily on the basis of questioned methodology and ethnocentric bias. But their general conclusions have also been defended by other researchers. Apparently Berlin and Kay have isolated some general truths about how people around the world talk about color and the possible evolutionary implications of language—even though neither they nor anyone else has been able to offer a suitable explanation for why languages seem to add words for color to their vocabularies in such an orderly sequence.

Nor is the way in which a speech community rounds off its numbers haphazard; rather it is explainable as an interplay between language and culture. Americans and Englishmen have traditionally expressed excellence in sports by certain round numbers—the 4-minute mile, the 7-foot high jump, the 70-foot shot put, the .300 baseball batting average. Once a speech community has established a general range of goals of excellence that are within the realm of possibility, the exact number chosen has little to do with the objective reality of measurable goals. Instead, the community chooses an exact goal that makes sense to it linguistically in terms of the measure it uses and the way it rounds off numbers. That is why Americans and Englishmen never talk about the 37/8-minute mile or the 69-foot shot put.

The American-British target for the 100-yard dash is 9 seconds, but the French speech community, which uses the metric system, expresses the target as 100 meters in 10 seconds. Simple arithmetic shows that the two goals do not refer to equal distance covered in comparable amounts of time. Allowing for 10 seconds of running time, the metric race would mean covering 109.36 yards and the American-British race would mean covering 111.1 yards., Obviously, the French goal for excellence speaks about a different real distance than the American or English— simply because a Frenchman rounds off his numbers for distances and for time in different ways than English-speaking peoples do. When speakers thus round off numbers to make them manageable, they give preference to those numbers that their speech community regards as significant. Americans see nothing wrong with rounding off numbers to 4 because they are familiar with that number for measurement, as in 4 ounces in a quarter pound or 4 quarts in a gallon. A Frenchman, however, would not regard such a number as round at all; because of his familiarity with the decimal system, he would round off to 5.

A speech community's method of rounding off its numbers often bears no relation to the real situation, and it may actually work against the best interests of the community. Fishing laws in some states specify, for example, that half a dozen trout larger than 10 inches may be caught in a day. Research by fish-management specialists might instead indicate that trout would thrive better if fishermen took 7 (not half a dozen) trout larger than 10½ (not 10) inches—but Americans round off to 6 and 10 not to 7 and 10½. The ideal speed for a stretch of highway, as scientifically determined by engineers, might be 57 miles per hour—but that number will be rounded off to a too-slow 55 or a too-fast 60 because it is customary for highway speeds to be based on the decimal system. Only one justification exists for the use of imprecise rounded numbers: The speech community has decreed that the linguistic ease of inexact combinations is preferable to the linguistic complexity of precise numbers.

That the way speakers round off numbers is often a linguistic convenience is clearly seen by comparing English with other languages. The ancient Greeks rounded off to 60 and 360 for their high numbers; and the old Germanic languages of northern Europe used 120 to mean "many." Most of the Indian tribes in primeval California based their numbers on multiples of 5 and 10. However, at least half a dozen tribes found great significance in the number 4, no doubt because it expressed the cardinal directions. Others emphasized the number 6, which probably represented the four directions plus the above-ground and below-ground worlds. The Yuki of Northern California were unique in counting in multiples of 8 and in rounding off high numbers at 64.

A misunderstanding about the way Chinese speakers round off their numbers has led many Europeans to state glibly that "in China you're a year old when you're born." That is because most European systems of stating one's age are different from the Chinese. In English, a speaker usually states his age as his most recent birthday followed by the measure *years old*. Exceptions are young children who often place their age between birthdays, as in *I'm three and a half years old*, and parents who usually express the age of the infants in months and weeks. Chinese also use a round number followed by the measure *swei* in place of the English measure *years old*. Confusion has resulted because *swei* is not exactly equivalent to the English measure but rather is closer in meaning to "the number of years during all or part of which one has been alive." In the case of newborn infants, they have, according to the *swei* measure, already lived for "part" of a year—and therefore their age is *yi swei*, which English translators usually render erroneously as "one year old" instead of as "part of one year."

Each language also encourages certain kinds of place names and makes difficult the formation of others. *Golden Gate* is a typical English place name, a noun *(Gate)* modified by an adjective *(Golden)*—but *Gately Gold* is an improbable construction in English and no place is likely to bear such a name. The importance of a language's structure in determining place names was pointed out by the anthropologist Franz Boas when he compared terms used by the Kwakiutl Indians and the Eskimos. The Kwakiutl are a seafaring people of British Columbia, Canada, whose survival is based almost solely on what they can wrest from the Pacific Ocean and the nearby rivers. So it is no wonder that their place names rarely celebrate history or myth but instead are descriptive in order to give practical benefits in navigation and in food-gathering, such as Island at the Foot of the Mountains, Mouth of the River, Having Wind, Place for Stopping, and so on. The Kwakiutl language makes it easy to form descriptive names because suffixes can be conveniently added to stem words. For example, a Kwakiutl speaker can discriminate among a great number of different kinds of islands—Island at the Point, Island in the Middle, and so on—simply by adding the suffixes for "at the point" and "in the middle" to the stem word for "island."

The nearby Eskimos also base their culture on the sea, and so they might be expected to name places in a similar way. But they do not—because the structure of their language makes it very difficult to do so. What are suffixes in Kwakiutl are in Eskimo the very words to which suffixes are added. Eskimos cannot create the name Island at the Point because in their language "at the point" is not a suffix but a stem word to which other words are added. To describe a place as Island at the Point, the Eskimo speaker would have to put together a circumlocution much too complicated for everyday use. Furthermore, the Eskimo language offers its speakers only a limited number of suffixes to attach to stem words, whereas Kwakiutl offers a great many. The result is that Kwakiutl possesses an extraordinarily rich and poetic catalogue of place names— such as Birch Trees at the Mouth of the River and Receptacle of the North Wind, names that make one's heart yearn to visit the places they identify—whereas the Eskimo list is considerably shorter and much less metaphorical.

Eskimos do not differ significantly from Kwakiutls in intelligence, imagination, the ability to abstract, or other mental capacities. Solely because of the structure of his language, the Eskimo fisherman is unable to talk easily about a place the Kwakiutl names Birch Trees at the Mouth of the River. If an Eskimo has no easy way to talk about a clump of birches at the mouth of the river, will he therefore be less alert to perceive that kind of place? And is it possible that language, instead of clarifying reality, forces the Eskimo to think about the world in ways different from speakers of Kwakiutl or other languages?

Such a connection between language and thought is rooted in common-sense beliefs, but no one gave much attention to the matter before Wilhelm von Humboldt, the nineteenth-century German philologist and diplomat. He stated that the structure of a language expresses the inner life of its speakers: "Man lives with the world about him, principally, indeed exclusively, as language presents it." In this century, the case for a close relationship between language and reality was stated by Edward Sapir:

> Human beings do not live in the objective world alone, nor alone in the world of social activity as ordinarily understood, but are very much at the mercy of the particular language which has become the medium for their society.... The fact of the matter is that the 'real world' is to a large extent built up on the language habits of the group. No two languages are ever sufficiently similar to be considered as representing the same social reality. The worlds in which different societies live are distinct worlds, not merely the same world with different labels attached.

About 1932 one of Sapir's students at Yale, Benjamin Lee Whorf, drew on Sapir's ideas and began an intensive study of the language of the Hopi Indians of Arizona. Whorf's brilliant analysis of Hopi placed common-sense beliefs about language and thought on a scientific basis—and it also seemed to support the view that man is a prisoner of his language. Whorf concluded that language "is not merely a reproducing instrument for voicing ideas but rather is itself the shaper of ideas.... We dissect nature along lines laid down by our native languages."

Whorf emphasized grammar—rather than vocabulary, which had previously intrigued scholars—as an indicator of the way a language can direct a speaker into certain habits of thought. The Eskimo speaker, for example, possesses a large and precise vocabulary to make exacting distinctions between the kinds and conditions of seals, such as "young spotted seal," "swimming male ribbon seal," and so on. But such an extensive vocabulary has less to do with the structure of the Eskimo language than with the fact that seals are important for the survival of its speakers. The Eskimo would find equally strange the distinctions that the English vocabulary makes about horses—*mare, stallion, pony, bay, paint, appaloosa,* and so forth. And both Eskimos and Americans would be bewildered by the seventeen terms for cattle among the Masai of Africa, the twenty terms for rice among the Ifugeo of the Philippines, or the thousands of Arabic words associated with camels.

Instead of vocabulary, Whorf concentrated on the differences in structure between Hopi and the European languages—and also on what he believed were associated differences in the ways speakers of these languages viewed the world. In his analysis of plurality, for example, he noted that English uses a plural form for both *five men* and *five days. Men* and *days* are both nouns, but they are otherwise quite different. A speaker can see with his own eyes a group of five men, but he cannot perceive five days through any of his senses. To visualize what a day looks like, the speaker of English has to conjure up some sort of abstract picture, such as a circle, and then imagine a group of five such circles. The Hopi has no such problem. He does not rely on his imagination to provide him with plurals that cannot be detected by his senses. He would never use a cyclic noun—one that refers to "days," "years," or other units of time—in the same way that he would use an aggregate noun ("men"). His language is more precise, and he has a separate category altogether for cycles. For him, cycles do not have plurals but rather duration, and so the Hopi equivalent for the English *He stayed for five days* is "He stayed until the sixth day."

Nor does the Hopi language possess tenses, which in most European languages stand time in a row as distinct units of past, present, and future. A speaker of English expresses an event that is happening in the present as *He runs* or *He is running*, but the speaker of Hopi can select from a much wider choice of present tenses, depending upon his knowledge, or lack of it, about the validity of the statement he is making: "I know that he is running at this very moment." "I know that he is running at this moment even though I cannot see him." "I remember that I saw him running and I presume he is still running." "I am told that he is running."

A further contrast between the two languages concerns duration and intensity. English employs such words as *long, short,* and *slow* for duration and *much, large,* and *high* for intensity. Speakers of English, accustomed to this usage, overlook the fact that these words refer to size, shape, number, or motion—that is, they are really metaphors for space. Such a situation is quite ridiculous because duration and intensity are not spatial. Yet speakers of English unconsciously use these metaphors for space in even the simplest utterances—such as *He SLOWLY grasped the POINT of the LONG story* or *The LEVEL of the assignment was TOO HIGH and so the student considered it A LOT OF nonsense.* The Hopi language is equally striking in its avoidance of metaphors of imaginary space for qualities that are nonspatial.

After his painstaking analysis of such differences between Hopi and European languages, Whorf asked the question that was central to his research. Do the Hopi and European cultures confirm the fact that their languages conceptualize reality in different ways? And his answer was that they do. Whereas European cultures are organized in terms of space and time, the Hopi culture, Whorf believed, emphasizes events. To speakers of European languages, time is a commodity that occurs between fixed points and can be measured. Time is said to be *wasted* or *saved;* an army fighting a rear-guard action tries to *buy* time; a television station *sells* time to an advertiser. People in the European tradition keep diaries, records, accounts, and histories; their economic systems emphasize wages paid for the amount of time worked, rent for the time a dwelling is occupied, interest for the time money is loaned.

Hopi culture has none of these beliefs about time, but instead thinks of it in terms of events. Plant a seed—and it will grow. The span of time the growing takes is not the important thing, but rather the way in which the event of growth follows the event of planting. The Hopi is concerned that the sequence of events in the construction of a building be in the correct order, not that it takes a certain amount of time to complete the job. That is why the building of a Hopi house, adobe brick by adobe brick, may go on for years. Whorf's comparison of Hopi and European languages and cultures—considerably more involved than the summary I have presented—convinced him that the contrasting world views of their speakers resulted from contrasts in their languages. He concluded that, linguistically speaking, no human being is born free; his mind was made up for him from the day he was born by the language of his speech community. Whorf questioned people's ability to be objective, and he threw into doubt the rationality of everyday utterances. He suggested that all their lives English speakers have been tricked by their language into thinking along certain channels—and it is small consolation to know that the Hopi has also been tricked, but in a different way.

Whorf's theories about the relationship between culture and language have been greeted enthusiastically by some scholars and attacked or treated warily by others. The weakness of the Sapir-Whorf Hypothesis, as it has come to be known, is the impossibility of generalizing about entire cultures and then attributing these generalizations to the languages spoken. The absence of clocks, calendars, and written histories obviously gave the Hopis a different view of time than that found among speakers of European languages. But such an observation is not the same thing as proving that these cultural differences were caused by the differences between Hopi and European grammars. In fact, an interest in time-reckoning is not characteristic solely of European cultures but can be found among speakers of languages as different as Egyptian, Chinese, and Maya. And, on the other hand, thousands of unrelated speech communities share with the Hopis a lack of concern about keeping track of time. To attempt to explain cultural differences and similarities as a significant result of the languages spoken is to leave numerous facts about culture unexplained. The great religions of the world—Judaism, Christianity, Hinduism, and Mohammedanism—have flourished among diverse peoples who speak languages with sharply different grammars. Mohammedanism, for example, has been accepted by speakers of languages with grammars as completely different as those of the Hamito-Semitic, Turkish, Indo-Iranian, Tibeto-Burman, and Malayo-Polynesian families. And the reverse is true as well. Cultures as diverse as the Aztec Empire of Mexico and the Ute hunting bands of the Great Basin spoke very closely related tongues.

Nevertheless, attempts have been made to prove the Sapir-Whorf Hypothesis, such as one experiment which used as test subjects bilingual Japanese women, living in San Francisco, who had married American servicemen. The women spoke English to their husbands, children, and neighbors, and in most everyday speech situations; they spoke Japanese whenever they came together to gossip, reminisce, and discuss the news from home. Each Japanese woman thus inhabited two language worlds—and according to the predictions of the hypothesis, the women should think differently in each of these worlds. The experiment consisted of two visits to each woman by a bilingual Japanese interviewer. During the first interview he chatted with them only in Japanese; during the second he carried on the same discussion and asked the same questions in English. The results were quite remarkable; they showed that the attitudes of each woman differed markedly, depending upon whether she spoke Japanese or English. Here, for example, is the way the same woman completed the same sentences at the two interviews:

> "When my wishes conflict with my family's...
> ... it is a time of great unhappiness." (Japanese)
> ... I do what I want." (English)
> "Real friends should...
> ... help each other." (Japanese)
> ... be very frank." (English)

Clearly, major variables in the experiment had been eliminated—since the women were interviewed twice by the same person in the same location of their homes, and they discussed the same topics—with but one exception. And that sole exception was language. The drastic differences in attitudes of the women could be accounted for only by the language world each inhabited when she spoke.

The Sapir-Whorf Hypothesis also predicts that language makes its speakers intellectually lazy. They will categorize new experiences in the well-worn channels they have been used to since birth, even though these channels might appear foolish to an outsider. The language spoken by the Western Apaches of Arizona, for example, has long had its own channels for classifying the parts of the human body, a system which ignores certain distinctions made in other languages and which makes different ones of its own. Then, about 1930, a new cultural item, the automobile, was introduced into the Apache reservation. An automobile, surely, is different from a human body, yet the Apaches simply applied their existing classification for the human body to the automobile. Figure Two lists approximate pronunciations of the Apache words for the parts of the human body, the way they are categorized—and the way their meanings were extended to classify that new cultural item, the automobile.

Figure Two

Apache Words for Parts of the Human Body and the Automobile

	Human Anatomical Terms	Extended Auto Meanings
External Anatomy:		
daw	"chin and jaw"	"front bumper"
was	"shoulder"	"front fender"
gun	"hand and arm"	"front wheel"
kai	"thigh and buttocks"	"rear fender"
ze	"mouth"	"gas-pipe opening"
ke	"foot"	"rear wheel"
chun	"back"	"chassis"
inda	"eye"	"headlight"
Face:		
chce	"nose"	"hood"
ta	"forehead"	"auto top"
Entrails:		
tsaws	"vein"	"electrical wiring"
zik	"liver"	"battery"
pit	"stomach"	"gas tank"
chih	"intestine"	"radiator hose"
jih	"heart"	"distributor"
jisoleh	"lung"	"radiator"

Many linguists nowadays are wary of the Sapir-Whorf Hypothesis. Research that has attempted to confirm the hypothesis, such as the experiment with the Japanese women or the study of Apache terms for the automobile, is usually regarded as producing fascinating examples rather than universal truths about the way speech communities view the world. Neither Whorf nor any of his followers has proven to everyone's satisfaction that differences between two speech communities in their capacity to understand external reality are based entirely or even overwhelmingly on differences in their languages. Whorf overemphasized one point (that languages differ in what *can* be said in them) at the expense of a greater truth (that they differ as to what is *relatively easy* to express in them). Languages, rather than causing cultural differences between speech communities, seem instead to reflect the different cultural concerns of their speakers. The history of language is not so much the story of people misled by their languages as it is the story of a successful struggle against the limitations built into all language systems. The Western Apache system for classifying the human body did not lock them into certain habitual patterns of thought that prevented them from understanding the automobile.

In fact, the existence of these patterns may have aided the Apaches in making sense out of that new cultural item.

The true value of Whorf's theories is not the one he worked so painstakingly to demonstrate—that language tyrannizes speakers by forcing them to think in certain ways. Rather, his work emphasized something of even greater importance: the close alliance between language and the total culture of the speech community. No linguist today doubts that language and culture interpenetrate one another; nor does any linguist fail to pay due respect to Whorf for emphasizing this fact.

References

Basso, Keith H. 1967. "Semantic Aspects of Linguistic Acculturation." *American Anthropologist*, vol. 69, pp. 471-477.

Berlin, Brent and Kay, Paul. 1969. *Basic Color Terms: Their Universality and Evolution.* University of California Press.

Brown, Roger and Lenneberg, Eric H. 1954. "A Study in Language and Cognition." *Journal of Abnormal and Social Psychology*, vol. 49, pp. 454-462.

Ervin-Tripp, Susan. 1964. "Interaction of Language, Topic and Listener." *American Anthropologist*, vol. 66, pp. 86-102.

Ferguson, Charles A. 1968. "Language Development." In Fishman, Ferguson, C.A., and Das Gupta, J., editors. 1968. *Language Problems of Developing Nations.* Wiley.

Fridja, N.H., and Van de Geer, J.P. 1961. "Codeability and Facial Expressions." *Acta Psychologica*, vol. 18, pp. 360-367.

Gleason, Henry A., Jr. 1961. *An Introduction to Descriptive Linguistics.* Holt, Rinehart & Winston, revised edition.

Hays, David G., et al. 1972. "Color Term Salience." *American Anthropologist*, vol. 74, pp. 1107-1121.

Heider, Eleanor R. 1972 A. "Universals in Color Naming and Memory." *Journal of Experimental Psychology*, vol. 93, pp. 10-20.

_____. 1972 B. "The Structure of the Color Space in Naming and Memory for Two Languages." *Cognitive Psychology*, vol. 3, pp. 337-354.

Heizer, R.F., and Whipple, M.A. 1951. *The California Indians.* University of California Press.

Hoijer, Harry, editor. 1954. *Language in Culture.* University of Chicago Press.

Hymes, Dell H., editor. 1964. *Language in Culture and Society: A Reader in Linguistics and Anthropology.* Harper & Row.

_____. 1961. "Functions of Speech: An Evolutionary Approach." In *Anthropology and Education*, edited by Frederick C. Gruber (1961), pp. 55-83. University of Pennsylvania Press.

Lotz, John. "On Language and Culture." In Hymes (1964), pp. 182-183.

Menninger, Karl. 1969. *Number Words and Number Symbols.* M.I.T. Press.

Nickerson, Nancy P. 1971. "Review of *Basic Color Terms.*" *International Journal of American Linguistics*, vol. 37, pp. 257-270.

Sapir, Edward. 1929. "The Status of Linguistics as a Science." *Language*, vol. 5, pp. 207-214.

Sartre, Jean-Paul. 1959. *Nausea.* New Directions.

Swadesh, Morris. 1971. *The Origin and Diversification of Language*, edited by Joel Sherzer, Aldine-Atherton.

Whorf, Benjamin L. 1956. *Language, Thought and Reality.* M.I.T. Press.

Wittgenstein, Ludwig. 1963. *Tractatus Logico-Philosophicus.* Humanities Press, second edition.

Questions For Discussion

1.　Is nonverbal behavior culturally determined? Discuss the answer on the basis of Irujo's article.

2.　In the article on nonverbal communication, the author makes a distinction between emic and etic approaches to the study of cultural issues. Review this section of the paper and attempt to give examples, in your own words, of both approaches.

3.　Give an example from your own experience or that of someone you know which illustrates the misunderstanding or embarrassment which can be caused by cultural differences in nonverbal behavior.

4.　Think of eight emblems of your culture (gestures which have specific meanings, such as the index finger on the lips to indicate "shhh"). Find out from a native of another country whether these gestures exist in his or her culture and whether they have the same meanings.

5.　In the article, "Communicative Competence, a Historical and Cultural Perspective," the authors examine the different notions of verbal competence. Outline the main distinctions made by them and state your agreement and/or disagreement with the different perspectives.

6.　The authors of the article "Communicative Competence" state the following in their conclusion: "Educators can view their task as one of providing children the experiential opportunity to exercise these [linguistic] competences in new areas rather than as having to 'eliminate bad spirits.'" What is the meaning of this statement? How do the authors justify it?

7.　In "What No Bedtime Story Means" the author makes the following comparison: "In Trackton children learn to talk, in Roadville adults teach them how to talk." What are the implications of these distinctions for the school achievement of these two cultural groups?

8.　On the basis of "What No Bedtime Story Means" compare your own socialization into language with the distinctions presented in the article.

9.　Does language shape our attitudes and perceptions or do the latter shape language? Speculate on the basis of the issues discussed in "Man at the Mercy of Language."

D. CULTURE AND THOUGHT

Cognitive Styles and Cultural Democracy in Action

by Manuel Ramirez III

The emphasis on acculturation in the melting pot ideology,[1] which has been adopted by most educational institutions, has contributed to the continuance of the assumption that values and life styles which differ from those of the middle class United States are inferior and must be abandoned. Cubberly, a renowned American educator, supported this belief. Referring to people of minority groups who had settled in urban centers of the East Coast, he stated:

> ...everywhere these people settle in groups or settlements, and ...set up their national manners, customs, and observances. Our task is to break up these groups or settlements, to assimilate and amalgamate these people as a part of our American race, and to implant in their children, as far as can be done, the Anglo-Saxon conception of righteousness, law and order, and our popular government, and to awaken in them a reverence for our democratic institutions and for those things in our national life which we as a people hold to be of abiding worth.[2]

This attitude has led to the use of the family-is-damaging model[3] in the development of educational programs for people of minority groups in this country. In fact, in the case of some ethnic groups, it would be more accurate to say that a *culture*-is-damaging model has been applied. That is, the cultures of some ethnic groups (particularly blacks, Indians, and peoples of La Raza) have been viewed by educational institutions as interfering with the intellectual and emotional development of children and hindering the development of life styles and values typical of mainstream U. S. culture.[4]

Chicano culture has long been viewed as inferior by educational institutions. The belief that Spanish interferes with the Chicano child's ability to learn English and that loyalty to his family and ethnic group competes with his loyalty to the "American way of life" is reflected in programs being implemented across the country, many of which are labeled "compensatory."

Many Mexican American children have been assigned to classes for the mentally retarded merely because they do not speak or understand English and/or because they are unfamiliar with information familiar to children of middle-class U. S. culture.

Rejection of Learning Styles

Institutional practices based on the assimilationist melting pot philosophy disregard the individual's experiences in his home and in his barrio. He must either conform to the demands of these institutions or leave them. Rejection of an individual's culture is accompanied by rejection of his established learning, incentive-motivational, human-relational and communication styles. Thus, he is being asked to abandon these styles and to adopt new ones. Instead of reinforcing and utilizing the culturally unique learning and communication styles of members of minority groups, educational institutions have chosen to ignore them and have attempted to impose styles of their own choosing.

Culturally Determined Learning Styles

Culturally unique learning styles represent a critical variable in the education of the culturally different. Lesser and his colleagues have shown that members of different ethnic groups exhibit different patterns of intellectual ability, each group performing better in some areas than in others.[5] The results showed that the intellectual patterns varied for each of four ethnic groups and that the patterns were similar for different socioeconomic groups within the same culture. These findings imply that intellectual patterns observed in these cultural groups, *are manifestations of culturally unique learning styles.* That is, each culture emphasizes the importance of achievement in certain areas. Parents and other agents of socialization employ culturally sanctioned teaching styles to develop certain interests and aptitudes in children.

Kagan and Madsen have compared the performance of Anglo, Mexican, and Mexican American children in cooperative and competitive situations.[6] When rewards could only be earned if the children participating in a task cooperated with each other, Mexican children were the most cooperative, Mexican American children next most cooperative, and Anglo children the least cooperative. When, in turn, the children were given a competitive set on the same task, Anglo children were more competitive than either Mexican or Mexican American children. The School Situations Picture Stories Technique (a variation of the TAT) was administered by Ramirez, Price-Williams, and Beman[7] to Mexican American and Anglo American fourth-grade children of the same socioeconomic status. When the stories were analyzed for need achievement as defined by McClelland and his colleagues[8] Anglo children scored slightly higher than Mexican Americans. When stories were analyzed for need achievement for the family (e.g., the child achieves so that members of his family benefit from his achievement and/ or are proud of him) Mexican American children scored significantly higher than Anglo children. These findings again document cultural differences in children's performance.

Cultural Democracy

Differences in learning styles between members of different ethnic groups are the result of socialization practices reflecting the values of these groups. Institutions which have followed the melting pot philosophy have favored that set of styles characteristic of the United States middle class. Hence, many people in this country have been denied academic, economic, and social success. Educational programs which are not based on the unique learning styles of the people they serve do not provide culturally relevant learning environments and are culturally undemocratic. They reject the cultural background of their students and create conflicts by forcing these students to question the values and learning experiences which they have acquired in their homes and neighborhoods. The results of these practices are reflected in school drop-out rates and in the low levels of educational attainment of members of minority groups. Schools are too often institutions of acculturation rather than of education. If we are to eliminate these undemocratic practices and ensure that educational institutions respect cultural differences evident in our society, we must encourage the adoption of a new philosophy, that of cultural democracy. The right of each individual to be educated in his own learning style must be explicitly acknowledged.

This implies that the individual has a right to maintain a bicultural identity, that is, to retain his identification with his ethnic group while he simultaneously adopts mainstream United States values and life styles. This philosophy encourages institutions to develop learning milieus, curriculum materials, and teaching strategies which are sensitive to the uniqueness each individual brings to the classroom. Because cultural democracy focuses on the importance of the teacher-learner relationship, it implies increased humanism in the educational processes.

Since cognitive styles subsume variables related to learning styles, they can be used to assess both the individual and the institution, permitting determination of the extent to which the institution reflects the styles of the students it serves.

Witkin and his colleagues have identified two cognitive styles—field-dependence and field-independence:

> In a field-dependent mode of perception, the organization of the field as a whole dominates perception of its parts: an item within a field is experienced as fused with organized ground. In a field-independent mode of perception, the person is able to perceive items as discrete from the organized field of which they are a part.[9]

We have selected field dependence/independence as the conceptual framework for our analysis of the relationship of Mexican Americans to educational institutions because it has been studied widely in a cross-cultural context, and because it clearly relates cognitive styles to unique cultural socialization practices.

Although Witkin's conceptual scheme is very useful in implementing cultural democracy in the school, there are some problems connected with it. Too much emphasis has been placed on the presumed advantages of field independence and the disadvantages of field dependence. Field independent socialization styles have been generally described in more favorable value-laden terms than field dependent child-rearing practices.[10] It is only a short step from such descriptions to the conclusion that some cultures are pathological because they interfere with the development of field independent characteristics in children. In fact, Witkin's theory of differentiation could easily lead to the aforementioned conclusion. The theory states that all people are field dependent or undifferentiated at birth. As they develop they become more field independent or differentiated. Relationships between parents and children which lead to field dependence in children are classified as interactions which interfere with the development of differentiation. The concept of differentiation, then, assumes that field dependence is a more "rudimentary" stage of development. Such a presumption excludes the possibility that a field dependent cognitive style may develop independently of a field independent style. In fact, cross-cultural research has shown that members of some cultures tend to be field dependent while people in other cultures tend to be field independent.[11] This would seem to indicate that cultures, through socialization practices, tend to encourage the development of either relatively more field dependent or field independent cognitive styles in children. The fact that most research shows that children in most cultures tend to do better on the Rod and Frame and Embedded Figures Tests[12] as they grow older does not exclude the fact that they may also be becoming more field dependent. There simply is no way to measure development of field dependence at present. That is, the Rod and Frame and Embedded Figures Tests may be adequate measures of field independence but not of field dependence.

The hypothesis that field independence and field dependence are two separate cognitive styles is supported by Cohen, who identifies two conceptual styles—analytic and relational—which are similar to field dependence and field independence:

> ...the analytic cognitive style is characterized by a formal or analytic mode of abstracting salient information from a stimulus or situation and by a stimulus-centered orientation to reality, and it is parts-specific (i.e. parts or attributes of a given stimulus have meaning in themselves). The relational cognitive style, on the other hand, requires a descriptive mode of abstraction and is self centered in its orientation to reality; only the global characteristics of a stimulus have meaning to its users, and these only in reference to some total context.[13]

The fact that field dependent and independent cognitive styles may be two separate cognitive styles should not be taken to indicate that a person cannot be both field dependent and field independent. In fact, our observations have led us to conclude that many adults and some children are indeed bicognitive and are able to function in the situationally appropriate style.

There is another caution which should be mentioned with respect to Witkin's conceptual framework, the use of the word "dependence." It is far too easy to make the assumption that what is meant by field dependence is dependent personality. In addition, the word "dependent" is value-laden. For these reasons we have decided to substitute the word "sensitive" for "dependent". (From this point on field sensitive will be used instead of field dependent.) As can be seen from the research reviewed below, the word "sensitivity" better describes the behavior of people with this cognitive style. It is their greater sensitivity to the social and physical environment which distinguishes them from field independent individuals on many tables.

Preferred Modes of Thinking, Perceiving, Remembering, and Problem-Solving

Early work by Goodenough and Karp,[14] and by Witkin,[15] uncovered an interesting pattern of correlations between measures of cognitive style and different subtests of the Wechsler intelligence scales. The subtests of the Wechsler scales cluster into three major factors: a *verbal* dimension, an *attention-concentration* dimension, and an *analytic* dimension. The only cluster of subtests found to correlate to a significant degree with measures of field sensitivity-independence was that of the analytic dimension. Thus, individuals scoring toward the field independence end of the dimension tended to score higher on such subtests as Block Design, Object Assembly, and Picture Completion. No difference was found between field sensitive and field independent individuals on the other two sub-sets of test items. The frequent finding that field independent individuals tend to score higher on measures of intelligence than field sensitive individuals may be interpreted to indicate an advantage held by field independent subjects in responding to items of the analytic dimension.

Research has also shown that when the test materials are characterized by an abstract or impersonal nature, field independent individuals appear to have an advantage. However, a markedly different pattern becomes evident when the test materials focus on social or human factors. Field sensitive individuals have been found to give longer and more complex stories to picture cards designed to assess verbal expressiveness.[16] Field sensitive individuals appear to remember faces and social words more often than field independent individuals, though their incidental memory for non-social stimuli is not generally superior.[17]

It appears, then, that in some form or another, field sensitive individuals are more influenced by, or more sensitive to the human element in the environment. Field independent individuals have an advantage in testing situations which de-emphasize the human element, situations in which the testing material is relatively more impersonal. They are more able to isolate parts from a whole and are less constrained by conventional uses of objects and materials.

Characteristics which differentiate field sensitive from field independent individuals then, are those which reflect preferred modes of relating to, classifying, assimilating, and organizing the environment. These descriptions do not represent "cultural disadvantage" or "deficiency."

Field Sensitivity-Independence and Incentive-Motivational Styles

The term, "incentive-motivational style" may be defined as a preference for a set of goals and rewards (incentives). These incentives are represented by changes in the environment which indicate, symbolize, or have become associated with support, acceptance, and positive recognition of behavior. Preferred incentives refer to those sets of environmental events which effectively influence behavior. Of concern here is how effectively different environmental events influence, modify, or reinforce behavior.

Examination of the research into differences in incentive-motivational styles again reveals that field sensitive persons are more influenced by the human element in the environment than are field independent persons.

Disapproval and approval (praise) exhibited by an authority figure appears to be more effective with field sensitive children than with field independent children. For example, it has been found that the performance of field sensitive children is depressed when an authority figure indicates disapproval by remarking, for example, "This doesn't seem like the kind of group that can do well; you're not as fast as the other groups." Conversely, field sensitive children are motivated more effectively under conditions in which the authority figure indicates approval through praise, "This is a very bright group; you certainly have caught on faster than most children."[18] The tendency for field sensitive children to seek approval from the authority figure is consistent with the observation that when stress was introduced into a testing situation, field sensitive children tended to orient, or look up to the face of the adult examiner about twice as often as field independent children.

One of the differences between the incentive-motivational styles of field sensitive and field independent individuals is related to the *interpersonal* dimension. For example, field sensitive individuals are more likely to be motivated by those forms of reward which offer personalized support and recognition or acceptance.

Field Sensitivity-Independence and

Interpersonal Perceptions

The concept of field sensitivity-independence provides some interesting and suggestive insights into the dynamics of interpersonal perceptions between student and teacher. In a recent study by Di Stefano,[19] five extremely field independent teachers and five extremely field sensitive teachers were asked to describe 11 students by means of 21 bi-polar semantic differential scales[20] and 25 single adjective scales selected from the Peabody. The students who were described were also classified as field sensitive or field independent, and were asked to describe the teachers in the same manner. Di Stefano's main conclusion was that "people with similar perceptual styles tend to describe each other in highly positive terms, while people whose perceptual styles are different have a strong tendency to describe each other in negative terms."[21] Three other findings are of special interest: (1) teachers tended to rate students of their own perceptual style as more successful than those of the opposite style; (2) field sensitive teachers tended to be slightly more lenient in their grading than field independent teachers, and field independent teachers were more critical in grading field sensitive students; and (3) field independent teachers tended to concentrate on the areas of science and mathematics.[22]

These results demonstrate the possible existence of a somewhat unusual form of professional discrimination. If teachers view students with perceptual styles similar to their own as being more successful, or potentially more successful, they are likely to offer these students more encouragement and possibly higher grades.

Assessing the Cognitive Style of

Mexican Americans

The initial discussion of field sensitivity-independence mentioned its relationship to socialization practices of cultures. Witkin and his colleagues[23] have identified socialization practices related to the development of field sensitivity in children. They have labeled these "the field sensitive socialization cluster."

When the socialization practices of Chicanos from traditional[24] communities are compared with those of the field sensitive socialization cluster, many similarities are found. This is especially true in the area of indicators concerning separation of the child from the mother and family. The Chicano child is encouraged to be responsible and independent, aggressive and assertive, as long as he is achieving for the family and/or protecting it. While the middle-class Anglo is typically encouraged to establish an identity independent of the family, the Chicano from a traditional community is encouraged always to view himself as an integral part of the family. He is reared in an atmosphere which emphasizes the importance of interpersonal relationships. Consequently, he develops great sensitivity to social cues and to the human environment in general. This would lead us to predict that Chicanos reared in traditional communities are likely to be field sensitive.

The results of two studies (one in Houston, Texas, and another in Riverside, California) confirm this prediction. In the Houston study, 120 fourth graders, 60 Mexican Americans, and 60 Anglo children of the same socioeconomic class and religion (Catholic) were tested with the Portable Rod and Frame Test. The results shown in Table 1 indicate that, as predicted, Mexican American children scored in a more field sensitive direction. In the Riverside desegregation study[25] 596 Mexican American and 571 Anglo children from grades kindergarten through six were tested with the Man in the Box, an instrument similar to the Portable Rod and Frame. The results, again, supported the hypothesis that Chicano children are more field sensitive than Anglo children.

TABLE 1

Mean Portable Rod and Frame Test Scores of Mexican American and Anglo American Fourth-Grade Students

	Mexican Americans (N=60)		Anglos (N=60)			
	X	SD	X	SD	t	P
Males	14.56	7.80	6.97	7.07	4.06	<.001
Females	17.26	6.80	9.51	8.71	3.84	<.001

The Field Sensitive Mexican American and the Field Independent Institution

I am hypothesizing that the primary reason for failure of educational institutions to fulfill the needs of the majority of Mexican Americans, and others in this country, is that they are not sensitive to the cognitive styles of these people. That is, these institutions are oriented toward serving the person who is relatively more field independent.

Fifty-three teachers and 711 students of several elementary schools in the Los Angeles metropolitan area, which have high concentrations of Mexican American students, were tested with the Portable Rod and Frame Test. The results presented in Table 2 show that teachers and Mexican American students differ greatly in cognitive style. The teachers are far more field independent.

TABLE 2

Mean Portable Rod and Frame Test Scores of Teachers and Mexican American Students

		Mexican American Students					
Teachers		Grade 1		Grade 4		Grade 6	
M	F	M	F	M	F	M	F
1.83	2.71	18.26	20.21	14.70	16.89	9.43	14.52

Cohen has also found that the curriculum, assessment instruments and learning environments in most schools are biased in the direction of the analytic style, similar to field independence.[26] When one considers the results of the Di Stefano study, it can be concluded that most schools represent culturally undemocratic learning environments for Mexican American children. That is, it could be predicted that Mexican American students are being viewed as less capable by their teachers and are being given lower grades.

Cognitive Styles as Vehicles for Developing Culturally Democratic Learning Environments

Cognitive styles may make it possible to implement the philosophy of cultural democracy in education. Preliminary observations we have made on the teaching strategies of a small sample of field sensitive and field independent elementary school teachers indicate that there is considerable difference in their approaches to teaching. Field sensitive teachers, for example, express more warmth in their relationships with students and appear to be more sensitive to personal feelings and interests of students. Field sensitive teachers also use social rewards, tend to humanize and personalize curriculum materials and are more likely to employ structured guidance and the deductive approach in presenting curriculum to students. Field independent teachers, on the other hand, appear to be more formal and aloof in their relationships with students. Field independents also tend to use more formulas and graphs (mathematical and scientific abstractions) in their class presentations, are more likely to encourage students to work independently and to use the inductive approach in presenting curriculum.

We hope that this research will lead us to techniques which we can employ to train teachers to teach in both styles and also to write curricula and develop assessment instruments which reflect both the field sensitive and field independent styles. The development of such educational environments would allow children of any cultural background to acquire the ability to function in either cognitive style and consequently increase their level of achievement.

This is a revision of a paper presented at the annual meeting of the American Psychological Association, Washington, D.C., September, 1971. The author is indebted to Barbara Goffigon for her help in preparing it. For a more extensive discussion of this topic see Manuel Ramirez and Alfredo Castañeda, *Cultural Democracy in Education and Mexican American Children*, published by Academic Press, 1974 *Editor's Note*: the author of this article chose not to hyphenate "Mexican American" and "Anglo-American."

[1] Alfredo Castañeda, "Melting Potters vs. Cultural Pluralists: Implications for Education" in Alfredo Castañeda, *et al.*, *Mexican-Americans and Educational Change* (Riverside, Calif.: Mexican-American Studies, U. C. R., 1971).

[2] Elwood P. Cubberly, *Changing Conceptions of Education* (Boston: Houghton Mifflin Co., 1909) pp. 15-16.

[3] Robert D. Hess, "Parental Behavior and Children's School Achievement: Implications for Head Start," *Critical Issues in Research Related to Disadvantaged Children* (Princeton, N.J.: Educational Testing Service, 1969).

[4] J. T. Chandler and J. Plakos, "Spanish-Speaking Pupils Classified as Educable Mentally Retarded," (California State Department of Education, 1969).

[5] G. S. Lesser, G. Fifer, and D. H. Clark, "Mental Abilities of Children from Different Social-Class and Cultural Groups," *Monographs of the Society for Research in Child Development,* 102 (1965).

[6] Spencer Kagan and M. C. Madsen, "Cooperation and Competition of Mexican, Mexican-American, and Anglo-American Children of Two Ages Under Four Instructional Sets," *Developmental Psychology*, 5 (July, 1971), pp. 32-39.

[7] Manuel Ramirez, Douglass Price-Williams and Alma Beman, "The Relationship of Culture to Educational Attainment," (Houston: Center for Research in Social Change and Economic Development, Rice University).

[8] D. C. McClelland, J. W. Atkinson, R. A. Clark, and E. L. Lowell, *The Achievement Motive* (New York: Appleton, 1953).

[9] H. Witkin, "A Cognitive Approach to Cross-Cultural Research," *International Journal of Psychology*, 2 (No.4, 1967), p. 236.

[10] Herman A. Witkin, R. B. Dyke, H. F. Paterson, D. R. Goodenough, and S. A. Karp, *Psychological Differentiation* (New York: John Wiley & Sons, 1962).

[11] Witkin, "A Cognitive Approach," pp. 233-250.

[12] The Embedded Figures Test (EFT) requires subjects to find a simple design within a complex one. The Rod and Frame test (RFT) requires subjects to adjust a rod to a position perceived as vertical within a square frame that is tilted. Thus, it is possible to obtain quantitative measures of the extent to which an individual's perception is influenced by, or is more sensitive to the surrounding field.

[13] Rosalie Cohen, "Conceptual Styles, Culture Conflict, and Non-Verbal Tests of Intelligence," *American Anthropologist*, 71 (Oct., 1969), pp. 828-856.

[14] D. R. Goodenough and S. A. Karp, "Field Dependence and Intellectual Functioning," *Journal of Abnormal and Social Psychology*, 63 (March, 1961), pp. 241-246.

[15] Witkin, *et al.*, *Psychological Differentiation*.

[16] *Ibid.*

[17] Samuel Messick and F. Damarin, "Cognitive Styles and Memory for Faces," *Journal of Abnormal Psychology*, 69 (March, 1964), pp. 313-318; and D. Fitzgibbons, L. Goldberger and M. Eagle, "Field Dependence and Memory for Incidental Material," *Perceptual and Motor Skills*, 21 (Dec., 1965), pp. 743-749.

[18] Norma Konstadt and Elaine Forman, "Field Dependence and External Directedness," *Journal of Personality and Social Psychology*, 1 (1965), pp. 490-493.

[19] Joseph J. Di Stefano, "Interpersonal Perceptions of Field Independent and Dependent Teachers and Students," Working Paper Series No. 43. (London, Ontario: University of Western Ontario, Nov., 1970).

[20] C. E. Osgood, G. J. Suci and D. H. Tannenbaum, *The Measurement of Meaning* (Urbana: University of Illinois Press, 1957).

[21] Di Stefano, "Interpersonal Perceptions of Field Independent and Dependent Teachers and Students."

[22] *Ibid.*

[23] Witkin, *et al.*, *Psychological Differentiation*.

[24] For example, Mexican American culture has been described as traditional, dualistic, and atraditional, the first of these being that which most closely identifies with Mexican culture and values, the last, that which has most adopted middle-class American values.

[25] D. Canavan, "Field Dependence in Children as a Function of Grade, Sex, and Ethnic Group Membership," paper presented at the American Psychological Association meeting, 1969, Washington, D. C.

[26] Cohen, "Conceptual Styles, Culture Conflict, and Non-Verbal Tests of Intelligence."

Cultural Thought Patterns in Inter-Cultural Education
by Robert B. Kaplan

The teaching of reading and composition to foreign students does differ from the teaching of reading and composition to American students, and cultural differences in the nature of rhetoric supply the key to the difference in teaching approach.

> ...Rhetoric is a mode of thinking or a mode of 'finding all available means' for the achievement of a designated end. Accordingly, rhetoric concerns itself basically with what goes on in the mind rather than with what comes out of the mouth.... Rhetoric is concerned with factors of analysis, data gathering, interpretation, and synthesis.... What we notice in the environment and how we notice it are both predetermined to a significant degree by how we are prepared to notice this particular type of object.... Cultural anthropologists point out that given acts and objects appear vastly different in different cultures, depending on the values attached to them. Psychologists investigating perception are increasingly insistent that what is perceived depends upon the observer's perceptual frame of reference.[1]

Language teachers, particularly teachers of English as a second language, are latecomers in the area of international education. For years, and until quite recently, most languages were taught in what might be called a mechanistic way, stressing the prescriptive function of such teaching. In recent years the swing has been in the other direction, and the prescriptive has practically disappeared from language teaching. Descriptive approaches have seemed to provide the answer. At the present moment, there seems to be some question about the purely descriptive technique, and a new compromise between description and prescription seems to be emerging. Such a compromise appears necessary to the adequate achievement of results in second-language teaching. Unfortunately, although both the prescriptivists and the descriptivists have recognized the existence of cultural variation as a factor in second-language teaching, the recognition has so far been limited to the level of the sentence—that is, to the level of grammar, vocabulary, and sentence structure. On the other hand, it has long been known among sociologists and anthropologists that logic *per se* is a cultural phenomenon as well.

> Even if we take into account the lexical and grammatical similarities that exist between languages proceeding from a common hypothetical ancestor, the fact remains that the verbal universe is divided into multiple sectors. Sapir, Whorf, and many others, comparing the Indian languages with the Occidental languages, have underlined this diversity very forcefully. It seems, indeed, as if the arbitrary character of language, having been shown to be of comparatively little significance at the level of the elements of a language, reasserts itself quite definitely at the level of the language taken as a whole. And if one admits that a language represents a kind of destiny, so far as human thought is concerned, this diversity of languages leads to a radical relativism. As Peirce said, if Aristotle had been Mexican, his logic would have been different; and perhaps, by the same token, the whole of our philosophy and our science would have been different.

> The fact is that this diversity affects not only the languages, but also the cultures, that is to say the whole system of institutions that are tied to the language...[and] language in its turn is the effect and the expression of a certain world view that is manifested in the culture. If there is causality, it is a reciprocal causality....

> The types of structures characteristic of a given culture would then, in each case, be particular modes of universal laws.[2]

Logic (in the popular, rather than the logician's sense of the word) which is the basis of rhetoric, is evolved out of a culture; it is not universal. Rhetoric, then, is not universal either, but varies from culture to culture and even from time to time within a given culture. It is affected by canons of taste within a given culture at a given time.

> Every language offers to its speakers a ready-made *interpretation* of the world, truly a Weltanschauung, a metaphysical word-picture which, after having originated in the thinking of our ancestors, tends to impose itself ever anew on posterity. Take for instance a simple sentence such as 'I see him....' This means that English and, I might say, Indo-European, presents the impressions made on our senses predominantly as human *activities*, brought about by our *will*. But the Eskimos in Greenland say not 'I see him' but 'he appears to me....' Thus the Indo-European speaker conceives as workings of his activities what the fatalistic Eskimo sees as events that happen to him.[3]

The English language and its related thought patterns have evolved out of the Anglo-European cultural pattern. The expected sequence of thought in English is essentially a Platonic-Aristotelian sequence, descended from the philosophers of ancient Greece and shaped subsequently by Roman, medieval European, and later Western thinkers. It is not a better nor a worse system than any other, but it is different.

...As human beings, we must inevitably see the universe from a centre lying within ourselves and speak about it in terms of a human language by the exigencies of human intercourse. Any attempt rigorously to eliminate our human perspective from our picture of the world must lead to absurdity.[4]

A fallacy of some repute and some duration is the one which assumes that because a student can write an adequate essay in his native language, he can necessarily write an adequate essay in a second language. That this assumption is fallacious has become more and more apparent as English-as-a-second-language courses have proliferated at American colleges and universities in recent years. Foreign students who have mastered syntactic structures have still demonstrated inability to compose adequate themes, term papers, theses, and dissertations. Instructors have written, on foreign-student papers, such comments as: "The material is all here, but it seems somehow out of focus," or "Lacks organization," or "Lacks cohesion." And these comments are essentially accurate. The foreign-student paper is out of focus because the foreign student is employing a rhetoric and a sequence of thought which violate the expectations of the native reader.

A personality is carved out by the whole subtle interaction of these systems of ideas which are characteristic of the culture as a whole, as well as of those systems of ideas which get established for the individual through more special types of participation.[5]

The fact that sequence of thought and grammar are related in a given language has already been demonstrated adequately by Paul Lorenzen. His brief paper proposes that certain linguistic structures are best comprehended as embodiments of logical structures.[6] Beyond that, every rhetorician from Cicero to Brooks and Warren has indicated the relationship between thought sequence and rhetoric.

A paragraph, mechanically considered, is a division of the composition, set off by an indentation of its first sentence or by some other conventional device, such as extra space between paragraphs.... Paragraph divisions signal to the reader that the material so set off constitutes a unit of thought.

For the reader this marking off of the whole composition into segments is a convenience, though not a strict necessity.... Since communication of one's thought is at best a difficult business, it is the part of common sense (not to mention good manners) to mark for the reader the divisions of one's thought and thus make the thought structure visible upon the page....

Paragraphing, obviously, can be of help to the reader only if the indicated paragraphs are genuine units of thought.... For a paragraph undertakes to discuss one topic or one aspect of a topic.[7]

The thought patterns which speakers and readers of English appear to expect as an integral part of their communication is a sequence that is dominantly linear in its development. An English expository paragraph usually begins with a topic statement, and then, by a series of subdivisions of that topic statement, each supported by example and illustrations, proceeds to develop that central idea and relate that idea to all the other ideas in the whole essay, and to employ that idea in its proper relationship with the other ideas, to prove something, or perhaps to argue something.

> A piece of writing may be considered unified when it contains *nothing* superfluous and it omits nothing essential to the achievement of its purpose.... A work is considered coherent when the sequence of its parts...is controlled by some principle which is meaningful to the reader. Unity is the quality attributed to writing which has all its necessary and sufficient parts. Coherence is the quality attributed to the presentation of material in a sequence which is intelligible to its reader.[8]

Contrarily, the English paragraph may use just the reverse procedure; that is, it may state a whole series of examples and then relate those examples into a single statement at the end of the paragraph. These two types of development represent the common *inductive* and *deductive* reasoning which the English reader expects to be an integral part of any formal communication.

For example, the following paragraph written by Macaulay demonstrates normal paragraph development:

> Whitehall, when [Charles the Second] dwelt there, was the focus of political intrigue and of fashionable gaiety. Half the jobbing and half the flirting of the metropolis went on under his roof. Whoever could make himself agreeable to the prince or could secure the good offices of his mistress might hope to rise in the world without rendering any service to the government, without even being known by sight to any minister of state. This courtier got a frigate and that a company, a third the pardon of a rich offender, a fourth a lease of crown-land on easy terms. If the king notified his pleasure that a briefless lawyer should be made a judge or that a libertine baronet should be made a peer, the gravest counsellors, after a little murmuring, submitted. Interest, therefore, drew a constant press of suitors to the gates of the palace, and those gates always stood wide. The King kept open house every day and all day long for the good society of London, the extreme Whigs only excepted. Hardly any gentleman had any difficulty in making his way to the royal presence. The levee was exactly what the word imports. Some men of quality came every morning to stand round their master, to chat with him while his wig was combed and his cravat tied, and to accompany him in his early walk through the Park. All persons who had been properly introduced might, without any special invitation, go to see him dine, sup, dance, and play at hazard and might have the pleasure of hearing him tell stories, which indeed, he told remarkably well, about his flight from Worcester and about the misery which he had endured when he was a state prisoner in the hands of the canting meddling preachers of Scotland.[9]

The paragraph begins with a general statement of its content, and then carefully develops that statement by a long series of rather specific illustrations. While it is discursive, the paragraph is never digressive. There is nothing in this paragraph that does not belong here; nothing that does not contribute significantly to the central idea. The flow of ideas occurs in a straight line from the opening sentence to the last sentence.

Without doing too much damage to other ways of thinking, perhaps it might be possible to contrast the English paragraph development with paragraph development in other linguistic systems.

For the purposes of the following brief analysis, some seven hundred foreign student compositions were carefully analyzed. Approximately one hundred of these were discarded from the study on the basis that they represent linguistic groups too small within the present sample to be significant.[10] But approximately six hundred examples, representing three basic language groups, were examined.[11]

In the Arabic language, for example (and this generalization would be more or less true for all Semitic languages), paragraph development is based on a complex series of parallel constructions, both positive and negative. This kind of parallelism may most clearly be demonstrated in English by reference to the King James version of the Old Testament. Several types of parallelism typical of Semitic languages are apparent there because that book, of course, is a translation from an ancient Semitic language, a translation accomplished at a time when English was in a state of development suitable to the imitation of those forms.

1. Synonymous Parallelism: The balancing of the thought and phrasing of the first part of a statement or idea by the second part. In such cases, the two parts are often connected by a coordinating conjunction.

    Example: His descendants will be mighty in the land
                and
                the generation of the upright will be blessed.

2. Synthetic Parallelism: The completion of the idea or thought of the first part in the second part. A conjunctive adverb is often stated or implied.

    Example: Because he inclined his ear to me
                therefore
                I will call on him as long as I live.

3. Antithetic Parallelism: The idea stated in the first part is emphasized by the expression of a contrasting idea in the second part. The contrast is expressed not only in thought but often in phrasing as well.

    Example: For the Lord knoweth the way of the righteous:
                But the way of the wicked shall perish.

4. Climactic Parallelism: The idea of the passage is not completed until the very end of the passage. This form is similar to the modern periodic sentence in which the subject is postponed to the very end of the sentence.

    Example: Give unto the Lord, O ye sons of the mighty,
                Give unto the Lord glory and strength.[12]

The type of parallel construction here illustrated in single sentences also forms the core of paragraphs in some Arabic writing. Obviously, such a development in a modern English paragraph would strike the modern English reader as archaic or awkward, and more importantly it would stand in the way of clear communication. It is important to note that in English, maturity of style is often gauged by degree of subordination rather than by coordination.

The following paper was written as a class exercise by an Arabic-speaking student in an English-as-a-second-language class at an American university:

> The contemporary Bedouins, who live in the deserts of Saudi Arabia, are the successors of the old bedouin tribes, the tribes that was fascinated with Mohammad's massage, and on their shoulders Islam built it's empire. I had lived among those contemporary Bedouins for a short period of time, and I have learned lots of things about them. I found out that they have retained most of their ancestor's characteristics, inspite of the hundreds of years that separate them.
>
> They are famous of many praiseworthy characteristics, but they are considered to be the symbol of generosity; bravery; and self-esteem. Like most of the wandering peoples, a stranger is an undesirable person among them. But, once they trust him as a friend, he will be most welcome. However, their trust is a hard thing to gain. And the heroism of many famous figures, who ventured in the Arabian deserts like T. E. Lawrence, is based on their ability to acquire this dear trust!
>
> Romance is an important part in their life. And 'love' is an important subject in their verses and their tales.
>
> Nevertheless, they are criticized of many things. The worst of all is that they are extremists in all the ways of their lives. It is their extremism that changes sometimes their generosity into squandering, their bravery into brutality, and their self-esteem into haughtiness. But in any case, I have been, and will continue to be greatly interested in this old, fascinating group of people.

Disregarding for the moment the grammatical errors in this student composition, it becomes apparent that the characteristics of parallelism do occur. The next-to-last element in the first sentence, for example, is appositive to the preceding one, while the last element is an example of synonymous parallelism. The two clauses of the second sentence illustrate synonymous parallelism. In the second "paragraph" the first sentence contains both an example of antithetic parallelism and a list of parallel nouns. The next two sentences form an antithetic pair, and so on. It is perhaps not necessary to point out further examples in the selection. It is important, however, to observe that in the first sentence, for example, the grammatical complexity is caused by the attempt to achieve an intricate parallelism. While this extensive parallel construction is linguistically possible in Arabic, the English language lacks the necessary flexibility. Eight conjunctions and four sentence connectors are employed in a matter of only fourteen "sentences." In addition, there are five "lists" of units connected by commas and conjunctions.

Another paper, also written by an Arabic-speaking student under comparable circumstances, further demonstrates the same tendencies:

> At that time of the year I was not studying enough to pass my courses in

school. *And* all the time I was asking my cousin to let me ride the bicycle, *but* he wouldn't let me. *But* after two weeks, noticing that I was so much interested in the bicycle, he promised me that if I pass my courses in school for that year he would give it to me as a present. *So* I began to study hard. *And* I studying eight hours a day instead of two.

My cousin seeing me studying that much he was sure that I was going to succeed in school. *So* he decided to give me some lessons in riding the bicycle. After four or five weeks of teaching me and ten or twelve times hurting myself as I used to go out of balance, I finally knew how to ride it. And the finals in school came *and* I was very good prepared for them *so* I passed them. My cousin kept his promise *and* gave me the bicycle as a present. *And* till now I keep the bicycle in a safe place, *and* everytime I see it, It reminds me how it helped to pass my courses for that year.

In the first paragraph of this example, four of the five sentences, or 80% of the sentences, begin with a coordinating element. In the second paragraph, three of the six sentences, or 50% of the total, also begin with a coordinating element. In the whole passage, seven of the eleven sentences, or roughly 65%, conform to this pattern. In addition, the first paragraph contains one internal coordinator, and the second contains five internal coordinators; thus, the brief passage (210 words) contains a total of thirteen coordinators. It is important to notice that almost all of the ideas in the passage are coordinately linked, that there is very little subordination, and that the parallel units exemplify the types of parallelism already noted.

Some Oriental[13] writing, on the other hand, is marked by what may be called an approach by indirection. In this kind of writing, the development of the paragraph may be said to be "turning and turning in a widening gyre." The circles or gyres turn around the subject and show it from a variety of tangential views, but the subject is never looked at directly. Things are developed in terms of what they are not, rather than in terms of what they are. Again, such a development in a modern English paragraph would strike the English reader as awkward and unnecessarily indirect.

The following composition was written, as a class exercise, by a native speaker of Korean, under the same circumstances which produced the two previous examples. Obviously, this student is weaker in general English proficiency than the students who produced the two prior examples.

Definition of college education

College is an institution of an higher learning that gives degrees. All of us needed culture and education in life, if no education to us, we should to go living hell.

One of the greatest causes that while other animals have remained as they first man along has made such rapid progress is has learned about civilization.

The improvement of the highest civilization is in order to education up-to-date.

So college education is very important thing which we don't need mention about it.

Again, disregarding the typically Oriental grammar and the misconception of the function of "parts of speech," the first sentence defines college, not college education. This may conceivably be a problem based upon the student's misunderstanding of the assignment. But the second sentence appears to shoot off in a totally different direction. It makes a general statement about culture and education, perhaps as *results* of a college education. The third sentence, presented as a separate "paragraph," moves still farther away from definition by expanding the topic to "man" in a generic sense, as opposed to "non-man." This unit is tied to the next, also presented as a separate paragraph, by the connecting idea of "civilization" as an aspect of education. The concluding paragraph-sentence presents, in the guise of a summary logically derived from previously posited ideas, a conclusion which is in fact partially a topic sentence and partially a statement that the whole basic concept of the assignment is so obvious that it does not need discussion. The paper arrives where it should have started, with the added statement that it really had no place to go to begin with.

The poorer proficiency of this student, however, introduces two other considerations. It is possible that this student, as an individual rather than as a representative native speaker of Korean, lacks the ability to abstract sufficiently for extended definition. In the case under discussion, however, the student was majoring in mathematics and did have the ability to abstract in mathematical terms. While the demands of mathematics are somewhat different from the demands of language in a conventional sense, it is possible to assume that a student who can handle abstraction in one area can also probably handle it at least to some extent in the other. It is also possible that the ability to abstract is absent from the Korean culture. This appears quite unlikely in view of the abundance of Korean art available and in view of the fact that other native speakers of Korean have not demonstrated that shortcoming.

The examples cited so far have been student themes. The following example is from a professional translation. Essentially, the same variations can be observed in it. In this case, the translation is from French.

> The first point to which I would like to call your attention is that nothing exists outside the boundary of what is strictly human. A landscape may be beautiful, graceful, sublime, insignificant, or ugly; it will never be ludicrous. We may laugh at an animal, but only because we have detected in it some human expression or attitude. We may laugh at a hat, but we are not laughing at the piece of felt or straw. We are laughing at the shape that men have given to it, the human whim whose mold it has assumed. *I wonder why a fact so important has not attracted the attention of philosophers to a greater degree. Some have defined man as an animal that knows how to laugh. They could equally well have defined him as an animal which provokes laughter,* for if any other animal or some lifeless object, achieves the same effect, it is always because of some similarity to man.[14]

In this paragraph, the italicized portion constitutes a digression. It is an interesting digression, but it really does not seem to contribute significant structural material to the basic thought of the paragraph. While the author of the paragraph is a philosopher, and a philosopher is often forgiven digressions, the more important fact is that the example is a typical one for writers of French as well as for writers of philosophy. Much greater freedom to digress or to introduce extraneous material is available in French, or in Spanish, than in English.

Similar characteristics can be demonstrated in the writing of native French-speaking students in English. In the interests of keeping this report within some bounds, such illustrations will be inserted without comment. The first example was written under circumstances similar to those described for the preceding student samples. The writer is a native speaker of French.

American Traffic Law as compared with Traffic law in Switzerland

At first glance the traffic law in United States appeared to me simpler than in Switzerland.

The American towns in general have the disposition of a cross, and for a driver who knows how to situate himself between the four cardinal points, there is no problem to find his way. Each street has numbers going crecendo from the center of the town to the outside.

There are many accidents in Switzerland, as everywhere else, and the average of mortality comparatively to the proportion of the countries is not better than in United States. We have the problem of straight streets, not enough surveillance by policemen on the national roads, and alcohol. The country of delicious wines has made too many damages.

The following illustration, drawn from the work of a native speaker of Latin American Spanish, was produced under conditions parallel to those already cited:

The American Children

In America, the American children are brought differently from the rest of the children in other countries. In their childhood, from the first day they are born, the parents give their children the love and attention they need. They teach their children the meaning of Religion among the family and to have respect and obedience for their parents.

I am Spanish, and I was brought up differently than the children in America. My parents are stricter and they taught me discipline and not to interrupt when someone was talking.

The next and last example is again not a piece of student writing, but a translation. The original was written in Russian, and the translation attempts to capture the structure of the original as much as possible, but without sacrificing meaning completely.

On the 14th of October, Kruschev left the stage of history. Was it a plot the result of which was that Kruschev was out of business remains not clear. It is very probable that even if it were anything resembling a plot it would not be for the complete removal of Kruschev from political guidance, but rather a pressure exerted to obtain some changes in his policies: for continuations of his policies of peaceful co-existence in international relations or making it as far as possible a situation to avoid formal rupture with the Chinese communist party and at any rate not to go unobstructed to such a rupture—and in the area of internal politics, especially in the section of economics, to continue efforts of a certain softening of "dogmatism," but without the hurried and not sufficiently reasoned experimentation, which became the characteristic traits of Kruschev's politics in recent years.[15]

215

Some of the difficulty in this paragraph is linguistic rather than rhetorical. The structure of the Russian sentence is entirely different from the structure of the English sentence. But some of the linguistic difficulty is closely related to the rhetorical difficulty. The above paragraph is composed of three sentences. The first two are very short, while the last is extremely long, constituting about three-quarters of the paragraph. It is made up of a series of presumably parallel constructions and a number of subordinate structures. At least half of these are irrelevant to the central idea of the paragraph in the sense that they are parenthetical amplifications of structurally related subordinate elements.

There are, of course, other examples that might be discussed as well, but these paragraphs may suffice to show that each language and each culture has a paragraph order unique to itself, and that part of the learning of a particular language is the mastering of its logical system.

> One should join to any logic of the language a phenomenology of the spoken word. Moreover, this phenomenology will, in its turn, rediscover the idea of a logos immanent in the language; but it will seek the justification for this in a more general philosophy of the relations between man and the world...from one culture to another it is possible to establish communication. The Rorschach test has been successfully applied to the natives of the island of Alor.[16]

This discussion is not intended to offer any criticism of other existing paragraph developments; rather it is intended only to demonstrate that paragraph developments other than those normally regarded as desirable in English do exist. In the teaching of paragraph structure to foreign students, whether in terms of reading or in terms of composition, the teacher must be himself aware of these differences, and he must make these differences overtly apparent to his students. In short, contrastive rhetoric must be taught in the same sense that contrastive grammar is presently taught. Now not much has been done in the area of contrastive rhetoric. It is first necessary to arrive at accurate descriptions of existing paragraph orders other than those common to English. Furthermore, it is necessary to understand that these categories are in no sense meant to be mutually exclusive. Patterns may be derived for *typical* English paragraphs, but paragraphs like those described above as being atypical in English do exist in English. By way of obvious example, Ezra Pound writes paragraphs which are circular in their structure, and William Faulkner writes paragraphs which are wildly digressive. The paragraph being discussed here is not the "literary" paragraph, however, but the expository paragraph. The necessities of art impose structures on any language, while the requirements of communication can often be best solved by relatively close adhesion to established patterns.

Superficially, the movement of the various paragraphs discussed above may be graphically represented in the following manner:

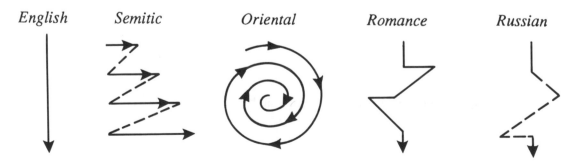

| *English* | *Semitic* | *Oriental* | *Romance* | *Russian* |

Much more detailed and more accurate descriptions are required before any meaningful contrastive system can be elaborated. Nonetheless, an important problem exists immediately. In the teaching of English as a second language, what does one do with the student who is reasonably proficient in the use of syntactic structure but who needs to learn to write themes, theses, essay examinations, and dissertations? The "advanced" student has long constituted a problem for teachers of English as a second language. This approach, the contrastive analysis of rhetoric, is offered as one possible answer to the existing need. Such an approach has the advantage that it may help the foreign student to form standards of judgment consistent with the demands made upon him by the educational system of which he has become a part. At the same time, by accounting for the cultural aspects of logic which underlie the rhetorical structure, this approach may bring the student not only to an understanding of contrastive grammar and a new vocabulary, which are parts of any reading task, but also to a grasp of idea and structure in units larger than the sentence. A sentence, after all, rarely exists outside a context. Applied linguistics teaches the student to deal with the sentence, but it is necessary to bring the student beyond that to a comprehension of the whole context. He can only understand the whole context if he recognizes the logic on which the context is based. The foreign student who has mastered the syntax of English may still write a bad paragraph or a bad paper unless he also masters the logic of English. "In serious expository prose, the paragraph tends to be a logical, rather than a typographical, unit."[17] The understanding of paragraph patterns can allow the student to relate syntactic elements within a paragraph and perhaps even to relate paragraphs within a total context.

Finally, it is necessary to recognize the fact that a paragraph is an artificial thought unit employed in the written language to suggest a cohesion which commonly may not exist in oral language. "Paragraphing, like punctuation, is a feature only of the written language."[18] As an artificial unit of thought, it lends itself to patterning quite readily. In fact, since it is imposed from without, and since it is a frame for the structuring of thought into patterns, it is by its very nature patterned. The rhetorical structures of English paragraphs may be found in any good composition text.[19] The patterns of paragraphs in other languages are not so well established, or perhaps only not so well known to speakers of English. These patterns need to be discovered or uncovered and compared with the patterns of English in order to arrive at a practical means for the teaching of such structures to non-native users of the language.

In the interim, while research is directed at the rhetorics of other languages, certain practical pedagogical devices have been developed to expedite the teaching of rhetorical structures to non-native speakers of English. An elementary device consists simply of supplying to the students a scrambled paragraph. A normal paragraph, such as the one cited from Macaulay above, may be arbitrarily scrambled, the sentences numbered, and the students asked to rearrange the sentences in what appears to them to be a normal order. Frequently, the results of such an assignment will demonstrate the diversity of views or cultures represented in the classroom. The exercise can be used effectively to point out the very disparity. The students must then be presented with the original version of the paragraph, and the instructor must be able to explain and justify the order of the original.

[INSTRUCTIONS: Arrange the sentences below into some normal order.]

[This is the order in which the author arranged his sentences. Can you detect his reason?]

Scrambled Order

Normal Order

1. A jackass brays; a turkey cock gobbles; a dog yelps; a church bell clangs.
2. The narrow streets and lanes leading into the market are crammed with Indians, their dark skins glistening like copper or bronze in the bright sun, their varicolored cloaks looking like a mass of palette colors smeared together.
3. There is the smell of animal dung mingled with the odor of carnations and heliotrope from the flower stalls.
4. In the open plaza outside the market the crowd mills about.
5. Mothers sit on the curb nursing their babies.
6. A kind of blending of Indian talk in various dialects creates a strange droning noise.
7. On the narrow sidewalks, merchandise is spread so haphazardly that in order to pass, pedestrians have to press against the wall or leap the displays.
8. Wrinkled old women squat over charcoal braziers cooking corn cakes, or black beans, or pink coconut candy.

The narrow streets and lanes leading into the market are crammed with Indians, their dark skins glistening like copper or bronze in the bright sun, their varicolored cloaks looking like a mass of palette colors smeared together. In the open plaza outside the market the crowd mills about. A kind of blending of Indian talk in various dialects creates a strange droning noise. A jackass brays; a turkey cock gobbles; a dog yelps; a church bell clangs. On the narrow sidewalks, merchandise is spread so haphazardly that in order to pass, pedestrians have to press against the wall or leap the displays. Wrinkled old women squat over charcoal braziers cooking corn cakes, or black beans, or pink coconut candy. Mothers sit on the curb nursing their babies. There is the smell of animal dung mingled with the odor of carnations and heliotrope from the flower stalls.[20]

[This paragraph is descriptive, presented in the present tense, and arranged perceptually in the order of sight, hearing, and smell.]

A second device consists of giving the students carefully written topic sentences, arranged in some convenient way such as that suggested below, and then asking the students to fill out the subdivisions of the topic sentence with examples and illustrations chosen to support the point. Depending upon the relative difficulty of the topic, the examples may be supplied by the instructor in scrambled order.

American Television

American commercial television appears to consist of three principal classes of material: programs of serious interest, such as news broadcasts and special features; programs intended primarily as entertainment, such as variety shows, situation comedies, and adventure tales; and the advertisements which link all of these.

I. Programs of serious interest:
    A.   News Broadcasts:
            1._____
            2._____
    B.   Special Features:
            1._____
            2._____

II. Programs intended primarily as entertainment:
    A.   Variety Shows:
            1._____
            2._____
    B.   Situational Comedies:
            1._____
            2._____
    C.   Adventure Tales:
            1._____
            2._____

III. Advertising:
    A._____
            1._____
            2._____
    B._____
            1._____
            2._____

IV. [Conclusion:]

[INSTRUCTIONS: The student is to supply contrasting examples for each of the spaces provided under items I and II. In item III the student must also supply the main subdivisions, and in item IV the point of the whole essay must also be supplied by the student. Obviously, item IV will vary considerably depending upon the kinds of illustrations selected to fill the blanks.]

The illustration constitutes a very simple exercise. Greater sophistication may be employed as the student becomes more familiar with the techniques. Obviously, too, the outline must be introduced and taught simultaneously. A simple technique for teaching the outline may be found illustrated in a number of texts for both American and foreign students.[21]

It is important to impress upon the student that "A paragraph is *clear* when each sentence contributes to the central thought...[and that] clarity also demands coherence, that is, an orderly flow of sentences marked by repetition of key ideas."[22]

While it is necessary for the non-native speaker learning English to master the rhetoric of the English paragraph, it must be remembered that the foreign student, ideally, will be returning to his home country, and that his stay in the United States is a brief one. Under these circumstances, English is a means to an end for him; it is not an end in itself. Edward Sapir has written:

> An oft-noted peculiarity of the development of culture is the fact that it reaches its greatest heights in comparatively small, autonomous groups. In fact, it is doubtful if a genuine culture ever properly belongs to more than such a restricted group, a group between the members of which there can be said to be something like direct intensive spiritual contact. This direct contact is enriched by the common cultural heritage on which the minds of all are fed.... A narrowly localized culture may, and often does, spread its influence far beyond its properly restricted sphere. Sometimes it sets the pace for a whole nationality, for a far flung empire. It can do so, however, only at the expense of diluting the spirit as it moves away from its home, of degenerating into an imitative attitudinizing.[23]

He is absolutely correct in pointing out the dangers of spreading a culture too thin and too far from home. However, in the special case of the foreign student learning English, under the conditions stipulated above, the imitation which would be an error in most cases is the sought aim. The classes which undertake the training of the "advanced" student can aim for no more. The creativity and imagination which make the difference between competent writing and excellent writing are things which, at least in these circumstances, cannot be taught. The foreign student is an adult in most cases. If these things are teachable, they will already have been taught to him. The English class must not aim too high. Its funtion is to provide the student with a form within which he may operate, a form acceptable in this time and in this place. It is hoped that the method described above may facilitate the achievement of that goal.

[1] Robert T. Oliver, "Foreword," *Philosophy, Rhetoric and Argumentation,* ed. Maurice Nathanson and Henry W. Johnstone, Jr. (University Park, Pennsylvania, 1965), pp. x-xi.

[2] Mikel Dufrenne, *Language and Philosophy,* trans. Henry B. Veatch (Bloomington, 1963), pp. 35-37.

[3] Leo Spitzer, "Language—The Basis of Science, Philosophy and Poetry,"*Studies in Intellectual History,* ed. George Boas *et al.* (Baltimore, 1953), pp. 83-84.

[4] Michael Polanyi, *Personal Knowledge: Towards a Post-Critical Philosophy* (Chicago, 1958), p. 9.

[5] Sapir, "Anthropology and Psychiatry," *Culture, Language and Personality* (Los Angeles, 1964), p. 157.

[6] *Logik und Grammatik* (Mannheim, Germany, 1965).

[7] Cleanth Brooks and Robert Penn Warren, *Modern Rhetoric,* 2nd ed. (New York, 1958), pp. 267-68.

[8] Richard E. Hughes and P. Albert Duhamel, *Rhetoric: Principles and Usage* (Englewood Cliffs, New Jersey, 1962), pp. 19-20.

[9] From *The History of England from the Accession of James the Second* (London, 1849-61).

[10] The following examples were discarded: Afghan-3, African-4, Danish-1, Finn-1, German-3, Hindi-8, Persian-46, Russian-1, Greek-1, Tagalog-10, Turk-16, Urdu-5, Total-99.

[11] The papers examined may be linguistically broken down as follows: Group I—Arabic-126, Hebrew-3; Group II—Chinese (Mandarin)-110, Cambodian-40, Indochinese-7, Japanese-135, Korean-57, Laotian-3, Malasian-1, Thai-27, Vietnamese-1; Group III—(Spanish-Portugese) Brazilian-19, Central American-10, South American-42, Cuban-4, Spanish-8, (French) French-2, African-2 (Italian), Swiss-1. Group I total-129; Group II total-381; Group III total-88. TOTAL-598. These papers were accumulated and examined over a two-year period, from the beginning of the Fall 1963 semester through the Fall 1965 academic semester.

[12] I am indebted to Dr. Ben Siegel for this analysis.

[13] *Oriental* here is intended to mean specifically Chinese and Korean but not Japanese.

[14] From *Laughter, An Assay on the Meaning of the Comic.* Trans. Marcel Bolomet (Paris, 1900).

[15] From S. Schwartz, "After Kruschev," trans. E. B. Kaplan, *The Socialist Courier* (April, 1965), p. 3.

[16] Dufrenne, pp. 39-40.

[17] Hans P. Guth, *A Short New Rhetoric* (Belmont, California, 1964), p. 205.

[18] Edward P. J. Corbett, *Classical Rhetoric for the Modern Student* (New York, 1965), p. 416.

[19] Important work in the rhetoric of the paragraph is being done by Francis Christensen, among others. See especially "A Generative Rhetoric of the Paragraph," *College Composition and Communication* (October, 1965), pp. 144-156.

[20] Hudson Strode, "The Market at Toluca," *Now in Mexico* (New York, 1947).

[21] At the risk of being accused of immodesty, I would recommend in particular the section entitled "Outlining" in Robert B. Kaplan, *Reading and Rhetoric* (New York, 1963), pp. 69-80.

[22] Francis Connolly, *A Rhetoric Casebook* (New York, 1953), p. 304.

[23] Edward Sapir, "Culture, Genuine and Spurious," *Culture, Language and Personality,* (Los Angeles 1964), pp. 113-14.

Questions For Discussion

1.   On the basis of your own socialization and experience speculate on whether you are field dependent or field independent.

2.   Speculate on the indirect implications that the article on cognitive styles has regarding the standardized testing of cultural minorities in Western and North American schools.

3.   Kaplan in his article states: "Each language and each culture has a paragraph order unique to itself, and that part of the learning of a particular language is the mastering of its logical system." Which types of paragraph orders does he identify and what are the implications of these to the education of people from different cultures?

4.   On the basis of Kaplan's article, examine which rhetoric or writing style may be yours.